973.7 Lyn
Lynn, Alvin R.
Kit Carson and the First
  Battle of Adobe Walls : a
tale of two journeys
                    $34.95
          ocn861676491
          09/03/2014

DISCARD

The Grover E. Murray Studies in the American Southwest

Also in the series

Brujerías: Stories of Witchcraft and the Supernatural in the American Southwest and Beyond, by Nasario García

Cacti of Texas: A Field Guide, by A. Michael Powell, James F. Weedin, and Shirley A. Powell

Cacti of the Trans-Pecos and Adjacent Areas, by A. Michael Powell and James F. Weedin

Cowboy Park: Steer-Roping Contests on the Border, by John O. Baxter

Dance All Night: Those Other Southwestern Swing Bands, Past and Present, by Jean A. Boyd

Deep Time and the Texas High Plains: History and Geology, by Paul H. Carlson

From Texas to San Diego in 1851: The Overland Journal of Dr. S. W. Woodhouse, Surgeon-Naturalist of the Sitgreaves Expedition, edited by Andrew Wallace and Richard H. Hevly

Grasses of South Texas: A Guide to Identification and Value, by James H. Everitt, D. Lynn Drawe, Christopher R. Little, and Robert I. Lonard

In the Shadow of the Carmens: Afield with a Naturalist in the Northern Mexican Mountains, by Bonnie Reynolds McKinney

Javelinas: Collared Peccaries of the Southwest, by Jane Manaster

Land of Enchantment Wildflowers: A Guide to the Plants of New Mexico, by LaShara J. Nieland and Willa F. Finley

Little Big Bend: Common, Uncommon, and Rare Plants of Big Bend National Park, by Roy Morey

Lone Star Wildflowers: A Guide to Texas Flowering Plants, by LaShara J. Nieland and Willa F. Finley

Myth, Memory, and Massacre: The Pease River Capture of Cynthia Ann Parker, by Paul H. Carlson and Tom Crum

Pecans: The Story in a Nutshell, by Jane Manaster

Picturing a Different West: Vision, Illustration, and the Tradition of Austin and Cather, by Janis P. Stout

Plants of Central Texas Wetlands, by Scott B. Fleenor and Stephen Welton Taber

Seat of Empire: The Embattled Birth of Austin, Texas, by Jeffrey Stuart Kerr

Texas, New Mexico, and the Compromise of 1850: Boundary Dispute and Sectional Crisis, by Mark J. Stegmaier

Texas Quilts and Quilters: A Lone Star Legacy, by Marcia Kaylakie with Janice Whittington

Truly Texas Mexican: A Native Culinary Heritage in Recipes, by Adán Medrano

The Wineslinger Chronicles: Texas on the Vine, by Russell D. Kane

Kit Carson

and the

First Battle

of Adobe Walls

Kit Carson

and the

First Battle
of Adobe Walls

A Tale of Two Journeys

Alvin R. Lynn
Foreword by J. Brett Cruse

Texas Tech University Press

This book is typeset in Minion. The paper used in this book meets the minimum requirements of ANSI/NISO Z39.48-1992 (R1997). ∞

Designed by Nicole Jones
Cover photograph/illustration by Barbara Werden

Library of Congress Cataloging-in-Publication Data
Lynn, Alvin R.
Kit Carson and the First Battle of Adobe Walls : a tale of two journeys / Alvin R. Lynn ; foreword by J. Brett Cruse.
pages cm.—(The Grover E. Murray studies in the American Southwest)
Includes bibliographical references and index.
ISBN 978-0-89672-861-5 (hardcover : alk. paper)—ISBN 978-0-89672-862-2 (e-book)
1. Adobe Walls, 1st Battle of, Tex., 1864. 2. Carson, Kit, 1809–1868. 3. Military archaeology—Texas. 4. Texas—Antiquities. I. Title.
E83.863.L96 2014
973.7—dc23
2014003529

Printed in the U.S.A.
14 15 16 17 18 19 20 21 22 / 9 8 7 6 5 4 3 2 1

Texas Tech University Press
Box 41037
Lubbock, Texas 79409-1037 USA
800.832.4042
ttup@ttu.edu
www.ttupress.org

Much of the credit for this book goes to my wife, Nadyne. It is hard to thank her enough for the contributions she made. She encouraged me, and without her support I probably would not have finished the book. It is with sincere thanks that I dedicate this writing to my wife.

Contents

Illustrations

Figures

Plates, following page 64

Maps

Artifact Description Tables

Foreword

Christopher "Kit" Carson is one of the best known frontiersmen of the American West. Indeed, few individuals of that time and place in American history have had as many books written about them as has Kit Carson, and for good reason. His adventures throughout the western United States made him famous as a mountain man and trapper, explorer, and soldier. From the time he was sixteen years old in 1825, when he signed on with a large merchant caravan heading to Santa Fe, until his death in 1868, Carson would spend his adult life as an explorer of the Rocky Mountains, as a scout and soldier, and as an Indian fighter.

As a young man, Kit Carson became one of the famed mountain men, trapping beaver and other animals throughout the western United States. At various times he worked with the Hudson's Bay Company as well as the renowned Jim Bridger trapping along the Yellowstone, Powder, and Big Horn rivers. Along the way, Carson learned to speak Spanish, French, and several Native American languages, though he never learned to read or write.

Carson lived among and married into the Cheyenne and Arapaho tribes. He married an Arapaho woman in 1835, but she died four years later after the birth of their second child. In 1840, Carson married a Cheyenne woman, but she stayed with him for only a short time. In 1843, he married his third wife, Josefa Jaramillo, the fourteen-year-old daughter of a prominent Taos family. They had eight children together.

In the summer of 1842 Carson met and was later hired by John C. Frémont as a guide to lead Frémont through much of California, Oregon, and the Great Basin area. In 1843 the two men surveyed the Great Salt Lake in Utah, and then moved further west to Fort Vancouver in the Pacific Northwest. Carson also guided an 1845–1846 expedition to California and Oregon. Through his association with Frémont, Carson made an important contribution to the westward expansion of the United States. Once Frémont's accounts of his explorations were published, Carson achieved national fame, and he became the hero of many dime novels.

Carson served as a scout during the Mexican-American War from 1846 to 1848. In 1853, he became the federal Indian agent for northern New Mexico, working with the Utes and Jicarilla Apache. While there, he advocated for the creation of reservations as a means to save the Indians from the onslaught of Anglo-American settlers. When the Civil War started, Carson joined the First New Mexico Volunteer Infantry Regiment, where he served as a colonel in support of the Union cause. In 1862, he and his men fought the Confederates at the Battle of Valverde. He later led campaigns against some of the Native American tribes in the region. Among these was the campaign to force the Navajo to Bosque Redondo, a reservation located some three hundred miles away at Fort Sumner, New Mexico. The forced relocation, known as the Long Walk, cost the lives of many Navajo.

Because of his participation in a large number of historical events it is easy to understand why Kit Carson became a favorite subject of novelists, historians, and biographers and why so many books have been written and a number of movies made about him. One event in his life, however, has received surprisingly little attention. It came just four years before his death in 1868. The event was his campaign against the Comanche and Kiowa Indians in the Texas Panhandle in 1864. The ensuing battle with those tribes at the ruins of the Adobe

Walls trading post on the Canadian River would be one of the largest battles with Native Americans in the history of the United States.

In November 1864, Carson was sent by General James H. Carleton to try to manage the Indians in western Texas in the hopes of lessening the harassment of travelers along the Santa Fe Trail to Fort Union, New Mexico Territory. Carson and his four hundred troopers and Indian scouts made their way to the central Texas Panhandle, where they met a combined force of Kiowa and Comanche warriors numbering perhaps as many as 1,500 at the ruins of the 1840s Adobe Walls trading post. The Indian force was led by the famous Kiowa Chief Dohäsan. Luckily for Carson, he had brought with him two mountain howitzers that were deployed and kept the Indians at bay. Carson realized soon enough that he was greatly outnumbered, and he made the wise decision to retreat. During their retreat the troopers burned Dohäsan's village.

Though Carson did not win the battle, the engagement with the Indians was significant. The Indians were caught off guard, and for the first time Carson demonstrated that the powerful Comanche and Kiowa tribes could be attacked within their own territory. Prior to this battle the idea of leading troops into the stronghold of the Southern Plains tribes was almost inconceivable and considered far too dangerous. Later similar attempts would be made by Lt. Col. George Armstrong Custer at the Battle of the Washita in 1868 and by Col. Ranald S. Mackenzie in 1871 and 1872 with little success. It would not be until the U.S. Army made a concerted effort with several columns converging all at the same time during the Red River Indian Campaign in 1874 that the Southern Plains Indians would finally be defeated.

Alvin Lynn's *Kit Carson and the First Battle of Adobe Walls: A Tale of Two Journeys*, takes a dramatically different approach in recounting this episode in Kit Carson's life than those taken by other authors. While other researchers have relied exclusively on the archival records, Lynn discovered that the archives contained a surprisingly small amount of information regarding Carson's 1864 Adobe Walls campaign. During his research, Lynn also became interested in the actual route that Carson and his troops took to reach Adobe Walls, and he found that some works by earlier authors contained definite mistakes regarding distances and locations. For this reason, and in order to avoid similar mistakes, Lynn decided he had to verify the route by walking its entire length from Fort Bascom, New Mexico, to Adobe Walls, Texas—some two hundred miles—following the same path taken by Carson in 1864. He also believed that the only way to actually verify the route would be if he could find and document artifacts that might be associated with Carson and his men along the route and at campsites where they stayed.

Beginning in 1995, Lynn spent a good portion of the next fifteen years identifying landowners and walking the Carson route. Along every step of the way he used a metal detector to locate metal artifacts that confirmed the route and the campsites used by Carson and his men. Lynn describes the route in detail, comparing landforms he observed with those described in the archival records. The locations of recovered artifacts were plotted on maps to reveal the actual route, the locations of camps, and ultimately the site of the first battle with the Indians at Adobe Walls. Lynn integrates the evidence from the artifacts with the archival records, and the result is a detailed recreation of the Fort Bascom to Adobe Walls route, which is richly described by Lynn. The artifacts recovered are described in detail and are profusely illustrated, which makes for a valuable resource for historical archeologists.

As a seasoned veteran of archeological prospecting with a metal detector, I know how difficult and time consuming the process can be. Having spent several challenging years searching for and documenting battle sites associated with the Red River War of 1874 in the Texas Panhandle, I was astonished that Lynn was able to work his way across eastern New Mexico and into the central Texas Panhandle locating, documenting, and recording artifacts associated with the Carson campaign the entire way. This was truly no small feat. With the wealth of information gathered and presented by Lynn, we now know precisely the route taken by Carson in 1864, and we have a much clearer understanding of the kinds of items, supplies, and weapons taken and used by Carson and his men during their campaign against the Southern Plains Indians.

Kit Carson and the First Battle of Adobe Walls: A Tale of Two Journeys will probably not be the final book written on Kit Carson or even on his Adobe Walls campaign, but this book provides a level of detail into the lives of Carson, his men, and the First Battle of Adobe Walls that is unsurpassed, and it is likely that it will remain so for a long time to come.

J. Brett Cruse

Prelude

It is a cold, crisp morning on December 4, 2004, and I am at the very place where Colonel Kit Carson sat astride his horse on Thanksgiving Day 1864. I stand in reverie as Carson's 1864 battle unfolds in my mind. I see the plain of battle in the distance, the red bluffs, the remains of Bent's trading post where the doctor set up his hospital, the valley pathway for warriors camped downriver. I imagine the silhouettes of a Kiowa picket and, farther over, young warriors whose taunt rings clear, "Come on over here!"

Soldiers set chase to a dust cloud that signals the Kiowas are speeding to alert their venerable chief, Dohäsan. Women and children scurry off to hide as the charge continues eastward through the Kiowa village.

On this hill, I am standing close to where Carson positioned the two howitzers. Closing my eyes, I see Comanche reinforcements join the Kiowas as they slow their mounts, turn, and face the New Mexico and California Volunteers. The First Battle of Adobe Walls, 25 November 1864, breaks out before me. Neither side realizes that they are engaged in one of the largest battles between Native American and U.S. Army forces west of the Mississippi River—335 soldiers pitted against roughly a thousand Kiowas and a sprinkling of Comanches, Apaches, and Arapahos. I marvel that Carson chose winter to engage the Kiowas and Comanches in battle.

This little-known battle came to my attention in 1992, while I was researching a contribution to *100 Moore Years, A History of Moore County, Texas*[1]. I discovered that a strip of land bisecting the Texas Panhandle along the Canadian River, including Moore County, had been a thoroughfare of activity for Native Americans, Spaniards, Mexican traders, buffalo hunters, California gold seekers, emigrants, and the military. Finding that the famed Kit Carson had traversed the area on his way to fight the Kiowas at Adobe Walls piqued my interest.

It seemed unusual that historians had written so little about this battle. I reflected on it often and had to dig deeper, at first by frequenting libraries and archives. What began as a curiosity became a mission—to recover and preserve this segment of Texas history. Fueling that undertaking was my disappointment that no author who had written about Carson's battle at Adobe Walls ever set foot on the trail or the battlefield.

Today, I know the movements and strategy of this battle well; I've studied every scrap of information and read every book I could find about it. But my certainty that I now stand at the place where the combatants faced off rests on the artifacts recovered from the thousands of acres I have crossed since 1992.

Most of these acres lie on twenty-six ranches whose present owners respect and safeguard what they steward and who permitted me on their lands. As I reminisce about the quest that brought me to Carson's battle site, I realize my good fortune in gaining access to all the land bedding the trail—open range when Carson's troops marched across it. More than forty men and women trusted me enough to let me through their gates and became friends in the process of my search. These landowners are the proprietors of the pieces I dug from their sod. A few kept the artifacts, but most entrusted them to me to present to the Panhandle-Plains Historical Museum, where they will be made accessible for research purposes.

In field and laboratory, I've practiced procedures I learned working for professional archeologists, the same techniques I applied on the Red River War Project, and ones that I teach as a steward for the Texas Historical Commission. I've cataloged every find by date, GPS location, field number, and site number; then I cleaned, identified, analyzed, and photographed each piece.

More than 1,800 items from these ranches fill my notes and my mind. I used the best resources available to me in determining which of the artifacts belonged to Carson's contingent and which belonged to some other group. The truth is in the artifacts: precious relics that reveal our past. Without these pieces, the story of Carson's battle is incomplete. With them, Carson's story takes credible shape.

My excitement and reverie begin to wrestle with more mundane recollections of unwrapping history: fatigue, aching feet, sore muscles, gnats, the endless sweat of manual labor. But what fulfillment walking that old road has given me. How it never ceases to stir me when I sit down to write about it. And write about it, I must. Whatever mistakes I fail to catch; whatever it may lack, my quest is a story no one else can tell.

Preface

The purpose of this book is neither to pass judgment on the campaign of Colonel Kit Carson and his soldiers nor to give an opinion on Native American's defense of their homeland. Rather, it is a tale of two journeys: Kit Carson's 1864 military expedition from Fort Bascom to Adobe Walls and my journey more than a hundred years later to find evidence of his campaign. The work straddles two scholarly disciplines of history and archeology, which, through the processes of fieldwork and research, bind them together as historical archeology.

The first section of the book is a narrative of Carson's march to Adobe Walls that culminated in a battle against Kiowas and Comanches, whose raids upon white travelers on the Santa Fe Trail were creating havoc. I paralleled Carson's story with my search for his route.

The second section of the book includes descriptions as well as charts and tables explaining the archeological field methods used, and analyses of the artifacts. Data obtained from the artifacts either challenged, corroborated, or enhanced the historical information I gleaned from documents in libraries and archives.

I owe my gratitude to archeologist Brett Cruse of the Texas Historical Commission for the opportunity to work as a crewmember on the Red River War Project in the late 1990s. The experience set my mind as to how I would go about my venture. Under Cruse's leadership, we spent long hours hiking over rough terrain in hot temperatures, swinging a metal detector—the best method for locating metal articles. After finding an artifact, we recorded it, marked its location using a Global Positioning System (GPS), and sent it to the laboratory for processing. The techniques we developed during the Red River War Project worked well in my fieldwork on Kit Carson's 1864 Adobe Walls campaign.

Unraveling Carson's 1864 military expedition, a forgotten part of Texas history, was exciting to me, and it naturally overflowed into my conversation. People listening caught my enthusiasm and encouraged me to write a book. Desiring to preserve my newly gained knowledge about Carson's Adobe Walls campaign, I determined to do that, though getting the information into book form was a formidable task for me and required the help of many people. To them I owe my appreciation.

Acknowledgments

Because of the large number of people who helped me in this undertaking, it is possible that I inadvertently missed someone. If so, please forgive me, for your input was important, and I thank you.

Foremost in my acknowledgements are the property owners. Without them, I could not have located the significant sites. Their ranches were at the core of my venture. An artist once told me, "You must sell yourself before you can sell your art work." My first task was selling the project and, thereby, myself to the landowners. I needed their help, so it was important for them to know what I was doing and why I was doing it. I found the ranchers to be gracious, generous, and extremely receptive in learning that their land played a part in a noteworthy historical event. Their ranches stretched from Quay County, New Mexico, to Hutchinson County, Texas, and included Ute Lake Ranch, Matt and Betty Irwin's Red Rock Land and Cattle Company, James Obar Ranch, Jeff and Ivy Ward Ranch, Bravo Ranch, Spring Creek Ranch, Griffin Ranch, Smith Ranches, Holt Ranch, Gordon Culwell Ranch, Burson Ranch, Jerry Rentfro Ranch, Jim and Kathleen Hill Ranch, Clint and Mindy Johnson and Brenda Michaels Ranch, LIT Ranch, George Brown Ranch, Mayo Ranch, Reimer Ranch, Brent Ranch, Coon Ranch, Sneed Ranch, Taylor Ranch, Lola Perky Starkey Ranch, McDowell Ranch, Herring Ranch, and Turkey Track Ranch. Special mention goes to the C. C. Whittenburg family and Board of Trustees of the Turkey Track Ranch for allowing me access to the 1864 Adobe Walls battle site; to Dale Scroggs for showing me around the Turkey Track; and to ranch manager Dennis Kern for his encouragement and assistance. To all the above ranchers, I owe my thanks for allowing me to traipse across their land.

Funding for my book came from the generous support of Joyce and Harold Courson and from the Texas Archeological Society Donor's Fund.

I extend my appreciation to Lola Jean Starkey, who was a great encourager and convinced me that I could—and should—write a book, and to her daughter Larri Jo Starkey, copy editor for American Quarter Horse Journal, who spent hours helping me put it in manuscript form.

Wyman Meinzer, State Photographer of Texas, and I spent three fun-filled days and two evenings capturing images of Carson's old road, campsites, battle site, and artifacts. Wyman uses light in a unique way to produce photographs that reach out to observers, inviting them to "come closer, and hear my story." I am grateful for Wyman's interest in my project and for his expert photography that enhanced my book about the history of the 1864 Adobe Walls Campaign. Thank you, Wyman.

Also thanks to Ken Pirtle for taking a photograph of the author to be used inside the book jacket.

The Carson family was generous with their time, knowledge, and resources. John Carson, great-grandson of Kit Carson, gave me a tour of Bent's Fort, Carson's last residence in Boggsville, Colorado; and the first burial site of Carson and his last wife Josefa. John supplied me with family information and photographs, including one of his great-grandmother, Josefa Carson. John introduced me to his aunt, Stella Carson Harrington, Kit Carson's granddaughter, who graciously talked with me about her life in Colorado. VeAnn Clark, Stella's granddaughter, furnished a photograph of Stella. I extend my gratitude to the Carson family.

I am indebted to two Kiowas. James Coverdale identified tools I found in the Kiowa village and created a ledger drawing, in the style of Kiowa artists, of the 1864 battle at Adobe Walls for my book. Sherman Chaddlesone of Anadarko, Oklahoma, allowed me to include a Kiowa tradition about Stumbling Bear at the First Battle of Adobe Walls. Each artist taught me about Kiowa culture in a way unique to his special interest.

Pilots Mickey Price, Jim Uselton, and Knut Mjolhus flew me over the Texas Panhandle to photograph the Fort Bascom–Adobe Walls Road. These aerial forays provided views impossible to get from the ground, saved wear and tear on my vehicle and feet, and helped me make an accurate map of the trail.

Meeting people was the most enjoyable part of fieldwork. I had meals with some ranchers in their homes; spent the night with a few; occasionally helped with ranch chores; and, with some, philosophized and drank tea as we sat on the tailgate of my pickup. Their memories flow through my mind and warm my heart, today, as I read my field notes.

Several folks at Fort Sill, Oklahoma, deserve credit for their contributions. Towana Spivey, Director and Curator for the Fort Sill National Historic Landmark Museum, furnished copies of the Millie Durgan letters and pictures of Millie Durgan Goombi and Stumbling Bear. Gordon Blaker, Director and Curator for the U.S. Army Field Artillery Museum, arranged for the firing of a twelve-pound mountain howitzer. Harry Shapell and his reenactment crew fired the artillery for a photograph shoot. Rod Roadruck, Exhibit Specialist of the U.S. Army Field Artillery Museum, provided photographs of the firing.

Clive Siegle, Professor of History at Richland College in Dallas, Texas, furnished ordnance information.

Alan Shields guided Jim Allison and me across his ranch in the Oklahoma Panhandle to old Camp Nichols, built by Kit Carson in 1865.

To all those individuals who shared my interest and helped me in ways distinctive to them, I owe my gratitude. The late Harry Myers of Santa Fe, New Mexico, had the unique ability to find documents related to my project and eagerly shared them with me. Rob Gromann, Amarillo Central Library, furnished sundry photographs. Duane Moore of Tucumcari, New Mexico, helped with fieldwork and provided photographs of Fort Bascom. Researcher, historian, and friend Scott Burgan shared information about Adobe Walls. Artist Richard Hogue furnished photographs of his paintings of the Adobe Walls battle. Doctor Douglas D. Scott, Department of Anthropology, University of Nebraska–Lincoln, analyzed and provided a report on bullets recovered from the 1864 Adobe Walls battle site. Doctor Scott Brosowske, Danny Witt, and James Coverdale of the Courson Archeological Research Laboratory helped identify metal artifacts.

I am grateful for artifact distribution maps created by Brett Cruse, Texas Historical Commission, and Luis Alvarado, Texas Parks and Wildlife Department; and colored battle maps developed by Roland Pantermuehl, Texas Historical Commission. All enhanced the presentation of my book.

Finding photographs of Adobe Walls battle participants proved difficult, and I am indebted to the people who assisted me. Descendants of Doctor George Courtright—Carolyn Lutz, Joann Runkle, and Marjorie Tudor—provided me with an image of the doctor, his diary, and a watercolor near the battle site made by an anonymous soldier on the day after the battle. Mike Kindt of Ashville, Ohio, sent me photographs of a display of Dr. Courtright and Colonel Carson from the Ashville Museum. Lorenzo Vigil, Chief Interpreter, Fort Union, New Mexico, provided a photograph of Nick Eggenhofer's painting, *First Battle of Adobe Walls.*

From June E. Bausman I received a photograph of her great-great-grandfather, Captain Charles Deus. I appreciate Christine E. White's permission to use excerpts from Deus's biography written by her father, Vernon H. Joyce.

Betsy Dunbar, Communication and Reader Services, American Baptist Historical Society, Atlanta, Georgia, furnished the Kiowa ledger drawings of the Battle of Adobe Walls.

For the first three or four years, I worked alone in the field, but later, Joe Faulkenberry, Rolla Shaller, Duane Moore, Todd Browning, Red Skelton, Danny Shipley, Mike Gilger, Wyman Meinzer, James Coverdale, John Carson, Walt and Isabel Davis, and Brett and Meg Cruse joined me in visiting sites, photographing, or swinging a metal detector. I appreciate their interest, company, and time.

I am indeed thankful for the fine institutions and societies where I did research and for interlibrary loan services.

Rolla Shaller, Joe Faulkenberry, and I cleaned, analyzed, and recorded hundreds of artifacts using the archeology laboratory at Panhandle-Plains Historical Museum. Other contributors from the museum were:

Doctor Jeff Indeck, Curator of Archeology (collections access and support); Michael R. Grauer, Associate Director for Curatorial Affairs and Curator of Art (ordnance information and photographs of paintings); Lisa Jackson, Curatorial Assistant, (computer work, scanning artifacts, and preparation of trail maps); Warren Stricker, Director, Research Center (archival work and photo scanning); Betty Bustos, Assistant Archivist (archival research); Mary Moore, collections access; and Paul McFadden, volunteer, ordnance division (identification).

I'm thankful for Judith Keeling, Editor-in-chief; Joanna Conrad, Assistant Editor and Journals Manager; Amanda Werts, Managing Editor; and Kellyanne Ure, Editorial Assistant, at Texas Tech University Press, who graciously welcomed me to their offices. I appreciate their patience, guidance, and assistance. Also, thanks goes to Dr. Eileen Johnson, Executive Director, Museum of Texas Tech University, for reading and commenting on the final copy of my manuscript.

I offer a heartfelt thanks to all of the readers for their time taken to carefully read the manuscript and offer suggestions to improve my presentation of the Carson Campaign.

Much thanks goes to my wife, Nadyne. She read my manuscript, made corrections, helped type sections of the text, worked on my computer when I messed it up, and listened to countless readings of my draft. She traveled with me to libraries, archives, and other resource centers, and while there, helped me search for documents and photographs. She located descendants of participants at the 1864 Adobe Walls battle, who shared photos and diaries of their ancestors. Nadyne did not go to the field and swing a metal detector, but she always showed interest when I brought in the rusty, metal artifacts, laid them out on the table, cleaned them, and told her their story.

Introduction

The rising sun glowed eerily across the fog-shrouded valley as I drove south toward the Canadian River. Here, in present-day Hutchinson County in the Texas Panhandle, William Bent, frontier trader, built the first Adobe Walls, an Indian trading post, in the mid-1840s. This is not to be confused with the second Adobe Walls built by buffalo hunters in 1874 a little over a mile to the north. It was here, in this valley, where Adobe and Bent creeks run into the South Canadian River, that Colonel Christopher Houston "Kit" Carson, Commander, New Mexico Volunteers, fought the Kiowas and Comanches in 1864.

On that early, fall morning, when I opened the ranch gate and stepped out into the heavy, damp air, I heard the moan of a pump jack pulling oil from a newly drilled well. In earlier days, *Comanchero carretas* and military wagons groaned as they cut ruts into the seepy, river flats of the Canadian, but today large oil field trucks roar up and down the network of caliche roads.

I closed the squeaky pipe-gate and continued south. Nearing the 1864 battle site, I slowed my pickup to take in the scene. The fog had lifted, except along the creeks where small wisps of mist danced above the water's surface. The penetrating sun shone brightly, exposing the

Fig. 1. Early morning fog near Adobe Walls. Photograph by author, 2004.

dusty valley in its brown, wintery coat. After parking my vehicle at the historical marker and climbing to the top of the prominent ridge behind it, I gazed at the panoramic view of the battlefield. I imagined Kiowa and Comanche warriors in full-war regalia charging toward the group of soldiers gathered around the ghostly remains of William Bent's adobe trading post. Time was the only barrier between the quiet, pastoral scene before me and the deafening action of that long-ago battle: Kit Carson barking orders, howitzers belching, guns firing, horses and mules squealing, Kiowas and Comanches yelling.

As I surveyed the battle site from the top of the ridge, I realized that the old seasoned scout had recognized its strategic advantage, for it was on this high area that he placed the two mountain howitzers.

The short engagement that Colonel Carson and his men had expected was not to be. As the day wore on,

more Indians appeared from down river and joined the fight. Lieutenant George Henry Pettis, Carson's artillery commander, estimated that, by mid-afternoon, at least three thousand warriors were fighting Carson's troops.[2] Carson, however, mentioned only one thousand Indians attacking his forces. The principal number was Kiowas with a small number of Comanches, Apaches, and Arapahos.[3]

Even though Carson's battle at Adobe Walls was a major engagement, historians have written little about it. Most people know Carson for his explorations as a mountain man; his adventures with John Charles Frémont, known as the Great Pathfinder, in California during the Mexican war; and his role in subduing the Navajos and Apaches in Arizona and New Mexico.[4] Perhaps the Adobe Walls battle received little attention because the numbing effects of the Civil War simply overshadowed it.

Fig. 2. Cannon Hill where Pettis placed two mountain howitzers used in the 1864 battle at Adobe Walls. *Foreground*: Adobe Walls battle monument. Photograph by author, 2010.

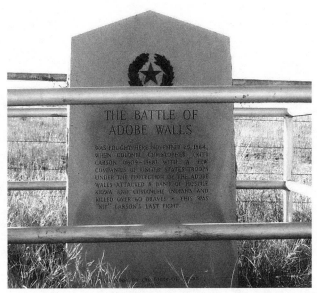

Fig. 3. First Battle of Adobe Walls monument erected by State of Texas, 1936. Photograph by author, 2004.

The surgeon assigned to the Adobe Walls campaign, Doctor George Stout Courtright, Assistant Surgeon, United States Army, wrote: "It will be remembered at this time, the war in the States was on in its intensity, and no thought was taken by the rank and file of what was doing in the territories and far west."[5]

The fact that chroniclers wrote little about Carson's campaign doesn't diminish its significance. Carson's strategy to penetrate deep into Indian Territory during the winter months helped reduce the loss of supplies and lessened the harassment of travelers along the Santa Fe Trail between the eastern states and Fort Union, New Mexico.

The early reading I did of other's writings lured me to the archives. Most of the information I found concerning the First Battle of Adobe Walls came from military and government records; Colonel Carson's report, which he wrote only a few days after the battle; the personal narrative Lieutenant Pettis wrote fourteen years after the battle; Dr. Courtright's memoir; and various descriptions of the conflict by Kiowas and Comanches.

Most historians who wrote about the 1864 Adobe Walls battle used the resources listed above. Of these, Edwin L. Sabin's *Kit Carson Days 1809–1868 Adventures in the Path of Empire—Revised Edition—Vol. II* (1935), and Tom Dunlay's *Kit Carson and the Indians* (2000) contain the most complete and accurate depictions of the battle.

To my knowledge, no author has written about Carson's route from Fort Bascom to Adobe Walls. For my information of the trail, I coupled the fieldwork I did with the journals of Lt. James W. Abert and François des Montaignes's notes about their expedition down the Canadian River in 1845. Abert and Montaignes chose the same route of approximately sixty miles and gave an excellent description of Carson's trail and camps in eastern New Mexico and the western Texas Panhandle.

Two books give an account of this trip. The first is *Through the Country of the Comanche Indians in the Fall of the Year 1845: The Journal of a U. S. Army Expedition Led by Lieutenant James W. Abert of the Topographical Engineers* (1970) by John Galvin. The second is *François des Montaignes: The Plains* (1972) coauthored by Nancy Alpert Mower and Don Russell.

Charles L. Kenner's *A History of New Mexican-Plains Indian Relations* (1969) gives a thorough background of the *Comanchero's* role, depicting the relationship of the populace of eastern New Mexico with the Indians of the Texas Panhandle. Most of the military Indian campaigns into Texas from New Mexico originated at Fort Union via Fort Bascom and down the Canadian River. Leo Oliva, in *Fort Union and the Frontier Army in the Southwest* (1993), provides an inside look at the Army of New Mexico's fort-life, ordnances, citizen relationships, and military expeditions.

Brett Cruse's *Battles of the Red River War: Archeological Perspectives on the Indian Campaign of 1874* (2008) is a practical guide to fieldwork methodology for historic military and Native American battle sites.

Fig. 4. *Battle of Adobe Walls,* oil, by Nick Eggenhofer (1896–1985). Courtesy of the National Park Service, Fort Union National Park.

Several other books proved useful as supportive references. Some contained useful information, while others exhibited unquestionable errors about events of the 1864 Adobe Walls battle. It is noteworthy that few versions of the battle are in complete agreement on troop movements, the number of Indian warriors, and the location of the Kiowa Indian village.

If you don't walk it, then don't write it came to me after reading authors whose works propagated mistakes, mainly because they did not combine their literary study with on-site surveys. To minimize this problem, I walked most of the distance of the trail, revisiting parts of it many times. In addition, my locating the Kiowa village makes my review the first account written from personal observation of the historic site and its relics. Also, the state's historical marker identified the general area of the battle site, but my survey was the first. Therefore, the unwelcome, yet inevitable, errors found in this narrative are mine alone. My intentional diligence was to avoid the mistakes made by some earlier writers: *I walked it, then I wrote.*

In addition, another cautious note is that Indians sometimes purposely gave incorrect information to whites. Case in point, Reverend Andrew Ellis Butterfield, a Methodist missionary to Apaches, Kiowas, and Comanches in Indian Territory in the 1890s, related one such incident from Stumbling Bear, a Kiowa interpreter for the famed ethnologist James Mooney:

"When Mr. Mooney had been gone about three weeks, Stumbling Bear said to me, [Butterfield]. 'Soon big Sunday paper will have big letters at top of page saying big story Stumbling Bear tell Mr. Mooney. Some big man like doctor, lawyer or preacher get paper, set on front porch, put his feet on board and set back in chair and read him, read him until he eyes almost go out, and all heap big lie.' Then his sides shook with laughter."[6]

The short supply of data that I collected from the archives was the catalyst that spurred me on. My goal was to find enough archeological evidence in the field to support my archival research.

As I trod the sod where Carson had traveled, a sense of duty enveloped me; I wanted to share what I had learned. I felt compelled to bring to light this piece of Texas Panhandle history. My plan was clear to me: I would walk the trail, do my fieldwork, and then write the story.

What began as a small venture turned into a fifteen-year project. Like the ardor of a first love, the more I learned, the deeper my passion grew. This undertaking, however, was not without disappointments, because human activity had obliterated the trail and a couple of the camps, and sometimes the trail and camps simply were not where I expected them to be. These setbacks made my eventual success even sweeter.

After driving about thirty thousand miles on highways and in the backcountry; walking a few hundred miles through yucca, sagebrush, grass burrs, and other sticky plants; suffering the bites of gray-back deer flies, gnats, and mosquitoes; dodging a few rattlesnakes; enduring hot weather, cold weather, and winds that could blow the bark off cedar posts, I often had to remind myself that I was there by choice.

The searches paid off, though. I located eighty percent of the wagon road from Fort Bascom to Adobe Walls and fourteen historic camps used by Indians, *Comancheros*, Carson's command, and other expeditions. A sufficient supply of identifiable artifacts confirmed that Colonel Carson and his men bivouacked in most of these camps.

Carson's campaign of 1864 was the focus of my project, but the stories of other travelers and the artifacts they left provided important details that I wove into the fabric of my story.

Abbreviations

ave average
CF center-fire
cm centimeter
dia diameter
dm depressed mark
dmdc depressed mark in depressed channel
EP external primed
gr grain
Ht, ht height

in inch
IP internal primed
Lgth, lgth length
RF rim-fire
rmdc raised mark in depressed channel
Thk, thk thick, thickness
Wdth, wdth width
Wt, wt weight

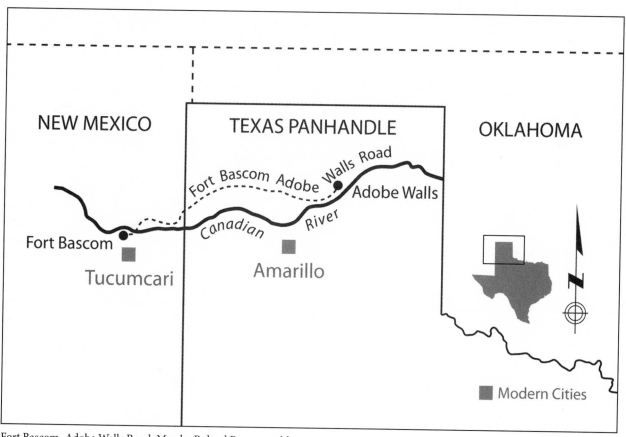

Fort Bascom–Adobe Walls Road. Map by Roland Pantermuehl.

Part I

Colonel Kit Carson's 1864 Adobe Walls Campaign

Chapter 1
Events Leading Up To the Adobe Walls Battle

During the summer of 1864, the United States Army at Fort Union was on high alert. The military was in conflict with the Kiowas and Comanches because of their raiding in eastern New Mexico and along the Santa Fe Trail. Apprehensive traders and settlers lived in fear. To ameliorate their anxieties and to keep trade open on the Santa Fe Trail (the lifeline for supplies coming from the east to Fort Union) it was imperative that troops quell the unrest.

As summer passed, incidents increased. In August, Indian raiders killed five Americans at Lower Spring on the Cimarron Route in southwest Kansas and took five wagons belonging to a Mr. Allison. Another train lost 130 mules. Over the next few months, other trains lost about a hundred oxen. Indians killed the wagon master of a government contract train and stole all the oxen.[1]

Indian raids, however, weren't the military's only problem. *Comancheros*—Spanish, Mexican, and Indian traders—who lived in the villages of northeastern New Mexico and along the Rio Grande, also thwarted the army's efforts. The term *Comanchero* first appeared in Spanish documents in 1813, replacing *vecinos* or "neighbors." The nomadic Comanches, who dominated the Plains, were the main patrons of this mixed bag of traders.[2]

Comancheros impressed early travelers with their slovenly habits of dress and hygiene. In 1839, Josiah Gregg (merchant, explorer, naturalist, and author),

Fig. 5. *Return of the War Party,* pastel, by Harold Bugbee, 1953. A common sight in northeastern New Mexico in the 1860s. #1650/21. Courtesy of the Panhandle Plains Historical Museum.

Fig. 6. *Comanchero Traders,* mural, by Ben Carlton Mead. Courtesy of the Panhandle Plains Historical Museum.

hauled his wares to Santa Fe, New Mexico. Some of those traders joined his group in what is now Oldham County, Texas, and traveled with him to Santa Fe. Gregg described them as being of the lower class of people in frontier villages. They travelled to the Plains with only a few dollars' worth of trinkets, a batch of hard bread, and a bag of *pinole*. According to Gregg, most *Comancheros* were satisfied to roam the Plains and trade their paltry goods for one or two head of livestock.[3]

A group of Mexican traders from Taos camped near Adobe Walls in 1845, coincidentally with John C. Frémont's third expedition. One lieutenant, James William Abert, wrote that the *Comancheros* dressed in jackets with stripes running transversely, large baggy breeches extending to the knee, long stockings, moccasins, and conical-crowned sombreros—exhibiting, altogether, a poor and shabby appearance.[4]

William H. Chamberlain, in his 1849 diary, presented a scenario of traders at Rocky Dell near the Texas-New Mexico state line. The overhangs in the bluffs afforded protection from the elements, making it a favorite site for *Comancheros* to hawk their goods to Comanches and other travelers along the Santa Fe Trail. When Chamberlain's train was at Rocky Dell, a group of *Comancheros* on a trading expedition to the Comanches

occupied the crude shelters. They offered to trade corn and hard crackers to the caravan.[5] Prior to the Civil War era and into the early 1870s, the involvement of the New Mexican traders with the Plains tribes was a knotty issue for the U.S. Army. The traders swapped contraband of lead shot, powder, guns, and whiskey for buffalo hides and stolen livestock.[6]

Not only did the *Comancheros* make a living by trading with the Indians, they also turned their allegiance to whatever other venture seemed profitable. Thus, in the early part of the Civil War, they acted as spies hired by the U.S. Army to gather information about Confederate soldiers in Texas. Conversely, near the end of the war they were informing the Plains Indians of the whereabouts of U.S. soldiers whose assignment was to suppress Indian uprisings.

This led General James Henry Carleton, commander of the military department of New Mexico, to place restrictions on the *Comanchero*–Native American trade and ordered the arrest of traders going to the Texas Plains. As expected, the order was hard to enforce because the *Comancheros* knew the land well and, thus, avoided military posts and pickets.[7]

The doomed trade restrictions suffered internally as well. Most of the troops along the eastern New Mexico

Fig. 7. Brigadier General James Henry Carleton, Commander, Department of New Mexico. #1986-11/11. Courtesy of the Panhandle Plains Historical Museum.

frontier were New Mexicans or longtime residents, and their sympathies lay with the traders, making it convenient to overlook orders to stop the trade.[8]

Carleton had Carson's troops occupied with the Navajo campaign in 1863, but by fall 1864, the U.S. government had placed the Navajos on a reservation along the Pecos River near Fort Sumner. With this action over, Carleton turned his attention toward an offensive operation against the Kiowas and Comanches to the east. He would send U.S. forces from Fort Bascom down the Canadian River and on to the plains of Texas.[9] Who better to lead the operation than his tried-and-true field commander, Kit Carson?

Carson, accustomed to marching orders, probably wasn't surprised to read that his next assignment was to organize an expedition under his command to "proceed against hostile Kiowas and Comanches."[10]

Since the late 1840s, Colonel Carson had been in the saddle most of the time, either serving his country or tending his personal ventures that required his being away from home, his wife Josefa, and their children.

The 1864 Kiowa-Comanche campaign came a little

harder for Carson because he was fifty-five years old and in uncertain health. He had just finished the Mescalero Apache–Navajo Expedition of 1862–1863, and the constant marching over torturous miles of rough terrain had inflamed an old wound suffered in a fall with a horse.[11] Carson knew a winter campaign would further aggravate his injury, but he never wavered in accepting his orders.

As early as August 1864, General Carleton initiated plans to get Colonel Carson and his troops into the field against the Kiowas and Comanches. He wrote Carson at Fort Sumner asking for at least two hundred Apaches and Navajos to go with troops to fight Comanches.[12] When this did not materialize, Carleton turned northward to a large landowner, Lucien Bonaparte Maxwell, who informed him that two hundred or more Utes were willing and ready to go out and attack the Indians on the Plains.[13]

Carleton had a dual motive in using Indians to complement the troops on this expedition. Many of the volunteer troops were due to muster out of the military in the fall, leaving a shortage in the infantry and cavalry.[14] Additionally, in case of an all-out war with the Plains

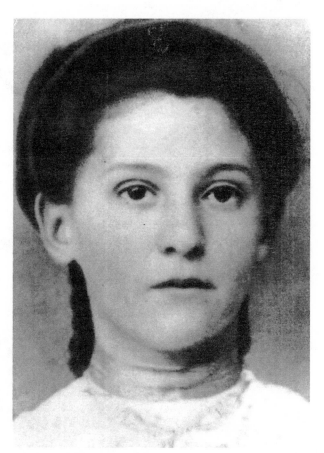

Fig. 8. Colonel Christopher Houston "Kit" Carson (1809–1868), commander of the First Battle of Adobe Walls, 1864. American frontiersman and legend, mountain man, trapper, explorer, scout, Indian agent, rancher, soldier. Son of Lindsey and Rebecca Robinson Carson. #1972/130. Courtesy of the Panhandle Plains Historical Museum.

Fig. 9. Josefa Jaramillo Carson (1828–1868), Kit Carson's third wife. Daughter of Francisco and Apolonia Vigil Jaramillo. Carson was thirty-four and Josefa was fourteen when they married on February 6, 1843, at Taos, New Mexico. Courtesy of the Jess Carson family.

Indians, Carleton wanted the Utes to commit themselves to the U.S. military and not ally with the Comanches and Kiowas.[15]

The directive that Carleton sent immediately involved Carson in negotiations with the Utes. He wrote: "Your knowledge of the haunts of the Indians of the plains, and the great confidence the Ute Indians have in you as a friend and as a leader, point to yourself as the most fitting person to organize, direct, and bring this enterprise to a successful issue."[16]

Carson replied that he had met with Kaneache, a Ute chief, who felt disposed to go with the military on this campaign against the Plains Indians. In return, the Utes needed blankets, shirts, arms, and ammunition, as many of them were virtually destitute.[17]

Later, Carson wrote Carlton that he had one hundred Utes and Apaches ready to go. They needed one hundred rifles with ammunition. To combat the cold

and snow, he requested 120 blankets and shirts, and for Kaneache, an extra horse. For the expedition, Carson requested two howitzers and three hundred mounted troops.[18]

By the last of October, Carleton finalized the arrangement for supplies needed by the Indians. He sent Carson a letter of authority to get one hundred rifles from Captain Shoemaker, who was in charge of ordnance at Fort Union.[19]

In addition to the logistics of men, supplies, and equipment for the campaign, was the question of the location of the winter camp of the Kiowas and Comanches. The answer to this came when Lieutenant Colonel Francisco P. Abreu reported that, on October 7, 1864, a corporal from Company K had received information from Mexicans recently returned from trading with the Indians, that the Comanches were camped beyond the North Palo Duro Creek about two hundred miles northeast of Fort Bascom. The traders estimated the Comanches number to be about three thousand.[20]

Carson set in motion his plan to move supplies by wagon to Adobe Walls on the Canadian River and to operate from there with pack mules toward the Palo Duro.[21] By November 10, all contingents of the expedition had arrived at Fort Bascom.[22] Seventy-five Utes and Jicarilla Apaches accompanied Colonel Carson. Sitting on ready at Bascom were fourteen officers, three hundred twenty-one enlisted men, twenty-seven wagons, an ambulance, and two mountain howitzers.[23]

Carson was soon to learn, at the battle at Adobe Walls, just how important these artillery pieces were. The mountain howitzer was lightweight and versatile. The barrel and carriage together weighed five hundred pounds, allowing disassembly and carriage by mule-back in mountainous country. In less-rough terrain, troopers secured the little howitzer to a prairie carriage behind a limber pulled by horses or mules. The cannons fired a twelve-pound spherical case shot, canister, or shell (all effective in short range).[24]

Serving in this campaign under Commander

Fig. 10. Ute chief Kaneache. Courtesy of Steve Keller, Keller Mining Bureau collection.

Fig. 11. Fort Bascom, New Mexico. The fort was in operation from 1863 to 1870. Established to control illicit trade between *Comancheros*, Comanches, and Kiowas. *Orientation*: Photograph taken looking northwest. Photographer: Lillie Gerhart Anderson, 1931. Courtesy of Duane Moore.

Fig. 12. Mountain howitzer on a prairie carriage, Fort Sill, Oklahoma. Similar to Carson's two cannons used in the battle at Adobe Walls. Photograph by author, 2010.

Colonel Christopher Houston "Kit" Carson, First New Mexico Volunteers, were Cavalry Commander Major William A. McCleave, First Regiment, California Volunteers; Infantry Commander Lieutenant Colonel Francisco P. Abreu, First New Mexico Volunteer Infantry; Artillery Commander Lieutenant George Henry Pettis, Company K, First Regiment of Infantry, California Volunteers; Doctor George Stout Courtright, Assistant Surgeon, United States Volunteers; and Lieutenant Charles Haberkorn, First Cavalry, New Mexico Volunteers, in charge of Ute and Jicarilla Apache scouts.[25]

New Mexico and California Volunteers made up most of Carson's command. The California troops marched into southern New Mexico in 1862 to shore up defenses against Confederate troops and Indians. The California Volunteers were well supplied and armed. The California military furnished each cavalryman with "a good horse, a good Sharp's carbine, a good revolver, Navy size, and a good sabre, ground sharp."[26]

The New Mexico troops were not as fortunate as their California cohorts were because New Mexico did not have the resources to equip a first-class army, as did California. Colonel Edward Richard Sprigg Canby, Commander, Department of New Mexico, in the spring of 1861, began raising an army of volunteers. The U.S. government supplied them with arms and equipment, but issued no clothing. Later, the army added a clothing allowance of $3.50 per month as an incentive.[27]

The arms distributed to the New Mexico Volunteers by the U.S. government were of assorted calibers, with some very old models. During the retreat at Adobe Walls in 1864, Dr. Courtright noted that some of the New Mexico troops had old muzzle-loading rifles, and they had become so dirty that it was almost impossible to load them.[28] The issuance of arms with a variety of calibers to the New Mexican volunteers caused problems in getting the right ammunition to the different companies.

The U.S. military, in signing up New Mexico recruits, advertised for "able-bodied men." It is interesting to note that the officials did not consider a "defective left eye" or a "slight injury to the left hand" to be disabling.[29]

Prior to the 1864 Adobe Walls campaign, both the California and New Mexico Volunteers had served admirably while engaged against the Confederate Army, the Mescalero Apaches, and the Navajos. These soldiers were experienced fighters, knowledgeable in the field of Indian warfare. Their attributes were of immeasurable worth to Carson during the Kiowa-Comanche expedition.

Carson's troops worked with excitement as they harnessed teams, packed and pulled canvas sheets over the loaded wagons, then made a final check of weapons before moving out on the long march to Adobe Walls. New recruits probably were somewhat nervous as they anticipated their first action against the Comanches and Kiowas on the plains of Texas. For Carson's contingency—all was ready and the action lay ahead.

Fig. 13. Remington Model 1858 "New Model" army revolver, .44-caliber revolver, *circa* 1865. Photograph by Ralph Duke, 2011. O. T. Nicholson Collection. Courtesy of Panhandle Plains Historical Museum.

Fig. 14. Colt Model 1851 Navy revolver, .36-caliber revolver, *circa* 1855. Photograph by Ralph Duke, 2011. O. T. Nicholson Collection. Courtesy of Panhandle Plains Historical Museum.

Fig. 15. Springfield Model 1842 U.S. percussion musket, .69 caliber, 1851. *Note*: New Mexico Volunteers also used a .58-caliber Springfield. Photograph by Ralph Duke, 2011. O. T. Nicholson Collection. Courtesy of Panhandle Plains Historical Museum.

Fig. 16. Sharps Model 1863 percussion rifle, .52 caliber. Photograph by Mike Oldham, 2011. Courtesy Mike Oldham Collection.

Chapter 2
Fort Bascom to Ute Creek

With wagons loaded, scouts out, troopers in their saddles, and infantry in formation, Carson, with a wave and a shout, ordered his command to commence down the Canadian River toward Comanche country. Soldiers yelled goodbyes to their compadres remaining at Fort Bascom as they marched off into the crisp, fall morning.

Cottonwoods along the river stood stark and leafless in the morning sun; bright green junipers on the bluffs contrasted with the red earth. After a few miles of struggling along the rough road, the mule teams, urged on by the teamster's commands, settled into a rhythmic motion. Supply crates jostled into their traveling spots as wagons bounced over rocks and ruts. Artifacts retrieved

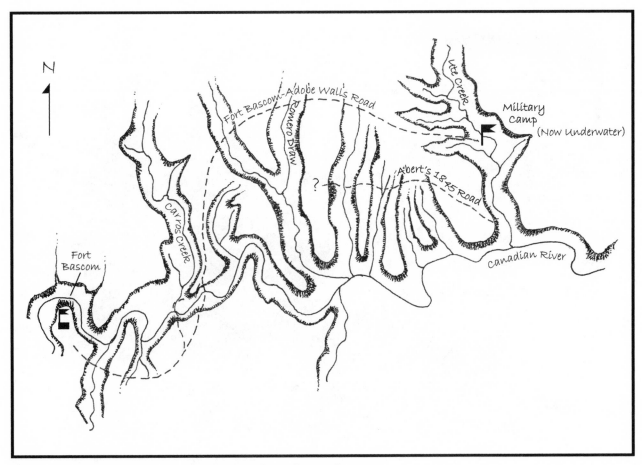

Map 2.1. Fort Bascom to Ute Creek. Illustrated by author and Lisa Jackson, 2011.

Fig. 17. Aerial view of Canadian River meanders near Texas-New Mexico state line. Photograph by author, 2010.

into Texas, forming meanders that have snake-like appearances. For eons, the river has followed its nine-hundred-mile course from the Sangre de Cristo Mountains of New Mexico to the Arkansas River, passing through the southeastern corner of Colorado, the northeastern corner of New Mexico, and on across the Texas Panhandle into Oklahoma.

A powerful force in its formative period, the high-energy flow of water of the Canadian River cut deep canyons into the sandstone and siltstone. In a few areas along the river's path, erosion or faulting removed the bluffs, allowing deposition of sand and gravel. Springs flowing from these deposits formed verdant oases that dotted the arid land.

The river has long served man and animal in its lengthy history as the lifeblood of natives, travelers, and fauna. Animals—deer, bear, beaver—in need of water, laid the first paths, followed by indigenous peoples whose trodden tracks gave way to horse trails. This highway-in-the-desert was crucial to the development of the ancient trading economy that existed between the

nearly a century and a half later attest that rough roads did, indeed, take a toll on wagons: bow staples popped out, bolts snapped, and harness chains tore apart.

Travel was difficult, but not impossible, along the Canadian River, which flows eastward from Fort Bascom

Fig. 18. *Carreta* at a pueblo, *circa* mid-1800s. *Comancheros* and *ciboleros* used this means of transportation while trading and hunting on the plains of Texas. From the Photographic Archives, Las Vegas Citizens' Committee for Historic Preservation.

Puebloans to the west and the fourteenth- and fifteenth-century Plains Village People living along the Canadian River and its tributaries in what is now the Texas Panhandle. The river's steep bluffs and side canyons made accessibility difficult and limited the number of places for crossings, yet those luxuriant spots have been trade sites for hundreds of years.

Later came the Plains Indians, having rounded up mustangs lost in the sixteenth century by Spanish explorers. Riding as though one with their horses, the Indians galloped into Spanish villages to trade or raid. In 1601, 263 years before Kit Carson's expedition to Adobe Walls, Don Juan de Oñate y Salazar (1550–1626)—also dubbed "the Spaniard" and "the Last Conquistador"—savored the shelter of the Canadian River. He wrote, "the *Magdalena* is the best river in all of the Indies."[1]

Then came the creaking *carretas* of *ciboleros* on bison-hunting trips and *Comancheros* on trading expeditions with Plains Indians. These capitalists found sanc-tuary in the same rest areas as earlier peoples. When it was time to travel, drivers walked beside their cumbersome, wooden-wheeled carts and cracked their whips mercilessly at the oxen, heading them out of the river bottom and up to the Indian paths along the headsprings.

Carson, adopting the ancient wisdom of those who had gone before, followed their early trails on his journey to Adobe Walls. Military records revealed neither the precise route of Carson's troops, nor the exact place they crossed the river. One thing is certain—the crusty, old colonel knew his men and animals could not survive without water, and for that reason, he either hung close to the river or camped at headsprings along the route.

Colonel Andrew Wallace Evans, commander of the Canadian River Expedition in the winter of 1868, reported that his column followed the same road Carson had taken in 1864. Evans, in describing his route on the trail, wrote that he traveled east, crossed to the left bank

Fig. 19. Aerial view of the Canadian River crossing between Carros Creek and Fort Bascom. Photograph by author, 2010.

of the Canadian at Bergman's Ranch four miles below Bascom then left the river at Red River Springs, and struck it again about twenty miles above Adobe Walls.[2]

In 1866, two years before Evans's trip, Lieutenant Colonel Silus Newton of Fort Bascom used the same crossing, which he said was three miles below the fort.[3] Duane Moore, of Tucumcari, New Mexico, told me in 2006, that on the Canadian River about three miles below the ruins of Fort Bascom, he had seen a natural rock crossing, and that, in 1960, ranchers were still using it.[4] I cite these three instances describing the same spot, because I think they pinpointed the place Carson's soldiers forded the river.

Crossing the river aroused the tempers of horses, mules, and men. Wagon drivers cracked their whips, wagon pushers grunted, and animals strained before the wagons finally landed on the opposite bank. With the bluffs behind them, the group paused only long enough to rest and make necessary repairs.

Pettis reported that after some difficulty in crossing to the north side of the Canadian River, the expedition was well on the warpath before noon.[5]

Carson, like previous travelers, moved far enough north to avoid most of the ravines and deep canyons feeding into the Canadian River. After leaving the river, near the mouth of modern-day Carros Creek, the column worked its way northeastward, up a valley and over gravel ridges, to Romero Draw, a distance of about four miles. There the command turned east and continued along the old road toward Ute Creek.

They likely traveled the same route that commander of the Comanche Expedition, Major Charles Frederick Ruff, took in 1860 on his way to Adobe Walls. Ruff followed a wagon road marked out the previous fall by Brevet Captain John Porter Hatch, Regiment of the Mounted Riflemen, New Mexico, which he found to be "a most excellent wagon road."[6]

Even on *a most excellent road*, travel was exhausting. Infantry, cavalry, wagons, horses, mules, cattle, and howitzers stretched into a long column, pounding the earth into powder that rose up and clouded the convoy. The choice position in this city-on-the-move was to the fore, ahead of noise, dust, and animal droppings.

This fact did not go unnoticed by army doctor, George Courtright, who declared, "In traveling on the march, I always rode with the first company, as it is so much more pleasant to be in the van or with the vanguard, and then I would be in position to choose a suit-

Fig. 20. Dr. George C. Courtright, Assistant Surgeon, U.S. Army. Carson's surgeon in 1864 at the First Battle of Adobe Walls. Image courtesy of Carolyn Lutz, great granddaughter of Dr. Courtright, 2011.

able place for my hospital, and often had time to take a good rest before the last of the troops would get into camp."[7]

By the end of the first day, the caravan had traveled thirteen miles from the Canadian crossing to Ute Creek. The long string of wagons rolled cautiously down the gravel slopes into the creek bottom. Lieutenant Pettis said the command bivouacked near the mouth of Ute Creek,[8] but neither he nor Carson described the camp. Today, it lies beneath the waters of Ute Lake with all evidence of human activity buried.

Lieutenant James William Abert, with the United States Topographical Engineers, described the area in 1845. "After descending 150 to 200 feet, we found ourselves in the bottom of the main river, just at the point where it is joined by the *Arroyo de los Yutas*. . . . Two deeply cut ruts gave to the trail the appearance of a wagon road, but the sometimes-variable parallelism showed that they were formed principally by the feet of passing animals. . . . The creek is well timbered, but the high rocks conceal it until we reach the very verge. . . . This must be the 'Spanish Crossing' where the people of New Mexico pass on their way to Comanche country."[9]

In Abert's account of vegetation growing along Ute Creek, he described *musquit* or *muskeet* as covered with long, saber-formed legumes. In addition to "mesquite," he mentioned grapevines, soapberries, hackberries, cacti, and sandburs.[10] All still grow near the creek, except where Ute Lake has encroached.

Trees, water, and concealment made the spot a fine camp. The territory was unfamiliar to most of Carson's troops because few had ever ventured east of Ute Creek. Some, though, had been unlucky in the past, and had drawn orders while at Fort Bascom to serve as pickets along the creek. In spite of the fineness of the site, Carson's soldiers had to deal with the annoying sandburs and cacti that Abert chronicled.

With lookouts stationed on nearby high points, livestock settled in, and equipment repaired, the soldiers, with grub in their stomachs, rolled up in their blankets for the night. Though fire logs burned to embers, sleep did not come easy, and for good reason. The Ute and Jicarilla Apache scouts enlivened the night with whooping and hollering as they performed war dances. Pettis said their chants were "intolerable" and lasted until nearly daybreak.[11]

Chapter 3
Ute Creek to Red River Springs

Soldiers awoke from a night that was too short. Cobwebs of slumber vanished as the men recollected the groaning, moaning Indians of the prior evening. The war dance that stirred the emotions of the seventy-five Utes and Jicarilla Apaches, awakening a profound sense of purpose, was, to the soldiers, a remarkable irritation. It was not the last night of disturbed sleep, but rather the first, as the nocturnal warpath rituals occurred every night and lasted until nearly daybreak. Until the troopers got used to the discordant war chants of so great a number of Indians, rest was difficult.[1]

Sleep-deprived and grumpy, the soldiers packed their bedrolls and ate breakfast. Each man tended his assignment in breaking camp: repacking gear, harnessing teams, and saddling horses. The scouts moved out first, followed by Carson and others in the prescribed order. Slowly, the contingent made its way up the slopes on the east side of Ute Creek to a flat prairie, traveling by easy stages on a practicable wagon road along the north bank of the Canadian River.[2]

The long train moved almost due east for five miles. Just beyond the point where Logan, New Mexico, now stands, the road bore to the northeast. It then led the caravan around a wide bow of the Canadian River, where three canyons intersected at the top of the bend.

This section of road was not one of the "easy stages" of travel mentioned by Carson. Mules labored under the weight of heavy-laden wagons. Wheels sank into the soft earth, making the load seem even heavier than it was and taxing the teams as they plowed across the irregular

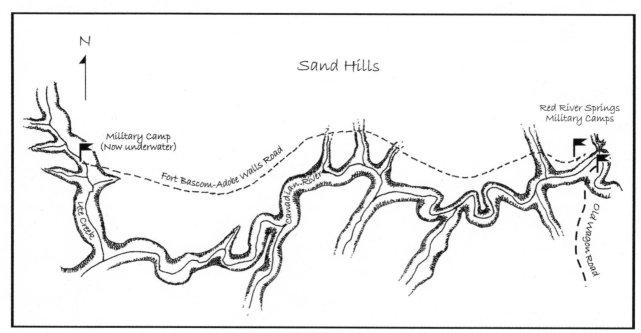

Map 3.1. Ute Creek to Red River Springs. Illustrated by author and Lisa Jackson, 2011.

terrain. After about three miles, the rough country gave way to an easier, firmer road on a short-grass prairie near the river.

Looking back to the west, Carson saw the familiar landmark, Tucumcari Mountain, disappear behind bluffs south of the river. As the column left the canyons and lost sight of the famous mountain, they were, without doubt, in unfamiliar territory.

Men, mules, and horses settled down while crossing five or six miles of a gently rolling plain flanked by a deep river canyon on the right and sand hills on the left. Other than the need to be ever watchful for Comanches and Kiowas, travel along this section of road was monotonous. Minds, freed from the demands of trudging through sand, pondered the morrow. *What would the day bring?*

In 1845, Lieutenant Abert travelled this same thoroughfare and described it as having scarcely any obstructions, although he observed several broken axle-trees of Spanish carts that had preceded him along the road. On the way, they found quantities of luscious plums on the sand hills, even though some wanted a little longer exposure to the ripening sun.[3]

The monotony for Carson's entourage did not last long. The road reverted to sand and rose gradually toward a deep canyon before turning away from the river to a point where the bluffs were not as steep. With brakes set and teamsters reining in hard, the wagons slid and rolled to the bottom of the incline. Today, a ranch road parallels the old wagon trail and crosses the canyon at the same spot. From the top of the hill down both sides of the canyon, broken parts—wagon bolts, nails, horseshoes, and horseshoe nails—litter the way, evidence of the price travelers paid for passage. Skeletal pieces of wagons and tack lie about, whispering a silent story from their dusty grave—a tale of strained muscles, sweat, and profanity.

Leaving the canyon, Carson's group veered to the southeast for a ways before turning back due east. Bluffs, high on the south side of the river, contrast the lower, north side, manifesting ancient geologic activity. The road Carson followed sloped downward onto a mile-long expanse of pleasant, level land. Gravel terraces, with springs flowing out of them, stretched to the river. At the northeast end of the flat, cottonwood trees grew in a

Fig. 21. Red River Springs still produces one hundred gallons of water per minute. Photograph by author, 2005.

small, spring-watered valley. As years passed, encroaching sand hills suffocated the spring.

Just beyond the valley, sandstone bluffs rise where the river makes a sharp bend to the southeast. At the base of the cliff, water flows from the porous sandstone, producing one hundred gallons of water per minute, almost one hundred fifty years after Carson's visit to the site.[4]

This Hilton-on-the-trail, a mile-long oasis, acquired the name Red River Springs by early travelers but locals today call it Ritter Springs. So much like a piece of Eden was it that denizens through the ages benefited from its offerings.

Visitors today observe stone hearths laid bare by modern road cuts and erosion, dotting the landscape. Manos and crude cutting tools lie scattered around the ancient hearths. In time immemorial, dwellers cooked wild game over the open fire pits, moving to the sandstone outcrops high above the river to grind grass seeds, hackberries, plums, and dried meats in bedrock mortars that are now ten to eighteen inches deep. Even today, wind blowing across the cliff affords an escape from buffalo gnats and deer flies that make a nuisance to humankind down near the river.

The prehistoric people vanished years ago, replaced by inhabitants that are more recent. Written and oral records, along with recovered artifacts, reveal that Native Americans, *Comancheros*, buffalo hunting *ciboleros*, Mexican *pastores*, cattlemen, rustlers, moonshiners, early ranchers, and the military have frequented these

Fig. 22. Bedrock mortars northwest of Red River Springs. Native Americans used these mortars for grinding seeds and nuts. Photograph by author, 2005.

springs. Each group contributed to the abundant proof that Red River Springs enjoyed a long history as a popular place to camp.

Abert, in his field notes for September 3, 1845, recorded that his group again camped in the Canadian bottom, near a Spanish camp of recent occupation. Remaining were a few poles upon which some withered leaves still remained, showing that they were of the present season. The pickets used to tie animals were still standing.[5] François des Montaignes, traveling with Abert, described their camp as being about a mile upriver from the spring emitting from the sand hills. He distinguished the old camp as being Indian, not Spanish.[6]

After setting up camp, Abert burned off an area for campfires, a customary procedure for prairie travelers. Men stood by with blankets ready to beat out flames that spread beyond the desired area, but this controlled burn got out of hand and blazed across the thick, dry growth like a demon. It raced from the grass to the tall, dry reeds below the camp and into the trees along the riverbank. Soon it roared through the brush on the bluffs. Dancing across the prairie, it devoured everything in its path.[7]

With extreme effort and a providential wind blowing away from their camp, the frantic flame-beaters prevented their tents and equipment from burning. After securing the camp, the men picked their way around boulders to the top of the bluff where they watched the hungry flames consume the prairie. By nightfall, the fire lit the sky with a red glow. Near the horizon, flames licked the night.[8]

Abert's contingent stood in amazement as dark clouds formed and the earth-bound inferno sent bright, red reflections onto the underside of clouds, forming a "chiaro oscuro, which would have charmed a lover of Rembrandt." Though they were out of the path of the firestorm, the unmistakable smell of burning grass wafted their way, and an occasional wave of heat touched their faces. The eerie, low murmuring of whirling eddies reached their ears. It was a scene of "grand sublimity."[9]

The area where Abert camped looks much the same today, its beauty marred only by a barbed wire fence and the crumbled remains of an early, rock ranch house beneath the large cottonwoods. Tall reeds, like those mentioned by Abert, still grow below the campsite in the backwater of the Canadian River. Green patches of

Fig. 23. The hill with boulders from which Abert's detail watched the prairie fire on November 26, 1845. Photograph by author, 2005.

grapevines, cottonwoods, hackberries, and other vegetation line the riverbank.

Carson and his troops marched into the historical drama surrounding this little haven of refuge. As the sun dropped low in the sky, men and animals trudged onto the grassy flat above the river. Canvas-covered wagons rolled along, passing in review to the inanimate audience of rocky cliffs to the south.

The wooded basin was too small to accommodate Carson's command, so his men corralled the wagons on the flats where they unhitched the mules and horses and watered them at the springs of the river. Troops stationed themselves and the stock close to camp because they were deep into Indian Territory. By nightfall, the Utes and Jicarilla Apaches returned from scouting and gave a negative report to Carson—*no Indians.*

Sergeants posted pickets along the fringe of the camp. The rest of the troopers, weary from the day's travel, and with their chores behind them, squatted around campfires. They prepared smokes and lit them with twigs from the fires, leaned back on rocks or huddled on their haunches, and rehashed the day or talked of other things.

Flames in the campfire turned to embers. With their smokes finished and their tales told, the soldiers turned in—except for the Utes and Jicarilla Apaches who were just warming up for their nightly war dance.

So much for a good night's sleep.

Fig. 24. Bluffs across the river from Carson's campsite at Red River Springs. Photograph by author, 2006.

November 14, 1864

Carson, for some reason, laid over an extra day at Red River Springs. Perhaps the troops needed time to rest before leaving the safety of the river on their march across the soft, troublesome sand hills.[10]

As the sun rose on their second day at Red River Springs, men rolled up their uncomfortable blankets, drew their rations, and bunched in small groups to cook breakfast. Standard fare was salt pork, hardtack, hot coffee, and an occasional can or ration of dried vegetables. Dipping hardtack into coffee made it more palatable. A custom of Hispanic troopers was to fry softened hardtack and sweeten it with shavings from a cone of *piloncillo* (unprocessed brown sugar).

As they stood or squatted to eat, the cold, heavy November air shrouded them in campfire smoke. The aromas of food cooking and coffee brewing mingled with the unmistakable twang of livestock and wafted through the camp.

With breakfast over, it was time to go to work. Lieutenant Haberkorn likely dispatched scouts to explore the country that lay ahead, as it was usual for the army, whether encamped or on the move, to reconnoiter each morning.

Noise rose from the camp as soldiers prepared for the next leg. Farriers checked and reshod mules and horses; teamsters repaired harnesses, adjusted supplies in wagons, and filled water barrels; cavalrymen fed and watered mounts; foot soldiers sought an opportunity to rest their weary feet while assisting with camp chores. Officers barked orders and looked important while overseeing these activities.

Evidence of military camp life presents itself today in the abundance of artifacts. Lying beneath the sod are harness buckles, worn horseshoes, horseshoe nails, unfired bullets, storage box bands, leaded cans, and military buttons—many of which I located with my metal detector and recovered from the site.

Mrs. White

During the stopover of the 1864 Adobe Walls contingence at Red River Springs, Carson told his men about a small group of white travelers attacked by Jicarilla Apaches in the fall of 1849. He described how the scouting group, of which he was a member, assailed the Indian village in an attempt to rescue Mrs. White. "In his usual graphic manner," Carson pointed out the site of the camp and the place they found Mrs. White's body.[11]

James M. White, husband of Ann Dunn White, was a merchant in Santa Fe. In 1849, he returned to his home in Warsaw, Missouri, to move his wife and small daughter, Virginia, along with two servants, a mulatto named Ben Bushman and an unnamed black woman, to New Mexico. They bought passage to Santa Fe on the wagon train of François Xavier "Francis" Aubry.[12]

Nearing Santa Fe in late September, they encountered cold, stormy weather. Aubry's wagon master, William Calloway, prepared to go on to Santa Fe for fresh mules. White, thinking it safe to separate from the main caravan and eager to get his family to safe, comfortable quarters, decided to go along, as did a German named Lawberger and two New Mexicans.[13]

On, or about, October 24, 1849, Apaches attacked the group of nine a few miles east of Point of Rocks on the Santa Fe Trail in northeastern New Mexico, killing the six men and taking the two women and the little girl captive.[14]

When news of the death of the men and the abduction of the women reached Santa Fe, Colonel John Munroe, Commander, Ninth Military Department, New Mexico, immediately sent Captain William Grier into the field with all available men.[15] Grier's combined force of ninety soldiers included the forty-two men in his company, Company I, First Dragoons, New Mexico; and forty men from Captain Valdez's Mounted New Mexican Volunteers. Three guides accompanied the soldiers: Robert Fisher; Antoine Leroux (Joaquin Antoine Leroux or Watkins Leroux), a famous scout from Taos; and Kit Carson, who joined them at Rayado.[16] The experience of these three guides—veterans in mountain and prairie life, trailing Apaches, and knowing the customs and cunning of Indians—made them invaluable to Grier's expedition.[17]

Some Pueblo Indians reported to James S. Calhoun, Superintendent of Indian Affairs in New Mexico, that they had been in the Apache camp and had seen an American woman and her daughter, whom Calhoun supposed to be Ann and Virginia White.[18] This news gave Grier's detachment of soldiers hope. They had one goal in mind—to rescue Mrs. White and little Virginia.

On November 4, Grier and his men left Taos, marching over the mountains eastward toward the Canadian and Arkansas rivers. On November 9, they located a camp on Palo Blanco, a small stream about nine miles

Fig. 25. Point of Rocks on the Santa Fe Trail in northeastern New Mexico. Near this site, Apaches killed James White and captured his daughter, Virginia, and wife, Ann Dunn White. Photograph courtesy of Faye Gaines.

east of the Point of Rocks. They followed the trail south toward the Canadian River, crossing a vast country covering several hundred square miles.[19]

The guides stayed in advance of each day's march and found, in almost every camp, evidence of Mrs. White, such as a piece of calico, a shoe, or a leaf of a book. Carson described this trail as being the most difficult he had ever followed, "for the rascally Apaches, on breaking up their camps, would divide into parties of two and three and then scatter over the vast expanse of the prairies to meet again at some preconcerted place, where they knew water could be had."[20]

The troops located the Apaches encamped in a

grove of cottonwoods near Red River, today called the Canadian.[21] Carson was out front on a small rise when he saw the village. At first galloping forward, but then realizing he was alone, he reined in and returned to the advance group. There he found Grier held up, hoping to parley with the Indians. His hesitation, instead, allowed the Indians to get away.[22]

With bravado, the mounted Indians dashed in front of the troops, allowing the Indian women and children time to escape.[23] One of the fleeing Apaches fired a shot that struck Grier in the chest, but the folded gloves stuffed inside his coat kept the ball from penetrating his flesh. With the wind knocked from him and gasping for

Fig. 26. Probable area where the Apaches killed Mrs. White at Red River Springs in 1849. Photograph by author, 2005.

air, he ordered his troops to charge the village, but it was too late. The Apaches were on the run.[24]

Troopers raced through the village in pursuit, but the Apaches' fresh horses easily outran the tired, cavalry mounts. Grier's men inflicted more damage on the village than on the Indians, destroying all thirty lodges with their contents. Accounts of the battle vary, ranging from one to six Indians killed.[25]

Soldiers came upon the body of Mrs. White, about three hundred yards from the lodges, clasping a prayer book.[26] "Her life was extinct, though her soul had but just flown to heaven. There was still warmth in the corpse when the men first discovered it. An arrow had pierced her breast. Evidently she had been conscious that friends were near and was trying to make her escape when the missile of death produced the fatal wound."[27]

Troopers also found in the Indian camp a novel describing Carson as an Indian fighter and hero. In his autobiography, Carson speculated that Mrs. White knew he lived not very far away and had prayed that he would appear and free her. He wished that it might have been so, but he consoled himself with the thought that he

had performed his duty. In his autobiography, Carson wrote of the certainty that, if they had attacked the Indians immediately, they could have saved Mrs. White. He stated that "the treatment she had received . . . was so brutal and horrible that she could not possibly have lived long" and that her friends should never regret her death.[28]

The soldiers buried Mrs. White at the site, concealing her grave by burning the materials from the Apache camp on top of it.[29] Grier's men found no sign of the Whites' daughter, little Virginia.[30] Eight years after the White massacre, however, Brevet Brigadier General John Gasland, in a letter to Colonel L. Cooper in Washington, D.C., wrote, "No occasion has been lost since my arrival in New Mexico, in 1853, to gain accurate information in relation to the painful occurrence" of Virginia White. Gasland speculated that the child shared the same fate as her parents. Another account was that an Apache bashed in the child's head and threw her body in a deep canyon or the river. One reported that the Indians pinned the child to the earth with a sharp stick.[31] Still others claimed that she was alive and living on the Jicarilla Apache Reservation as late as 1918, dying in 1935.[32]

A follow-up to Gasland's letter conveyed the finality of the tragedy. A merchant of Mora, Mr. Bransford, had offered two American horses and one-half of the goods in his store for the recovery of the little girl, but the answer was, "The child is dead."[33]

Who can say why Carson recounted this event? Was it because it affected him deeply? Perhaps he made it a habit to talk with his soldiers about his experiences and the history of the places he had travelled. As hardened as Carson's soldiers were, the tale of Mrs. White's murder surely left them in a somber mood as they thought about the safety of their families back home and contemplated their own personal risk in the task before them. Perhaps, that was Carson's purpose in bringing up Mrs. White—to ignite his forces to fight with might in the task that lay ahead.

Chapter 4
Red River Springs to Nara Visa Springs (Cañada de Los Ruedos)

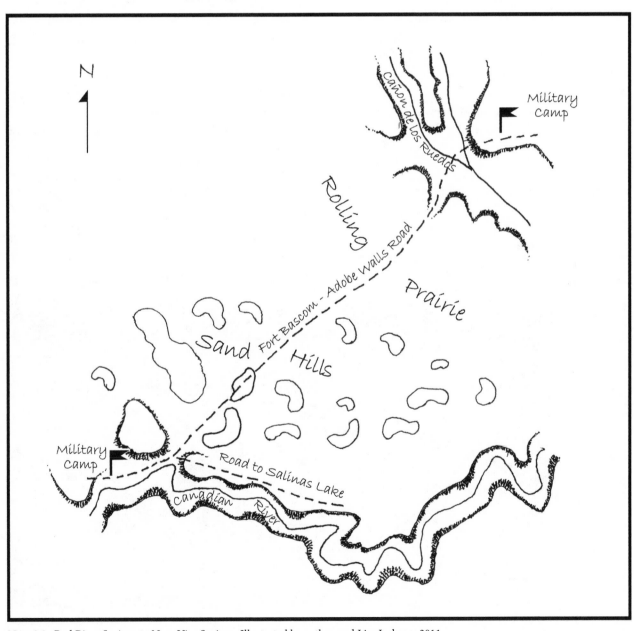

Map 4.1. Red River Springs to Nara Visa Springs. Illustrated by author and Lisa Jackson, 2011.

Indian scouts had been out of camp several hours before Carson's long column of men, animals, and wagons set out in a slow, northward procession up a sandy valley from Red River Springs on the Canadian River. Movement commenced with the vanguard and worked its way back through the column. For those in the rear guard, it was a long stretch of time before they started out. The elongated, sinuous line crept up the slope, away from the camp, toward Adobe Walls.

The wagon road divided in the valley, and Carson took the trace that bore northeast toward Nara Visa Springs, twelve miles away. He knew, from Major Ruff's 1860 expedition, that it was a shorter, less-difficult road than the one following the river.

The road not taken continued downriver fifteen miles to Salinas Lake, a clear, briny pond that provided salt—a commodity prized by soldiers at Fort Bascom, as well as local Indians and Mexicans. An example of its frequent utilization comes from Lieutenant Colonel Silus Newton of Fort Bascom, who reported in 1866 that thirty men loaded six wagons with eleven thousand

pounds of salt from the lake in one day.[1] So important was it that a village called Salinas built up nearby.

Back to Carson

When Carson's troops topped out of the Canadian River Valley, they saw enormous, bare sand hills, elongated by the prevailing southwest wind. The dunes appeared to be adrift in a sea of desert foliage: sage, plum bushes, skunkberry sumac (*Rhus trilobata*), yucca, and long-stemmed grasses. Mesquites grew where wind had swept away the sand, exposing solid soil.

Carson had seen these sand dunes in 1849 while chasing the Jicarilla Apaches who killed Mrs. White. Most of the men, however, were not aware of the formidable stretch of terrain that lay beyond them.

At first, men, animals, and wagons moved with ease along a high ridge, and then the ridge played out. From there, with a little more effort, they followed the wagon road through corridors sandwiched between great dunes. Travel went well for a short distance. Then, the

Fig. 27. Salinas Lake. Much smaller today than when the Indians and military mined salt in the mid to late 1800s. Photograph by author, 2002.

Fig. 28. Sand hills northeast of Red River Springs. Photograph by author, 2010.

road disappeared into pure sand, sand so deep that wagon wheels sank, and the teams strained to pull the heavy wagons. Teamsters goaded their animals; whips lashed and, most likely, expletives electrified the air. Foot soldiers pushed and grunted, while cavalry mounts tugged ropes attached to the wagons. The work was hard and hot, and even though it was late fall, I suspect sweat poured from men's brows. I imagine the accumulation of perspiration and sand irritated their skin with every wipe of the forehead.

About halfway between the river and Nara Visa Springs, the sand hills gave way to a barren, rolling, sandy ground. Travel, though still hard, did not tax the soldiers and animals as much.

In the summer of 1845, Lieutenant Abert moved along the same route with a similar complaint—that the deep sand yielded under the feet of the mules, making their progress slow and toilsome. The day was scorching, and as they held their course over the barren waste

without any sign of water, the men languished and feared they should not find that necessary article. Coming upon a thicket of wild plum bushes, they greatly alleviated their sufferings with the refreshing fruit. Plum trees grew everywhere, in abundance, and the men found the fruit equal to any of the cultivated varieties that they had tasted in the United States.[2]

Perhaps the summer of 1845 was a rainy year allowing the plum bushes to produce an abundant crop. When dry years come, sand hill plums do not get enough water, and most of the plums dry up and fall to the ground. The plums that do hang on in dry years are stunted and too tart to eat—inferior and aptly called hog plums. I think it possible that the men's hunger overpowered their palate because, two days later, the Frenchmen in this group made a meal out of a polecat.[3]

The terrain on this stretch of the route is, today, much the same as it was one hundred fifty years ago. Bare sand hills still abound amid brush and grass. Plum thickets thrive in the sand and occupy a large part of an acre. The ornery thorn bushes are a deterrent to men and livestock, and in the early days, wagon routes detoured around them. There is yet evidence of the old wagon road in places the sand has not covered.

When Abert left the higher sand hills, he saw the tops of tall, green cottonwoods—a sign of water that greatly encouraged his men. Upon reaching the lush valley ahead, they found a clear, cold spring.[4] Carson, nineteen years after Abert, observed these cottonwoods in November. They were not as noticeable without leaves, but his keen eyes picked them out as a marker for the valley.[5] After their trek through the sand hills, which took a toll on both man and beast, the springs were a welcome sight to the troops. Livestock drank freely, quenching their mighty thirst. Men filled and emptied their canteens until they were satisfied.

The wagon road entered the valley from the southwest, crossed the stream at the confluence with a western branch, and then exited up a high terrace on the east side of the creek. The artifacts I recovered indicate that Carson and most travelers camped on the high ground east of the creek. Abert, however, in 1845, described his camp as being between the creek and some small buttes.[6]

Abert kept meticulous notes during his expedition but did not give this creek a name, though it has a history of many names. Lieutenant Pettis, Carson's artillery officer in 1864, dubbed it Cañada de Los Ruedes, or Wheel Gulch, because the Mexican traders used the abundant cottonwoods to repair the crude, wooden wheels of their *carretas* before striking out onto the Plains.[7] Colonel Evans spent two nights there during a severe snowstorm in 1868 and called it Navais Spring.[8] Some early maps cited it as Nervice Spring, but on today's maps, it is Nara Visa Springs. By whatever name, it has been a favorite camping ground for at least one hundred fifty years of recorded history and long before that by earlier people.

Carson's men had been fortunate in having good weather.[9] The warm, pleasant conditions combined with

Fig. 29. Wagon road leading into Nara Visa Springs (Cañada de los Ruedos). Photograph by author, 2003.

hard physical exertion and the resulting sweat, sand, and grime may have enticed some to bathe in the springs, or at least, to do a bit of face splashing.

Refreshed with food, warmed by the fire, and pleasured with a good smoke, the troops unwound. Relaxation erased some of the effects of the day's trek through those frazzling sand hills. Even the dancing of the Utes and Jicarilla Apaches probably was not as bothersome on this night, when the tired soldiers rolled out blankets and turned in.

Chapter 5
Nara Visa Springs (Cañada de Los Ruedos) to Hay Creek

Before break of day, the soldiers had eaten breakfast, hitched up their mounts, and moved out. On this day, they would leave the Mexican cart road they had traveled since their departure from Fort Bascom. The cart road continued northward from Nara Visa Springs to Frio Creek in the northern Texas Panhandle. Carson's scouts, however, searched for the route going toward Adobe Walls and soon found it, a dim Indian trail heading east.[1]

The morning air was crisp. The night's rest had reinvigorated both men and animals. The march out of the valley was more pleasant than the previous day's sand-

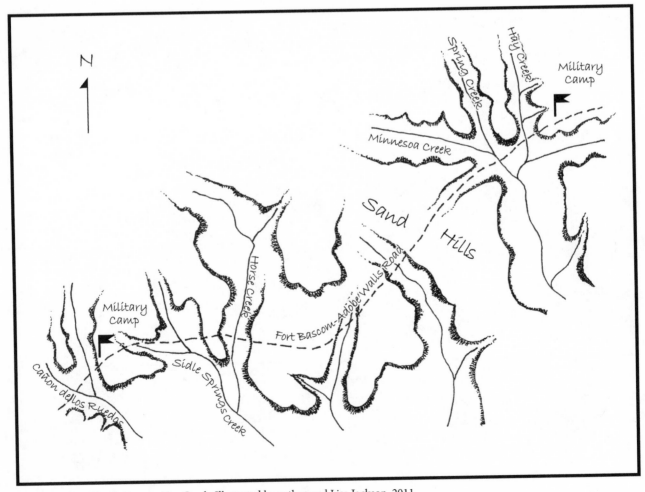

Map 5.1. Nara Visa Springs to Hay Creek. Illustrated by author and Lisa Jackson, 2011.

infested travel. Small, rounded, gravel hills gave way to rolling, sandy land that was firm enough not to impede travel. After about two miles, the troops entered Texas, though the event, likely, went unnoticed. According to Abert, the eastbound road changed into a bridle path at this point.[2] Surveyor John H. Clark marked it on his 1859 survey of the Texas-New Mexico boundary.[3] I believe the trail Carson's scouts came upon was the one recorded by Clark, and I base my confidence on two evidences: Clark's survey notes and an existing inscribed rock.

The marked stone lies near the junction of the Bascom Trail and the Texas-New Mexico state line. On one side "TEX" is inscribed, while the other side is incised with "NM 67M 09." "TEX," of course, stands for Texas and "NM" for New Mexico. The numeral "09" signifies 1909, the year of a resurvey. The mark "67M" indicates sixty-seven miles from the northwest corner of the Texas Panhandle.

Fig. 31. Survey rock near New Mexico-Texas state line, Texas. Photograph by author, 1996.

Surveyor D. D. Kirkpatrick, in his 1911 resurvey notes, described this point as Monument 18, marked by stones, and near an old Indian trail. He gave the distance from Monument 17 on the Canadian River to Monument 18 as seven miles and eight chains, situating the monument in the same vicinity that I found the inscribed rock originally put there by the 1909 surveyor.[4]

Beyond the stone marker, just inside Texas, Carson's troops approached a wide valley requiring the teamsters to edge their wagons down its sandy slopes. In the valley, they passed a flowing spring, today called Sidle Spring. Since they were just three miles from the previous night's lodging and their water barrels were full, they, in all probability, sated their thirst and travelled on.

About a mile due east of the spring, a high north-south ridge separates Sidle Springs Creek from Horse Creek. Carson's men headed directly toward the depression in the middle of the ridge, which they crossed. The east side of the saddle was steep, causing a difficult descent. Teamsters set brakes. Men strained with ropes attached to the wagons to keep them on course and to prevent capsizing as they slid down the gravel-covered incline. Artifacts retrieved from the slope—military buttons, horseshoes, broken bolts, and small wagon parts—are evidence of the physical exertion required to get the wagons down the grade.

At the bottom of the ridge, the road changed to a red pavement-like surface and then to a sloping formation of sandstone that made entering Horse Creek easy. Exiting the creek was more difficult, because the east slope was softer and steeper. Deep swales and eroded ruts defined the route out of the creek.

Fig. 30. Survey rock near New Mexico-Texas state line, New Mexico. Photograph by author, 1996.

Fig. 32. The Fort Bascom–Adobe Walls Road passed just north of this spring known today as Sidle Springs. Photograph by author, 1996.

For the next few miles, the undulating topography and sturdy soils made Carson's travel trouble-free, except for having to dodge thorny mesquites. Carson's troops recognized these prickly plants, which they learned to avoid while campaigning in the Southwest. Abert, in 1845, described *musquit* as being abundant, scrubby bushes no more than five feet tall.[5]

Carson, himself, had experienced first-hand, the effects of thorns and stickers on the body during the Mexican-American War. During the 1846 Battle of San Pasqual in California, when he was with General Stephen Watts Kearny, Commander, Army of the West, the Mexicans had the U.S. troops pinned down on a rocky, cactus-infested hill. Kearny dispatched three couriers—Carson, Beale, and an Indian—to San Diego for help. Under cover of night, Carson, along with Lieutenant Edward Beale, a young naval officer, and a California Indian, crept out of camp and slithered down the loose, rocky slope through the Mexican camp. Beale and Carson removed their boots and fastened them under their belts to keep from making too much noise. At the

bottom of the hill, they discovered, to their dismay, that both had lost their boots while crawling through the brush—and there were thirty miles of prickly pear, brush, and rocks between them and San Diego.

Understanding the extreme gravity of Kearny's situation, the three couriers split up, with the hope that at least one would get through with Kearny's message. Carson and Beale headed out barefooted, and the Indian's moccasins offered little more protection. Amazingly, all three men arrived at their destination. Each suffered greatly from sticks, pricks, and lacerations. Carson could not walk for a week, and Beale stayed in sickbay for about a month. According to some reports, the Indian eventually died from the effects of the march.[6]

Thorny, scrubby mesquites still thrive in the Texas Panhandle, and men are still trying to avoid their pricks. The painful punctures of their needle-like thorns contain a mild poison and can cause infection in living creatures. Mesquites are an ecological ranching nuisance, taking over the acreage and stealing moisture from native grasses vital to cattle. The early Anglo travelers described motts of mesquites as early as the 1840s. However, over-grazing by ranchers and fire control allowed the density of mesquites to increase to where some of the land became almost unusable.

Three miles east of Horse Creek, the road crossed a ravine at the head of a deep canyon. Old maps show a spring below the road. Perhaps Carson's men nooned there, for they had gone seven miles from the previous night's camp—about a half-day's journey. Men and livestock needed rest before heading into the hilly country ahead. Today, all evidence of military presence is gone—obliterated by cattle traffic. Corrals and a windmill stand on the west side of the creek at what was once a favorable camping spot.

A look around the area reveals stony logs that tell of a time millions of years ago when forests populated the area. Tree trunks, replaced by silica, formed petrified wood. In a still-later geologic time, iron oxide encrusted the petrified wood, giving it a dark color. While camped in nearby canyons, Abert described these oxide-coated, petrified logs as looking like huge chunks of iron ore.[7] Marching along this same route in 1866 with the Third Cavalry from Fort Smith, Arkansas, to Fort Union, New Mexico, Thomas Abram Muzzall, Hospital Steward First Class, First Missouri Cavalry recorded seeing a large petrified tree miles off on the prairie and not a tree or bush in sight.[8]

After leaving Cañada de Los Ruedes, the road bore almost due east and skirted the heads of canyons three to four miles north of the Canadian River. One mile east of Carson's noon camp, the road turned and proceeded northeast up the valley of Chisum Canyon.

Abert, in 1845, left the road at this point and headed directly south to travel along the Canadian River.[9] This was unfortunate for historians studying Carson's route, because Abert kept a detailed diary of his travel describing the route and events of each day. Carson, Pettis, and Courtright were, however, silent concerning the next one hundred miles of their journey along the Bascom Road. There is one exception; Carson mentioned that snowstorms caused them to lay over an extra day on two separate occasions.

Carson's troops and livestock labored as they plodded northeast to a high divide, across a deep valley, and then through sandy country for three more miles to another valley where a windmill stands today. Modern-day cowboys say that early ranchers mistakenly thought this road was the Santa Fe Trail, so they named the mill Santa Fe. After another mile's climb through sandy terrain, the troops descended into Minneosa Valley. The road followed the south side of a high ridge to the creek, which, today, is dry, sandy, and several hundred yards wide. Spring Creek, a live-water tributary, is just a quarter-mile upstream. Minneosa Creek is fourteen miles, a good day's march, from Carson's previous camp. Carson's men would have been tired when they arrived there, but the few metal artifacts I found on either side of the stream, do not represent a sufficient quantity for an overnight stay. The creek could have been dry in 1864, or, it's possible that floods washed away all evidence of the military's ever having been there.

Still looking for a campsite, the long line of men, livestock, and wagons trudged on, crossed the sandy creek, pivoted a bit more easterly, and continued for another mile to Hay Creek, a welcome sight after the dry Minneosa. Clear water flowed from springs upstream, and still flows during the winter months. Grass flourished along treeless banks, making it a good place for troops to camp and for horses and mules to drink their fill, graze, and recuperate. Deep swales are still visible in the bank delineating where the road crossed Hay Creek and continued eastward. I found enough metal artifacts along the creek and on the upper, east side to confirm it as a military campsite.

The absence of trees sent soldiers out on the prairie searching for buffalo chips or chance woodchips, so important for food preparation and warmth on that late fall evening. With fuel gathered and fires lit, the men huddled around the flames to knock off the November chill and to breathe in the pleasant aroma of boiling coffee.

Chapter 6
Hay Creek to Romero Creek

The road leaving Hay Creek was the best Carson and his men had been on since leaving Fort Bascom. Compacted, gravel-covered soil gave way to sturdy prairie sod as they made their way up the gradual incline out of the valley. Except for a few small creeks, this fine thoroughfare continued for four miles, and then disappeared into a stretch of badlands. It looked as if someone had opened the gates to Hades. Small islands of grass struggled for life in the eroded, barren basin. Straight-banked arroyos cut into the dark clay of the valley floor. In some places, erosion-formed tunnels lay beneath the surface, giving the illusion of solid ground. Travel was perilous

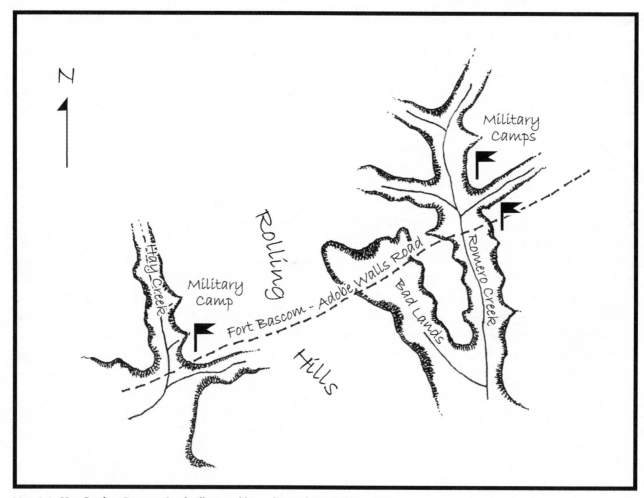

Map 6.1. Hay Creek to Romero Creek. Illustrated by author and Lisa Jackson, 2011.

Fig. 33. Road on solid ground leaving Hay Creek. Photograph by author, 2004.

because riders were uncertain as to when the ground might collapse under the weight of wagons and animals.

I walked across this inhospitable tract on a hot summer day, and the heat was stifling as it radiated off the bare, clay soil. Today the road is no longer visible at this point, but broken mule shoes and pieces of metal mark the route where it exits on the east side of the barren valley.

After Carson's troops picked their way across the bleak terrain, they again came to a firm road. Upon leaving the badlands, they crossed the divide into Romero Valley.

As I trekked across the valley following the wagon road, I imagined the troops' excitement when they reached this point. Looking across the grass-covered hills surrounding Romero Creek, their eyes took in the rough canyon-lands to the south, paused to see the prominent hill in the northeast, and gazed upon the cottonwoods growing near the springs that fed Romero Creek. It was a splendid panorama.

Cowboys told me that these springs once gushed volumes of water. Even today, they produce several gallons per minute, but the water stops short of the wagon-road crossing. There are, however, seasonal holes of water near the confluence of West Romero Creek and Main Romero Creek. Nearly 150 years ago, in 1866, Muzzall opined that Romero was a beautiful stream with plenty of fish in it. I must agree; it is a nice creek with fish in the holes.[1]

Fig. 34. Eroded badlands between Hay Creek and Romero Creek. Photograph by author, 2004.

Military buttons and percussion rifle and pistol bullets found around these waterholes date back to the 1860s, when Carson was there. Other relics scattered for almost a mile along the creek, imply that campers ranged from early Indians to late-nineteenth-century ranchers.

Ruff-Kiowa Fight

Of note is a battle that occurred near this vicinity a few years before Carson's 1864 campaign. Commander Major Charles Frederick Ruff, Regiment Mounted Riflemen, Department of New Mexico, with 225 mounted riflemen, attacked and destroyed a large Comanche village. The troops left Camp Jackson, New Mexico, on July 11, 1860. Five days out, their Mexican scouts reported that a favorite camping place of the Indians was about two miles to the north.[2]

After a quick march, the troopers spotted a large encampment of Comanches, and shortly, everyone was in rapid motion—soldiers charging, Indians fleeing. The villagers divided into three groups. In the first group,

more than two hundred women and children, with a few men, escaped to the northwest. In the second group, fifteen to twenty men drove off about two hundred head of horses. In the third group, about eighty warriors fled to the northeast while being pursued by the military.[3] Ruff chased the warriors for twelve miles across a high prairie to Rita Blanca Creek before giving up. Even though his soldiers made a valiant effort, their horses were in such poor shape that they had no chance of catching the Indians. It was midday in July, and Ruff said that it was one of the hottest days of the year. By the time troops arrived at the southwest side of the creek on their lathered mounts, the Indians were ascending the steep hills on the northeast side.[4]

After the chase, the soldiers led their tired horses down the slopes to Rita Blanca Creek to water, strip, and rest them. Later in the day, about thirty men rode back to the Indian village and burned it, destroying 180 buffalo robes; many lodges made of dressed skins and canvas; a large number of tin, iron, and brass kettles still hanging over the fires with meat in them; several sacks of

Fig. 35. Romero Creek. Photograph by author, 2003.

salt; and more than twenty-five saddles. The soldiers burned a dozen or more rifles and guns; powder horns filled with powder; piles of arrows, bows, and shields; and some thirty axes. The large amount of possessions burned indicated the presence of a very large party supplied with all the necessities of life. Ruff noted that the soldiers burned a most unusual amount of articles that may be termed luxury items of Indian life—tin cups and pans, ornamental mats, beadwork, dressed skins, and children's dolls and playthings.[5]

That night, while camped on the Rita Blanca, the Indians attempted to steal the military's horses, but the alert guards fired upon them, killing three Comanche warriors.[6] For the next five days, Ruff's troops dogged the Indians until they reached Bent's Trading Post, the site of Carson's eventual encounter with the Comanches and Kiowas four years later. By the time Ruff's command arrived there, his horses were exhausted and the Indians gone, so he returned to New Mexico. Though Ruff lost no men or animals, he attributed his lack of capturing Comanches to his worn-out horses and inept guides who were not willing to trail at night.[7]

Concerning Carson's 1864 campaign and his mention of holding up on two occasions because of snow,[8] the layover could have been at any two of the five camps between Hay Creek and Mule Creek. If it were Romero Creek, it would have been a miserable place to last out a snowstorm, for it was treeless with few protective hills.

Snow or not, Carson's contingent spent time in this valley and survived it. Like the camp on Hay Creek, soldiers found very little firewood at Romero Creek, so buffalo chips again served as fuel. Private Eddie Matthews, Company L, Eighth Cavalry, Fort Union, while on a scout in 1872 with Commander Colonel John Irvin Gregg, described gathering and cooking with buffalo chips: "Our wood ran out. All hands took sacks and scattered over the prairie picking up 'buffalo Chips' (buffalo manure) to cook by. These chips make a very good fire, but the odor arising after they burn sometime does not smell as sweet as 'new mown hay', But then soldiers are not particular about the smell, something to appease their appetites is more in their minds, than any thing else, and little difference to them it makes whether their victuals are cooked by coal, wood or buffalo chips."[9] A soldier's attitude about heating was probably the same as about cooking—the kind of fuel didn't matter. I can envision small specks of light glowing in the darkness along Romero Creek as night fell. Carson's men, seeking refuge from the cold night, wrapped up in overcoats and blankets trying to absorb the last bit of heat from their buffalo-chip fires.

Chapter 7
Romero Creek to Punta de Agua Creek

With morning camp activities finished, the procession stretched northeast along the undulating short-grass prairie. After about a mile, the terrain changed to a rougher landscape, and the column followed an arroyo up a gradual ascent to an elevated plain.

About three miles from Romero Creek, where Texas Highway 767 runs today, the contingent left the valley and proceeded around the east side of the prominent hill they gazed upon the previous day. As they topped the slope, their wagons bounced over a narrow caprock. Added strain on wagons and men is evidenced by the broken bolts and one military button found on the road.

Beyond the caprock, the troops turned more to the east, skirting a gently rolling plain for the next two miles to the head of Pedarosa Creek. The Bascom Road on which they travelled was the only road in 1864, but by

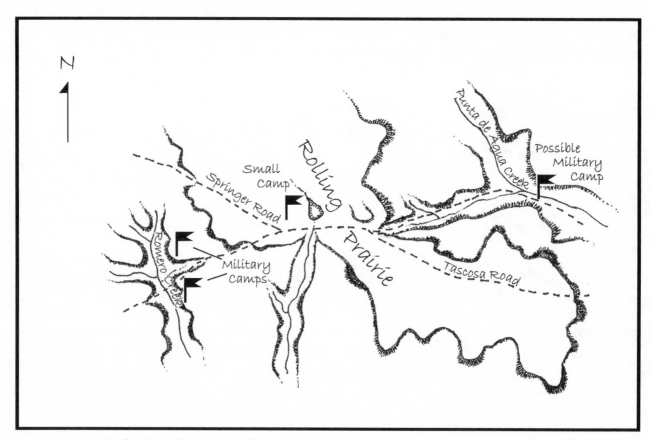

Map 7.1. Romero Creek to Punta de Agua Creek. Illustrated by author and Lisa Jackson, 2011.

Fig. 36. Fort Bascom–Adobe Walls Road near Playa Lake site. *Orientation*: looking west. Photograph by author, 1996.

the time I surveyed the area, a second, more recent, road was on the scene—constructed twelve years after Carson passed that way. After Casimero Romero established Tascosa, Texas, in 1876, a newly developed wagon road from Springer, New Mexico, to Tascosa joined the Bascom Road.[1] On the plain that divided the valleys of Romero and Punta de Agua creeks, the two roads met and ran congruently for a couple of miles. For a few years, heavy traffic on that section of road left deep swales and ruts. When I walked the trail in 1995, I measured a washout that was five feet deep and twenty-five feet wide, the result of erosion on the ruts.

Carson's men came upon a playa lake (a natural shallow lake found on the Texas high plains) about two hundred yards northeast of the head of Pedarosa Creek. They were just five miles out from Romero Creek, where they had camped the previous night. Their march had been uphill and was difficult, so it is likely that they turned off the main road onto a branch leading to the playa lake to check their gear and water the animals.

The branch rejoined the main road a short distance to the east.

I collected artifacts all along the south and southwest sides of the playa, leading me to believe Carson stopped there on his way, both, to and from Adobe Walls. On his homeward journey, with battle-weary men and wounded soldiers, Carson needed to stop and rest at every water source, and this playa lake was a good prospect for such a camp.

The Springer–Tascosa Road split from the Bascom Road just south of a high hill two miles due east of the playa lake. An old XIT map shows this intersection to be in League 209. Surveyors, while surveying this land for the XIT Ranch in the late 1870s and early 1880s, made notes of man-made structures and the wagon roads they encountered. Surveyor J. Summerfield, in 1879, described the area surrounding the forks as a gently rolling mesquite prairie of good grazing land with a fine valley on the north side of a hill. The location of the fork in the roads from his survey marker: *"3 hard flint*

Fig. 37. Survey marker rocks near intersection of Fort Bascom–Adobe Walls Road and Springer–Tascosa Road. Photograph by author, 1996.

rocks, 14x12x14 . . . Thence south at 140 road E&W. Cross it 40 vrs. west of forks. The Tascosa Road going SE and old Bascom Trail NE."[2]

I followed the surveyor's directions and walked forty varas along the road west from the fork and one hundred forty varas north, where I found a pile of rocks with a pipe driven in the center. I believe these to be the rocks set as the survey point of 1879. Later surveyors added the short, rusty pipe. The vara is a unit of length measurement that varies in different states and countries. The Texas vara is 33.33 inches or 2.778 feet, equaling 1900 varas per mile.

In December 1998, helicopter pilot Knut Mjolhus flew photographer Wyman Meinzer, author John Graves, and me to the site. Mjolhus, hovering the helicopter above the road, allowed Meinzer and me to snap photographs of the old road. From the air, the ruts looked like long, dark red ropes stretching across the prairie. Little bluestem, a fast-recovery grass and the first vegetation to grow in eroded areas, had filled the ruts, highlighting the trail. That winter day the reddish-brown hue of little

bluestem illuminated the trail against the backdrop of other grasses.

Eight miles into the day, Carson's men followed the route selected by his scouts, which led them from the high divide and down a valley to Punta de Agua Creek. Travel was easy until they reached the main creek. There, brush-covered sand hills lined the south bank of Punta de Agua at the confluence with the valley. To the east, the dunes played out, and grassy meadows replaced them.

Even though much of the road on this leg of Carson's journey was easy to find, I found no military camps. Without records from Carson or Pettis, determining where and even whether, Carson camped along the Punta de Agua or Rita Blanca Creek was difficult. One historic site where the troops entered Punta de Agua from the southwest contained a few metal artifacts. It was a small camp with good water, but its small size precluded use by the military; perhaps *pastores* used the site.

Speculation leads one to ask, did Carson take his men down creek or even to the next creek to bivouac?

Fig. 38. Fort Bascom–Adobe Walls Road along tributary of Punta de Agua Creek. Photograph by author, 1996.

Chapter 8
Punta de Agua Creek to Los Redos Creek

For almost three days, Carson's command had marched northeast away from the Canadian River breaks. At Punta de Agua Creek, the route changed to an east-southeast orientation down the creek for approximately five miles. The troopers marched a short distance down the south side of Punta de Agua and soon reached its confluence with Rita Blanca Creek. There, the terrain opened into a wide valley of meadows scattered with cottonwoods along a clear stream.

For years, this protected valley had served as a favored camping spot for Native Americans. The metal arrowpoints, ornaments, and tools found along the ridge between Rita Blanca and Punta de Agua suggest that the camp was a *Comanchero*–Indian trading site. One branch of the Bascom Road ran directly through the village, and *Comancheros* traveling farther east toward Adobe Walls more than likely traded there when they passed through.

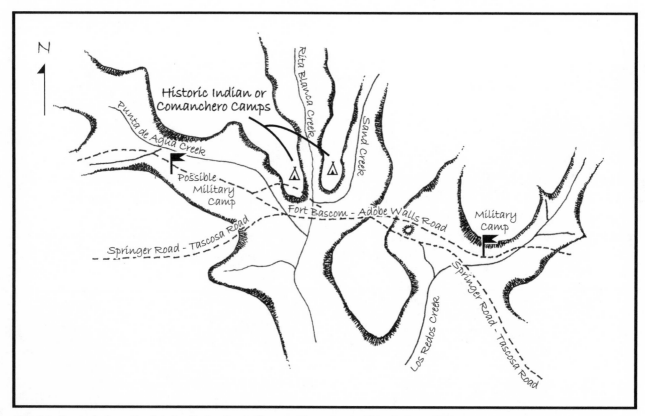

Map 8.1. Punta de Agua Creek to Los Redos Creek. Illustrated by author and Lisa Jackson, 2011.

Fig. 39. G. F. "Red" Skelton standing next to a *pastore* ruin on Punta de Agua Creek. Photograph by author, 1996.

According to Carson, he wrote his report of the military's return trip to Fort Bascom while camped on Rita Blanca Creek,[1] but I have searched the Rita Blanca for his campsite to no avail. Floods might have inundated the area, or Carson, thinking he was on the Rita Blanca, may have camped four miles to the east on Los Redos Creek, where there are remains of a large military camp. It is worthwhile to note that some later maps, in fact, do mistakenly identify the Los Redos as Rita Blanca Creek.

A traveler to the area today would see rock foundations and the crumbling walls of stone houses and sheep pens, reminders of Mexican *pastores* who entered the valley a little more than a decade after Carson passed through. These sheep men, or the older members of their families, may have been *Comancheros* or *ciboleros,* like the *pastores* who in the mid-1870s settled on the Canadian River to the south.[2] Some of them, perhaps, hunted bison on the Llano Estacado or traded with the Indians that Carson pursued in 1864.

These early traders and hunters knew this country well and noted the lush, stream-fed valleys. When not out on the plains trading with the Comanches, many of the *Comancheros* were farming and herding sheep along the Pecos River in New Mexico. After trade with the Indians ended in the mid-1870s, some of these agrarian people moved down the Canadian to the green pastures in the Texas Panhandle.[3] The coming of the cattlemen into this region in the late 1870s and early 1880s, pushed several of the *pastores* back to New Mexico. Some, however, stayed and have descendants living in the Texas Panhandle today.

In my search for a camp, I noticed two places where Carson could have crossed Punta de Agua and Rita Blanca Creeks. One place, the lesser possibility, was below the confluence of the two streams. Today, this area on the Rita Blanca is a sandy, half-mile-wide stretch. After walking across it, I realized that if the creek were then wide and sandy like it is today, it would have taken a lot of effort to cross it. The other, more-likely route to the north, was longer and traversed two narrow creeks, but was the easier way.

While surveying the area in 1875, W. D. Olmstead

Fig. 40. Aerial view near confluence of Rita Blanca and Punta de Agua creeks. Photograph by author, 1996.

mentioned crossing the north route twice in Survey 20, Block 49, H&TCRR Co. (Houston and Texas Railroad Company): "Beginning at the SW corner of survey no. 19, a mound. Thence E crossing Mustang Cr. 1900 Vrs to a mound (in which is buried a pickle bottle containing a big '50' cartridge shell and a Smith and Wesson do) . . . Thence S 1900 Vrs a mound. Thence W crossing Mustang Cr. and the Fort Bascom & Dodge City Trail twice, 1900 Vrs. to beginning."[4]

I envision Carson's troops upon leaving the protection of the wooded valley of the Rita Blanca, hunkered tight in their saddles, trying to expose as little flesh as possible to the cold. They struck out across the windy prairie toward a wide swale in the line of hills separating Rita Blanca Creek from the next valley to the east. The gradual slope and short prairie grass made an easy route for the soldiers to pass over the divide and down to a flowing creek.

Carson did not give a name to the stream, but four years later, Colonel Andrew Evans reported it as Bonita Creek.[5] Like most creeks along the Canadian River, name changes were common. This one was no

exception—at first called Bonita Creek, later mislabeled on maps as the Rita Blanca, and finally named Los Redos, which is a corruption of the Spanish *Las Ruedas*, meaning "the wheels."

"The Wheels"

The history of how the beautiful little creek, the Bonita, evolved to Las Ruedas or "The Wheels" is interesting and the cause of much speculation. C. E. "Buck" MacConnell wrote that when he was an employee of the XIT Ranch, in the early part of the twentieth century, he repaired the windmill on the creek. One of the cowboys told him that both the windmill and the creek were named Las Ruedas from a pair of broken-down wagon wheels found there when the well was drilled.[6] Bennie Trujillo, descendent of an early Spanish settler in the region, told Red Skelton of Channing, Texas, that there used to be several old wagon parts down on Los Redos, which he had found when he was a child and believed they were the remains of an Indian massacre. Red was not sure about the massacre, but, in relation to the wagon parts, he mentioned a blacksmith in Channing, a Mr. Kimbell, who gathered iron from an old wagon on this creek to use in his shop, and Red noted that Mr. Kimbell picked up every piece he could find.[7] The wheels, simply, may have come from a wagon that broke down, or perhaps left behind when a traveler's mules played out. Teamsters commonly abandoned wagons on military campaigns, especially in winter.

Vincent Colyer, U.S. Special Indian Commissioner, in 1869, journeyed westward along the south side of the Canadian River to Fort Bascom. On his way, he crossed the route Colonel Evans took on the 1868 Indian Campaign. Colyer derided the waste of military expeditions, mentioning items he saw strewn along Evans's 1868 route—the skeletons of dead horses from which the wolves had devoured the flesh, along with cast-away saddles, bridles, axes, camp coffee kettles, and so on. Especially moved was he when they passed Antelope Hills and came across the remains of several army wagons in so good a condition that he most heartily wished he had the wheels on his farm at home.[8] In whatever way

the wheels came to be on this creek, they memorialized the junkyard they created by giving it the name Las Ruedas, anglicized to Los Redos.

Los Redos Creek is an ideal place for a winter camp. It runs east-west for a short distance. On the north, gravel hills form the backdrop of a flat terrace that stretches a few hundred yards along the creek with a north-south ridge crossing it at the east end.

The Bascom Road is visible on the flat ground today. The bank has eroded where it enters the creek, and the trail manifests itself as a swale at the top of a small bluff. There is a good spring at the east end of the terrace where the creek bends to the north. Water from this spring flows some distance down the creek in the winter.

A large cottonwood mott grows along the south side of the creek near the camp. Farther east, large cottonwoods scattered along the creek appear to be old enough to have been there when Carson passed this way—and indeed, Thomas Muzzall, in 1866, described the creek as a well-timbered stream.[9] Indian, military, and Mexican artifacts give proof to extensive occupation of this camp.

Fig. 41. Los Redos Creek. *Center:* The flat where Carson set up camp. *Orientation:* looking north. Photograph by author, 1996.

Fig. 42. Remnant of wagon road near Los Redos Creek. Photograph by author, 1996.

Civil War–era military buttons and bullets of the vintage of Carson's 1864 campaign give credence to his camping at Los Redos.

I believe this site, Los Redos, is where Carson wrote his report when he stated that he was on Rita Blanca Creek, four miles to the west. It is not likely that troops marched only four miles unless hampered by weather or some other event. Muzzall, with Colonel Marshall Saxe Howe, Commander, Third Cavalry, camped at this site on Los Redos in 1866, and then passed by Rita Blanca and Punta de Agua creeks before camping on Romero Creek, a distance of twenty-two miles.[10] It is possible that Carson did the same.

Carson's men settled near the east end of the terrace. The gravel hills to the north and the ridge to the east protected them from the cold wind. This creek may have been one of the places where the troops laid over a day because of snow. Los Redos, unlike Romero Creek, afforded protection and an abundant supply of wood for cooking and warming.

Soldiers, cold and weary from their ninth or tenth day of marching, finished their usual camp chores and then enjoyed, as best they could, their warm fire and a smoke before another cold night on the ground, accompanied by Indian dances.

Chapter 9
Los Redos Creek to Rica Creek

Heavy, cold air held the campfire smoke low in Los Redos Valley as teamsters hitched reluctant mules to wagons and soldiers readied cavalry mounts for the day's march. Carson, as usual, sent his scouts out ahead. More than likely, he sent some of the scouts as flankers along the hills, because the first part of the march that morning was up a deep valley, an excellent place for Indians to attack from the surrounding bluffs.

The single-file descent into the creek bottom was slow, but not a problem, for it was only a few feet from the slope down to the stream. The creek had several meanders above the camp, so the caravan had to cross it three times during the first mile of the march before exiting the valley.

The troops inched upward along a sandy tributary until they reached a small tongue of the Plains that extended a short distance toward the Canadian River Valley. After the steep climb out of Los Redos Creek,

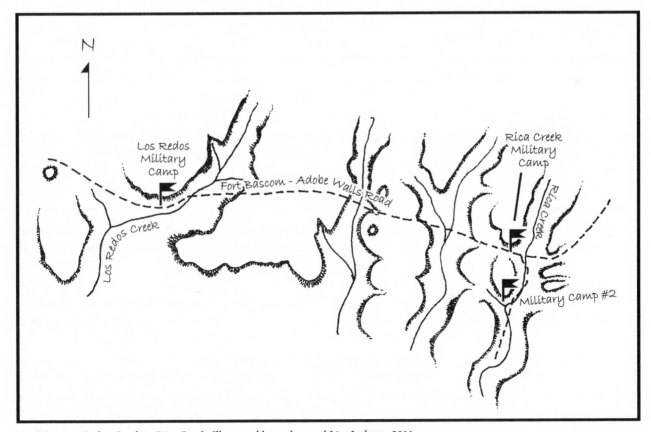

Map 9.1. Los Redos Creek to Rica Creek. Illustrated by author and Lisa Jackson, 2011.

Fig. 43. Fort Bascom–Adobe Walls Road near Cheyenne Creek. Photograph by Wyman Meinzer, 2009.

crossing the narrow section of the Plains that continued east for about two miles was a relief for the entourage. They then veered northeast to skirt the steep headers of narrow valleys. Highway U.S. 385 crosses the trail one and three-quarter miles south of Channing, Texas.

After circumventing the deep ravines, Carson's men descended into rolling country dissected by present-day Middle and East Cheyenne creeks. Between these creeks, two mesas form landmarks easily recognized by travelers—freighters, Indians, *Comancheros*, and military troops alike.

The Bascom Road runs between the mesas, and the troops found the traveling easy until they reached East Cheyenne Creek. From there, teams toiled as they lugged the heavy wagons up a mile-long slope through yucca, sage, and skunkberry sumac. Once the column reached the summit of the high divide, the soldiers had an unobstructed view across Rica Creek Valley to the light-colored caliche brow of the Plains five miles to the north-

east. The absence of trees in the valley and on the rolling hills to the east accentuated the vastness of the area.

In a short time, the long line of men, horses, mules, and wagons advanced two miles on a good road from the divide to the creek. Carson's scouts found a suitable campsite on a flat terrace near the wagon crossing. The troops had marched only eleven miles before they bivouacked. This could have been due to inclement weather, or perhaps the scouts reported to Carson that it was twenty-two miles to Agua Azul (Blue Creek), too far to reach that day.

Like Romero Creek, Rica Creek offered minimal protection from the weather. Small, rounded hills lined the east bank. A curved ridge about fifteen feet high along the west side of the terrace afforded a little shelter, but the creek was oriented north-south and funneled the cold, north wind through the camp.

There is, today, no permanent water in Rica Creek, but current resident Red Skelton told me that a small spring flowed during the mid-1940s.[1] An early sojourner left a fishhook and a weight made from flattened lead—good evidence that the creek had holes of water at one time.

Thomas Muzzall, traveling with the Howe expedition from Fort Smith, Arkansas, to Fort Bascom in 1866, called the campsite on Rica Creek Camp Jackson.[2] I don't know where Muzzall got the name, as I have not found it on any maps. Perhaps he mistook it for Camp Jackson in New Mexico, a site occupied by the military before they constructed Fort Bascom.

The campsite on Rica Creek, near the intersection of the Bascom Road and a wagon road that came up from the Canadian River to the south, was a popular stopover. Artifacts I recovered indicate Carson's troops and other travelers camped on the west side of the creek near the wagon crossing.

There were also military and Indian camps about a half-mile to the south where a rounded promontory extended from the northwest toward Rica Creek. A sagebrush-covered flat spread from the high ground to the creek. The Indian camp extended along the top of the ridge while the soldiers occupied the southwest side and the protected flat below. I believe Col. Andrew Evans camped in the protected flat area on his expedition in November 1868, because both .50/70 and Spencer cartridges found at this site were the type used by his command.[3]

About one hundred yards southwest of the encampment, a sandstone outcrop served as a signature rock for travelers. In 1995, I recorded names and dates from 1854 to 1993 inscribed on the small bluff. One carving was of particular interest to me, "D. Comstock, Dec. 16, 1868," because December 1868 to January 1869 was the time teamsters hauled supplies to Evans's depot farther down the Canadian River. It is probable that D. Comstock was a teamster hired by Evans.

Carson did not record his stay on Rica Creek, or most other stops on his expedition to Adobe Walls. The archeological evidence I found and military reports

Fig. 44. Cowboy Rock near Rica Creek. Names inscribed on rock date back to 1854. Photograph by author, 1996.

Fig. 45. Cowboy Rock inscription: "D. Comstock, Dec. 16, 1868." Some of Evans's teamsters camped near here during the 1868 Canadian River Expedition. Perhaps Comstock was a teamster with that expedition. Photograph by author, 1996.

(other than Carson's), nevertheless, give insight into his activities along the trail.

In my mind's eye, I see Carson's troops getting a little crusty after having marched over a hundred miles, suffering through cold snowstorms, and trying to sleep within earshot of the scouts' continuous chants. Most of Carson's men were seasoned soldiers, having fought at Valverde and in the Apache and Navajo campaigns. They were combat-hardened, tired of marching, and ready for action. Little did they know that the fight for which they were looking was only three days in the future.

Chapter 10
Rica Creek to Blue Creek

Carson's column marched up a shallow, grassy valley onto the low, rolling hills between Rica Creek and the brow of the Plains to the northeast. Wagons bounced over chert cobbles in the road near the head of the valley.

Ever on the lookout for Kiowas and Comanches, troopers doubtless paid little attention to the circular arrangement of the cobblestones, remnants of tepee rings left by earlier Indians. I suspect the teamsters cursed the rocks

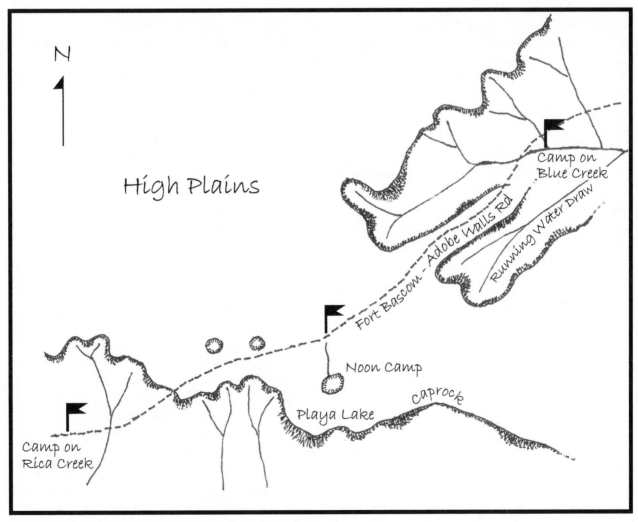

Map 10.1. Rica Creek to Blue Creek. Illustrated by author and Lisa Jackson, 2011.

Fig. 46. Wagon road on caprock east of Rica Creek. Photograph by author, 1996.

as the iron wheels of their wagons dislodged the stones, jostling everything in the laden wagons, including the drivers.

In the early 1990s, a cowboy from the LIT Ranch told me about the tepee rings. Of the eleven rings I mapped, all were incomplete. Wagon traffic over the old trail, along with natural processes, had displaced many stones, though a sufficient number remained in place to reveal generally circular outlines roughly twelve feet in diameter. I found no artifacts around the tepee rings, so it would be difficult to date them.

It didn't take Carson's command long to cross the three-mile expanse of rolling hills before they reached the steep slope bordering what is known today as the High Plains of Texas. Following the path set by their scouts, the contingent advanced through a gap where erosion had beveled the caliche caprock into a rough, but passable, opening. As was customary, the column halted after the wagons had ascended the hill, to allow the animals a brief respite and the teamsters time to make repairs on their wagons.

A great panoramic view of the vast expanse of flat land lay before them. To the south, at least twenty miles

across the Canadian River breaks, they saw the *ceja* (brow), of the Llano Estacado. Looking back to the west, the troopers observed nearly the entire route they had traveled the last two days.

It would have been interesting to hear the conversation of Carson's men describing the Plains upon seeing them for the first time. Since they didn't leave a written record, the impressions of other travelers will have to suffice.

Captain Randolph Barnes Marcy, Fifth U.S. Infantry, laid out the Marcy Trail from Fort Smith, Arkansas, to Santa Fe, New Mexico, in 1849. He was negatively impressed by that immense sea of grass called the Plains, the dreaded Llano Estacado. "It is a region almost as vast and trackless as the ocean—a land where no man, either savage or civilized, permanently abides; it spreads forth into a treeless, desolate waste of uninhabited solitude, which always has been, and must continue, uninhabited forever."[1]

Private Eddie Matthews, from Fort Union, recorded his thoughts in 1872, as he entered the Plains south of the Canadian River. Like Marcy, his impression of the flat lands was not favorable.

Fig. 47. High Plains of Texas Panhandle. Photograph by author, 2011.

We ascended a high hill then found ourselves on the 'famous staked Plains' of Texas. Famous for wild game of all kinds including Kiawa (sic) and Comanche Indians . . . As far as the eye can see is nothing but the bare plain, not the least hill or anything to obstruct one's view . . . What a pity some poor man could not own about forty miles of this land in some eastern city. It would then be worth something, but as it is, it is not worth one cent an acre at the present time. And it never will be worth anymore.[2]

Marcy and Matthews, both in the military, had immediate interests when crossing the Plains—water and forage for the livestock, and there was usually too little of both.

Jules Marcou, a geologist with First Lieutenant Amiel Weeks Whipple's survey in 1853, had more foresight and could see a promising future for the Plains. Whipple, commander of a survey for a proposed transcontinental railroad from the Mississippi River to the Pacific Ocean (1853–1856), noted in his daily report: "Mr. Marcou thinks that here, as upon the prairies crossed since leaving the Canadian, artesian wells might easily be made to afford plenty of water. Indeed; the numerous springs issuing from the sides of its bluff edges seem to prove the fact."[3]

Mr. Marcou was almost correct in his predictions. The water doesn't flow from artesian wells, but farmers today pump water from the Ogallala Formation and, thereby, grow a large amount of the world's food and fibers, such as corn, wheat, cotton, milo, and vegetables.

Carson's contingent, with horses and mules rested, wagons checked, and loads adjusted, was soon in motion again. Teams pulled with ease across the flat, grassy surface, not having to dodge clumps of sage and worrisome clusters of yucca. The troops' concerns about an ambush lessened because there were no hills to hide the Indians.

Easy travel and the diminished possibility of an Indian attack allowed troopers to relax and reflect on their homes and the loved ones waiting for them. Whether from a crude, adobe hut or finely furnished officers' quarters at Fort Union, memories of warm, pinion fires and home-cooked food likely drifted through their minds. Married men remembered their wives and children, while single troopers probably conjured up visions of a different segment of society—denizens of Taos and Santa Fe at the plaza ready for a fandango. Soldiers could almost hear the music resonating from the strings of the musician's fiddles and *guitiarras* (guitars) as dark-eyed *señoritas* sallied across the dance floor, bright skirts flowing, *cigarritos* dangling from their mouths, warm bodies moving to the beat of the music.

Keen-eyed Carson, frail from injuries and other health problems, could not help from knowing what his men were thinking. He might have wished for the warm hearth of his own adobe *hacienda*, with his children nestled in their beds and beautiful Josefa—the wife he had said goodbye to so many times as he departed on military campaigns.

Carson's passion for duty had placed his military service above his personal needs. Approximately twenty years earlier, in the Mexican-American War, Lieutenant Colonel John Charles Frémont, California Battalion, had dispatched Carson from California to Washington, D.C., with important letters. After suffering the hardships of passing through the southwest desert, the thought of seeing Josefa excited Carson; he would pass through Taos, rest, and spend a few days with his beloved wife before continuing.[4] But, it was not to be. Before Carson reached Taos, he met Brigadier General Stephen Watts Kearny traveling to California. Kearny and his troops of the Army of the West had captured New Mexico without firing a shot. After leaving some of his troops to keep order in Santa Fe, Kearny and the rest of his command began the long trek to California to participate in the actions against the Mexicans. When the contingent of soldiers met Carson, the general commanded him to

Fig. 48. *Fandango,* oil on canvas, by Theodore Gentilz (1819–1906), undated. SC05.047. Yanaguana Society Collection, Daughters of the Republic of Texas Library.

turn around and lead his troops to California, while sending another soldier on to Washington with the correspondence. Carson, although not pleased with his new responsibility, acquiesced to the realization that his action was necessary to help the United States defeat the Mexicans in California. Old Kit and his mule were on the scout again.[5]

Back to the Adobe Walls March

Carson's column relaxed only briefly to gaze across the plains of Texas on that cold November day in 1864. After proceeding about two miles, vigilant attention set in as they passed a deep ravine on the south and two playas on the north side of the road—excellent places for ambush. However, this day the troops would not fight Indians—they observed no other humans as they passed the gulley and lakes.

Somewhere near this area, Josiah Gregg, in 1839, came upon the old trail and penned in his journal the geographic wonder of the Canadian River Valley, presenting it as one of the most magnificent sights he had ever beheld. He described the perpendicular cliffs in all their majesty with the deep canyons below. Gregg, fascinated with the river valley, commented that it was so curiously formed that it could easily be mistaken for a work of art, and the Canadian River constituting a kind of chaotic space where nature seemed to have indulged in her wildest caprices.[6]

Carson's troops continued east across the prairie for two more miles. They arrived at a shallow ravine that ran a mile to the south and broadened into a large, natural lake. The site was ten miles east of the last camp on Rica Creek and may have been a noon stopping place, as confirmed by several military artifacts I found at the crossing. Travelers other than Carson may have gone south to the lake and camped there during dry years, for historic metal artifacts litter the lower terraces near the north shoreline.

When traveling west along this route in July 1866, Thomas A. Muzzall, with Colonel M. S. Howe's Third U.S. Cavalry, mentioned that he had seen a great deal of mirage that day.[7] A mirage is a naturally occurring, optical phenomenon in which different temperatures of air bend light rays to produce displaced images of distant objects or sky. Most residents of the Plains, even today, have witnessed the lake-that-wasn't-there or objects inverted and projected above the earth's horizon.

Many thirsty adventurers who crossed the prairie experienced mirages, usually in a desperate way, because of the illusion that a lake of water was ahead. Josiah Gregg, an experienced traveler on the Plains, called them false ponds. These phantom lakes were the most dangerous of any mirage, rendering many a man exhausted after jogging ahead to the lake and then realizing it did not exist at all.[8]

Carson's column, after leaving the noon camp, found it necessary to strike a more northward route to avoid deep canyons along the Canadian River. Abert had tried to cross the canyons about twenty years earlier and had contemplated abandoning his wagons because the terrain was so rough.[9]

The Ute and Jicarilla Apache scouts led Carson's command past a deep playa before leaving the Plains. There, the dim trail continued down the divide between Blue Creek on the north and Running Water Draw on the south. Today, U.S. Highway 87-287 crosses the old trail two miles south of Blue Creek. The comfort of traveling on the flat prairie vanished as Carson's men neared Blue Creek, where yucca, sage, plum thickets, bunchgrass, and small arroyos hampered their movement. The long train inched its way down the rough, gradual slope to the creek.

Carson must have carefully scanned the area for a suitable campsite. On the north side of the stream, a broad plain seemed an ideal place to camp, but Carson did not stop there. He continued down the creek for three-quarters of a mile, stopping at the base of steep bluffs, which offered a good defensive position and refuge from the late fall weather. There his troopers bivouacked, camping on both sides of the flowing creek where it curved eastward on its course. It was from this clear, running water that the creek got its name, Agua Azul (blue water), now known as Blue Creek.

At this site, today, bald eagles and turkeys roost among the rustling leaves of the cottonwood trees. Deer and quail hide in the plum thickets. Rabbits and other wildlife dwell in the underbrush. The valley, however, was not always as luxuriant, as trees have not always been present. This was almost certainly the case when Carson stopped there in 1864. Colonel Howe substantiated the lack of fuel two years after Carson's encampment there. In his report, Howe wrote that they had plenty of grass and water but no wood."[10]

Blue Creek, with its crystal-clear water and proximity to the Bascom Road, was a common gathering place,

Fig. 49. Fort Bascom–Adobe Walls Road near Blue Creek. Photograph by author, 1996.

in spite of the lack of trees. *Comancheros* set up their wares along the banks of the Blue, where they dickered with Comanches for the best deal.

Blue Creek has long been a hunting ground, sustaining a host of hunters over the years. Billy Dixon, in 1874, discovered camps abandoned by Mexican hunters.[11] John Cook, in *The Border and the Buffalo,* wrote about hunting bison with a group of *ciboleros* in the valley.[12]

That night, as the soldiers bedded down, they didn't realize how important this night's rest would be, for the next night there would be no sleep. In the ensuing forty-eight hours, the scouts, cavalry, and artillerymen would march fifty miles and fight a full day's battle with the Indians without benefit of sleep or food.

Carson, knowing his command was nearing its destination, remained vigilant. He stationed lookouts on the high bluffs to the north where they had a good view of the countryside. As they looked down at the warm campfires, they could see soldiers sleeping fitfully in bedrolls thrown upon the cold ground and, just beyond them, the shadowy figures of Utes and Jicarilla Apaches executing their nightly war dances in preparation for battle.

This would be the last night Carson would allow the Indians to dance, for the subsequent night his command would be on the trail of Comanches and Kiowas, and they would operate under an order of silence—"*no noise and no sleep.*"

Chapter 11
Blue Creek to Probable Mule Creek

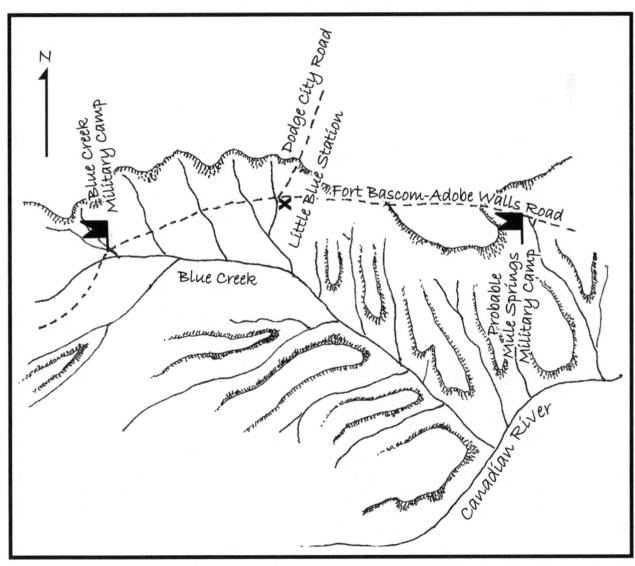

Map 11.1. Blue Creek to Probable Mule Creek. Illustrated by author and Lisa Jackson, 2011.

The morning of November 24, 1864, began as other mornings for Carson's command on the expedition to Adobe Walls, but the wind of change was blowing. The monotony of the long march was about over. Carson sent the scouts out early. After a quick breakfast, soldiers, stiff from another night on the cold ground, harnessed cantankerous mules. Wagons stood packed and ready to roll. Cavalrymen mounted their horses. The column was ready to move out, ever eastward, toward Adobe Walls. As in most of their earlier camps, it was an uphill march out of the valley.

Lugging the heavy wagons in the early morning shaved the edge off the livelier animals, and soon the horse and mule teams united in a rhythmic pull. Iron wheels crushing sagebrush and bushes, slapping wagon spokes, played out a familiar tune for the teamsters.

A mile out from Blue Creek, the column came upon a deep canyon that bisected the countryside. Men and animals wrestled their way across the brushy gorge, beyond which travel eased again as the topography changed to low, rolling hills and shallow valleys, some with flowing springs. A little farther down the trail, Carson's forces crossed modern-day Ludlow Creek. Today it is a dry crossing, but in all probability, it once ran water, for a spring still flows a short distance down the creek.

To the south, within walking distance of the spring, a sandstone outcrop tops a small knoll. On a bygone day, five Mexicans strolled by and lingered long enough to carve their names into two flat stones. There, they left their calling cards neatly etched in the rocks: *Juan Sandoval, Suarez, Cana, Rafel,* and *Juan M.* Perhaps they

Fig. 51. Mexican names incised on a rock on a Blue Creek tributary. Photograph by author, 2007.

were *ciboleros* who had ridden the Bascom Road to hunt bison or perhaps *Comancheros* who had journeyed there to trade.

Carson's retinue marched along the Bascom Trail over rounded hills and across dry, shallow valleys. Seven miles out from the previous night's camp, the group passed through two branches of a grassy valley. The year following Carson's passage through this valley, buffalo hunters, freighters, and the military established a road from Fort Dodge in Kansas to the plains of Texas and on to New Mexico. The new road intersected the Bascom Trail at this point and followed it to New Mexico. Colonel Evans's 1868 military map shows the valley as Wolf Creek. During the next decade, the westward movement pushed the frontier into the area, resulting in the establishment of Little Blue Stage Station, the result being that the spot was renamed Little Blue Creek, its present name.

One of my disappointments in mapping the Bascom Road is its elusiveness beyond Little Blue Creek eastward into Hutchinson County. There, it is so faint as to be invisible for most of the fifteen-mile stretch. Two factors figure in the absence of physical evidence. One is that without Dodge City traffic, the Bascom Road had fewer wheels rolling over it to cut deep ruts. Another is the destruction of virgin prairie by modern oilfield activity, where well pads dot the land and caliche roads have obliterated the dim wagon ruts.

In my quest to find the road, I thought I might spot it easier from the air, so I employed a pilot out of Dumas, Texas, Mickey Price and his small, top-winged plane. November 17, 1995, dawned clear and cool. I donned insulated coveralls, as suggested by Price. We met at

Fig. 50. Mexican names incised on a rock on a tributary of Blue Creek. Photograph by author, 2007.

Fig. 52. Probable area of Mule Springs camp. Photograph by author, 2011.

Moore County Airport west of Dumas. Price removed the right door to allow me an unobstructed view from which to photograph, but with the door off, the Federal Aviation Administration regulation required us to wear parachutes—a senseless requirement, since we flew very near the ground.

From the air, the trail was visible from south of Dumas to Little Blue Creek. Price crabbed the plane at an angle, allowing me several good shots. In the air, however, as on land, we lost the trail east of Little Blue Creek, and I saw no indication of the old road from the air.

Making a second stab at locating the road from the air, Amarillo pilot Jim Uselton flew me over the route in the spring of 2007. Again, to my frustration, I did not spot the obscure, fifteen-mile stretch of trail.

Even though my map is blank on this span of the ghost-trail, history has not been silent. While Army records contain nothing about Carson's previous nine days, they document the troop's activities for the next few days when they would have been on the intangible trail. These reports helped me locate small sections of an old trace that may be the Bascom Road. If Lieutenant George Pettis's calculations are correct, and if Carson's troops traveled eighteen miles from Blue Creek to Mule Springs, as Carson stated in his report, I hope, eventually, to find the camp.[1]

Carson's contingent, on November 24, 1864, camped at Arroya de la Mula (Mule Creek), which was located somewhere along the baffling fifteen-mile strip. Mule Creek was the jumping-off place for the last leg of Carson's march to battle.[2]

Chapter 12
Probable Mule Creek to the Canadian River

On the evening of November 24, 1864, the troopers had performed their usual camp duties before sunset. Some had begun to eat supper. It was no feast, nor were there special activities to celebrate that eve of the second official, national Thanksgiving Day. It likely passed unnoticed, perhaps even unknown, by Carson's contingent preparing for battle on a lonely prairie in Texas.

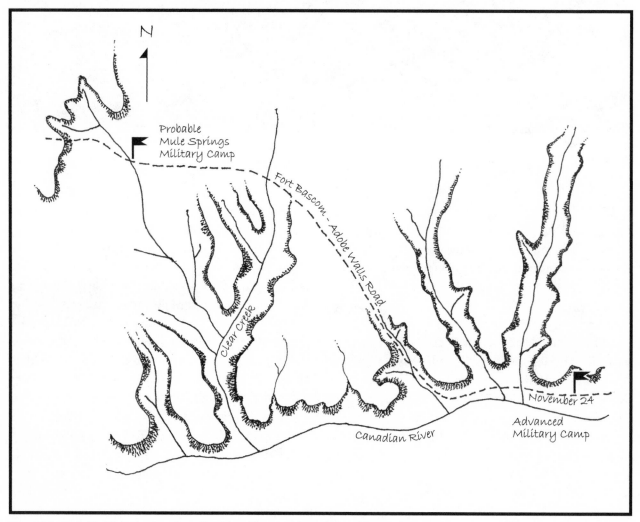

Map 12.1. Probable Mule Creek to Canadian River. Illustrated by author and Lisa Jackson, 2011.

Carson's Indians were lying about camp, some gambling, some sleeping. Others were waiting for something to eat from the soldiers' mess, when, suddenly, the Indians as a unit, sprang to their feet and gazed intently to the east, speaking excitedly in their own tongue.[1]

The surprised soldiers inquired of Carson, who comprehended the Indian languages, the cause of the commotion. Carson replied that the two Indian scouts he had dispatched that morning were then returning, and that the keen-eyed Indians in camp had spotted their barely discernible mounts on the horizon. Lieutenant Pettis, in his report, confessed that he had failed to see the tiny specks moving toward them on the hillside until an Indian pointed them out to him. Pettis said that what was more remarkable, was that the scouts, with a single shout into that rarefied, electrical atmosphere, had conveyed the intelligence that they had found the enemy and that work was to be done.[2]

A short time elapsed before the two scouts arrived. They rode through camp without answering any questions or giving any information until they found the colonel. To Carson, they reported that, about ten miles in advance, they had found indications that a large body of Indians with a very large herd of horses and cattle had moved that morning, and that the troops would have no difficulty in finding all the Indians they desired.[3]

Upon learning that Kiowas and Comanches were near, Carson immediately set his plan in motion. He split his troops, leaving the wagon train in camp. He ordered the dismounted cavalrymen and the foot soldiers of Company A, First California Infantry, under the command of Colonel Francisco Abreu, to remain in camp that night and to escort the wagon train on the morrow.[4]

The scouts would lead Carson, the artillery, and the mounted troops onward. Instead of rolling out their sleeping blankets, the scouts, cavalrymen, and troopers with the two mountain howitzers readied for a night march toward the Canadian River.[5] They filled their canteens, replenished their cartridge boxes and pouches, and stuffed their haversacks with food raided from the wagons.

Fig. 53. Wagon route through caprock to the Canadian River. *Orientation*: looking southeast. Photograph by Wyman Meinzer, 2009.

As night fell, the column followed the Indian trail that the scouts had discovered earlier in the day. Pettis reported that a heavy frost fell, so the night was probably moonlit and clear.[6] The soldiers' horses trudged across the rough terrain of several tributaries. As they neared the Canadian River, moonbeams revealed impassable red bluffs that dropped several hundred feet to another tributary of the Canadian.

A corridor opened to the tributary below. In bygone years, the hand of nature had carved a sandy arroyo through the bluffs. The gap was about ten miles out from camp, where the remainder of Carson's contingent lay sleeping, and approximately twenty miles west of Adobe Walls, where Kiowas and Comanches slumbered in their tepees.

This pass gained a place in United States court records when J. M. Robinson of Channing, Texas, mentioned it in a deposition thirty years later. A United States judge traveled to various Texas settlements to gain testimony from buffalo hunters and settlers concerning stream and wagon road locations in the Texas Panhandle to settle a boundary dispute between the United States and the State of Texas. When the judge questioned Robinson, Robinson stated that one wagon road came up out of the river bottom twenty miles west of Adobe Walls and joined the Bascom Trail at the head of Little Blue Creek.[7] The old road used the natural cut in the red bluffs for access to higher ground from the river.

Even with light from the moon, the descent into the Canadian River Valley was tedious. After picking their way down the steep, rough passage, the troopers followed a fresh Indian trail spotted by the scouts. Carson called a halt until daylight, following a march of about ten miles. Wanting to get a more precise notion of where the Comanches and Kiowas were, Carson sent his scouts back out.

It was a miserable stop. The soldiers were tired, not having slept since the previous night. Their fatigue added to the loathing they felt for their situation, including the hateful *no smoking and no talking* order. A heavy frost settled on them as they stood beside their horses, reins in hand, for the duration of the night. Their one consolation was that they did not have to endure the wailing and moaning of the Utes and Jicarilla Apaches doing their war dance, as Carson forbade it.

Chapter 13
Down River to Adobe Walls: The First Battle of Adobe Walls

Colonel Carson's scouts returned from down river just as the last hold of darkness gave way to daylight. At that time of day, during the winter, the temperature falls to its lowest point, and on a clear night, the heaviest frost forms. Troopers were almost numb from standing and holding their mounts for several hours. They welcomed Carson's order to saddle up and move out. The previous night, when the troops had descended into the river bottom, they were about a mile from the main channel, but as they moved eastward, the bluffs closed in on the river. By the time the column made its late night halt, it was right on the riverbank.

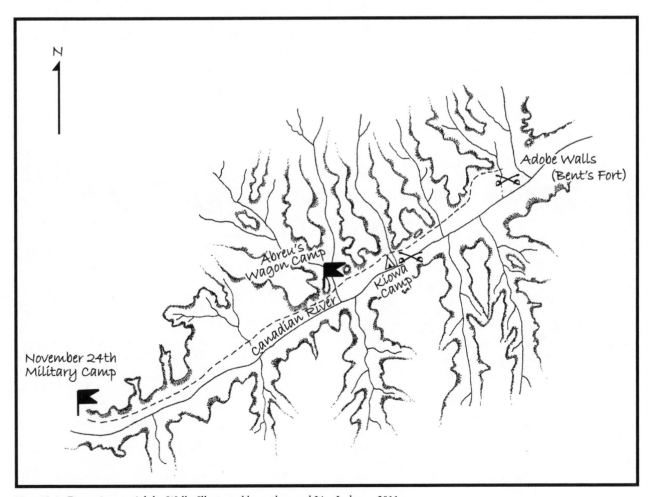

Map 13.1. Downriver to Adobe Walls. Illustrated by author and Lisa Jackson, 2011.

The troops were in the river channel when they marched out in the early hours of morning. Cane grasses were so tall that Pettis and Carson, who were riding side by side, had a hard time seeing each other.[1] Many years earlier (fall 1845), Lieutenant Abert wrote that the banks were, everywhere, covered with tall cane grass from six to eight feet high.[2]

Continuing their early morning march, they rode in order, with the scouts, Carson, and Pettis up front. About half of the cavalry rode behind the scouts, with the section of mountain howitzers close behind the cavalry. The remainder of the cavalry brought up the rear.[3]

The contingent of men and animals must have presented a strange, rather comical, sight. Indian scouts, knees pulled up high, and wrapped in conical buffalo robes, appeared as small tepees on horseback.[4] Horses and soldiers labored through tall cane grass, with their breath producing vaporous images like mythical creatures that disappeared and reappeared with each new breath.

After marching about two miles, the troops came to the end of the bluffs, and the terrain opened into about a three-mile-stretch of low, rolling hills cut by small valleys and rivulets. Red hillocks, scattered across the rolling land, brightened the drab, winter landscape. The column left the sandy riverbed and moved up, out of the tall cane grass, onto the undulating topography where the more-solid ground made travel easier.

The Battle Begins

About halfway across the broad expanse, soldiers heard *"Bene-acá! Bene-acá!*—Come here! Come here!"[5] The call from Kiowa pickets on the opposite side of the river broke the constant clamor of troop movement.[6]

Why did the Kiowas call?

Perhaps the Indians thought the passing riders were *Comanchero* traders, not recognizing them as soldiers. If the Indians knew they were soldiers, and the call was a challenge to the troops, then they got what they wanted. Whatever the reason, the ever-alert Carson hastily ordered Cavalry Commander Major William McCleave, with B Company, California Cavalry, and Captain Charles Deus, First Cavalry, New Mexico Volunteers, across the river in pursuit of the Kiowas.[7]

In a short time, shots rang out from the detachment Carson had sent to chase the Indian pickets. The shots rapidly multiplied to thousands, as the torturous events of the day unfolded into the First Battle of Adobe Walls.

Carson's Ute and Jicarilla Apache scouts, eager to fight, charged into the chaparral brush, shed their buffalo robes, and quickly emerged half-naked and deco-

Fig. 54. Near this point Carson made contact with the Kiowa Indians. Photograph by author, 2011.

Fig. 55. Colonel William A. McCleave, First California Cavalry. McCleave held the rank of major at the 1864 Adobe Walls battle. #ZIM CSWR Pict. Colls. PICT 000-742. Courtesy of Center for Southwest Research, University of New Mexico.

Fig. 56. Captain Charles Deus (1822–1904) in later years. Courtesy of June E. Bausman, great-great granddaughter of Charles Deus.

rated with war paint and war feathers. Pettis wrote of his amazement at the wonderful transformation of Carson's Indians dashing wildly into the river towards the enemy.[8]

Carson continued his march down the Canadian River until he approached a large, red bluff on the west side of Mustang Creek, (present-day Moore and Bugbee creeks). From a foothill at the base of the bluff, Carson could see the Indian village about five miles in the distance. At this point, he sent Captain Emil Fritz, First Cavalry, California Volunteers, with Company B on ahead to join Major McCleave. After hearing more gunshots, Carson ordered additional troopers to advance while he stayed back with a few mounted troops to protect the two howitzers.[9]

The foot soldiers made a gallant effort to keep the artillery rolling across the flood debris scattered among the cane, grasses, and weeds in the confluence of the Red (Canadian) River and Mustang Creek. The mountain

howitzers, placed on narrow frames, overturned easily. Setting them right delayed progress, and crossing the riverbed wilderness took about an hour. Relieved and exhausted, with no time to rest, the sound of rifle shots propelled the men onward.[10]

Trying to make up distance and time, the officer gave the command "trot-march" to the fatigued foot soldiers. I imagine a few choice words spewed forth under their breath, and even while making every effort to obey the command, some fell back. To the stragglers' relief came the order, "walk-march," allowing them to catch up. This sequence of orders continued as the battery moved down river. Even at this fast pace, the sound of battle grew fainter as the fighting moved eastward.[11]

The artillery battery entered a meadow where the Kiowas' horses grazed, just east of an isolated mesa. There the Ute and Jicarilla Apache scouts were busy cutting out their personal groups of ponies. Part of their agreement to serve with Carson was permission to keep any horses and other loot they could capture. Though

Fig. 57. *Carson's Howitzers on the Way to Adobe Walls,* oil on canvas, by Richard Hogue, 1985. Courtesy of Richard Hogue.

Fig. 58. Cattle grazing at the probable site of Kiowa remuda. Photograph by Wyman Meinzer, 2009.

Stella Carson Harrington. Granddaughter of Christopher "Kit" Carson. Born December 18, 1916. Courtesy of VeAnn Clark, Stella's granddaughter.

1864 Adobe Walls Battle, Kiowa ledger drawing, 1997. Courtesy of James Coverdale.

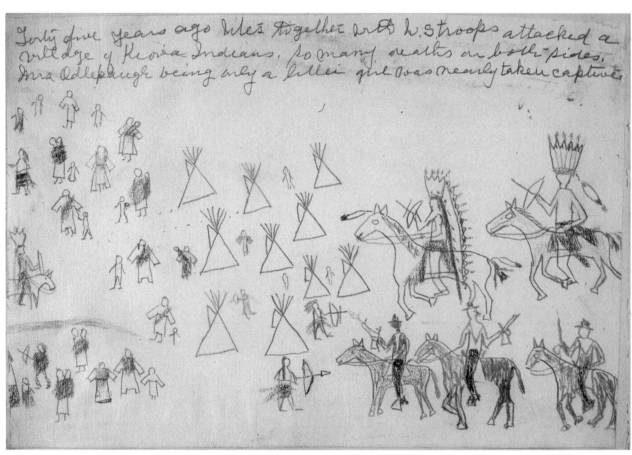

U.S. Troops and Ute Scouts Attacking a Kiowa Village, ledger drawing, *circa* 1909, from Isabel Crawford Collection. Crawford was a Methodist missionary to the Kiowas in Indian Territory. Courtesy of the American Baptist Historical Society, Atlanta, Georgia.

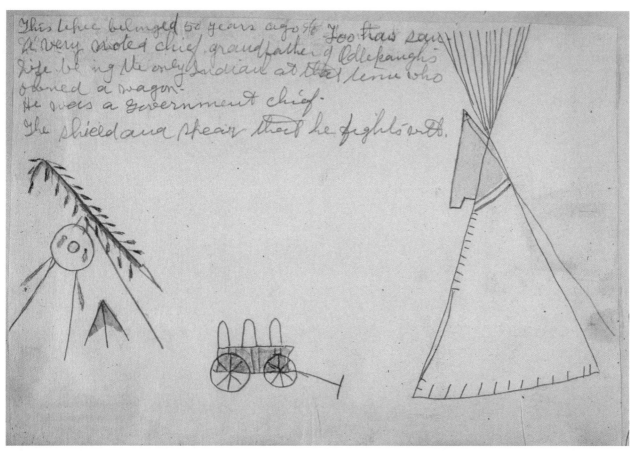

Chief Dohäsan's Wagon, Tepee, and Shield, ledger drawing, *circa* 1909, from Isabel Crawford collection. A Methodist missionary, Crawford served the Kiowas in the late 1800s and early 1900s. Courtesy of the American Baptist Historical Society, Atlanta, Georgia.

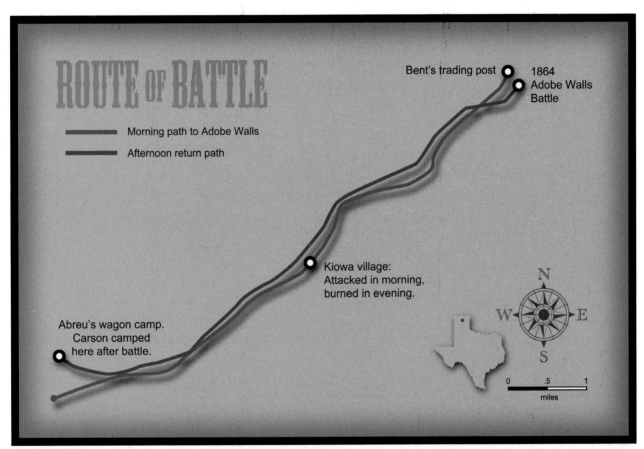

First Battle of Adobe Walls; route of battle from morning campsite to Adobe Walls and back to Abreu's wagon camp. Illustration by Roland Pantermuehl.

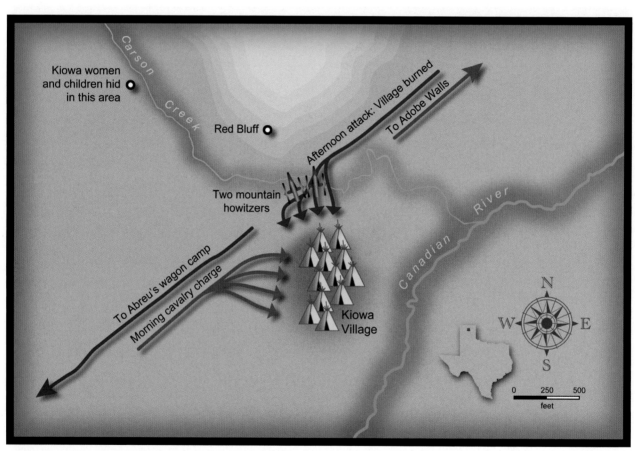

Battle site at Kiowa village. Illustration by Roland Pantermuehl.

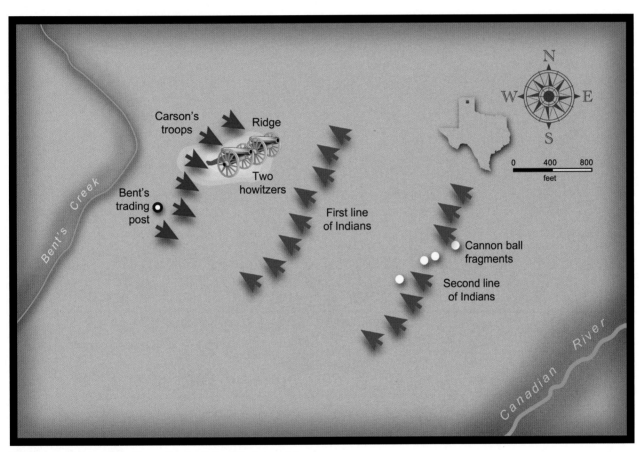

Battle site at Adobe Walls. Illustration by Roland Pantermuehl.

Day after the Battle of Adobe Walls, watercolor, by an unnamed soldier with Carson's command. Dated November 26, 1864. Given to Dr. George C. Courtright. Courtesy of Carolyn Lutz, great-granddaughter of Dr. Courtright.

Firing mountain howitzer. Re-enactment squad, Fort Sill, Oklahoma, 2011. Photograph by Rod Roadruck.

Teh-toot-sah (*circa* 1795–1866), oil on canvas, by George Catlin, 1834. *Teh-toot-sah* was also known as Tohausen, Dohäsan, Little Bluff, and Sierrito. His name translates as "Little Mountain," "Little Bluff," or "Top of the Mountain." First Chief of the Kiowa from 1833 until his death. He was from the Kata band of Kiowas. #1985.66.62. Smithsonian American Art Museum, Gift of Mrs. Joseph Harrison, Jr.

John Carson, great-grandson of Kit Carson, receiving a gift from James Coverdale, great-great-grandnephew of Chief Dohäsan at site of Dohäsan's Kiowa village. Photograph by author, 2009.

Red River Springs area. Carson's camp was west of trees along north side of Canadian River. Photograph by author. 2004

Nara Visa Springs. Carson's camp was on a hill across the creek. Photograph by author. 1996

Hay Creek. Site of Carson's camp. Photograph by Wyman Meinzer, 2009.

Romero Creek. Site of Carson's camp. Photograph by Wyman Meinzer, 2009.

Los Redos Creek. Carson's camp was on flat behind windmill. Photograph by Wyman Meinzer, 2009.

Rica Creek. Site of Carson's Camp. Photograph by Wyman Meinzer, 2009.

Blue Creek. Site of Carson's camp. Photograph by Wyman Meinzer, 2009.

Canadian River Valley. *Orientation*: Looking southwest from the caprock. Photograph by Wyman Meinzer, 2009.

Moore Creek. *Orientation*: Overlooking Carson's campsite from a high mesa. Photograph by Wyman Meinzer, 2009.

Kiowa village site at Red Bluff (*Guadal Doha*). *Orientation*: looking north from village site. Photograph by Wyman Meinzer, 2009.

Red Bluff military campsite where Billy Dixon received Medal of Honor on Christmas Eve Day, 1874. *Orientation*: looking east from *Guadal Doha*. Photograph by Wyman Meinzer, 2009.

Cannon Hill where Lt. George Pettis placed the two mountain howitzers. Photograph by Wyman Meinzer, 2009.

Battlefield, First Battle of Adobe Walls, 1864. Photograph by Wyman Meinzer, 2009.

Wyman Meinzer and Alvin Lynn. On a bluff overlooking Canadian River. Photograph by Joe Faulkenberry, 2009.

Night fire. Lt. James Abert observed such a fire near Red River Springs in 1845 and penned, "It is a scene of great sublimity." Photograph by Wyman Meinzer, 2009.

Fort Bascom–Adobe Walls Road. Aerial view. Photograph by Wyman Meinzer, 2009.

Texas button (1836) found at Red River Springs. Photograph by Wyman Meinzer, 2009.

Medallion (1861) for shoulder strap. Found at Red River Springs. Photograph by Wyman Meinzer, 2009.

Indian lance blade found in Kiowa village campsite. Photograph by Wyman Meinzer, 2009.

Gun-cleaning brushes found at Los Redos Creek. Photograph by Wyman Meinzer, 2009.

Brass Indian earring found at Rica Creek. Photograph by Wyman Meinzer, 2009.

Small brass crucifix found at Romero Creek. Photograph by Wyman Meinzer, 2009.

Brass buttons found at Los Redos Creek. Photograph by Wyman Meinzer, 2009.

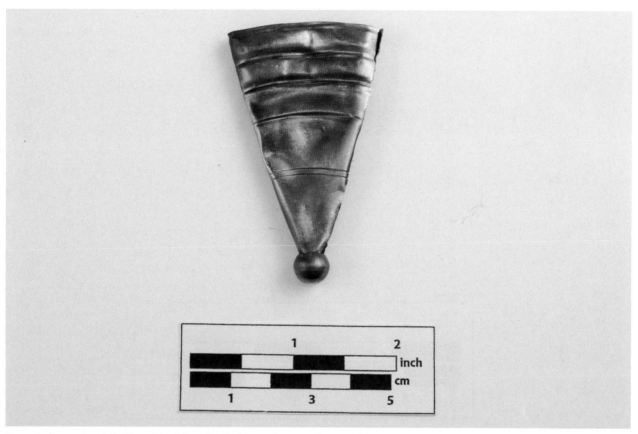

Brass tip from a Bowie knife scabbard found at Red River Springs. Photograph by Wyman Meinzer, 2009.

Lead bead necklace found at Romero Creek. Photograph by Wyman Meinzer, 2009.

Brass rifle trigger-guard found in Kiowa village campsite. Photograph by Wyman Meinzer, 2009.

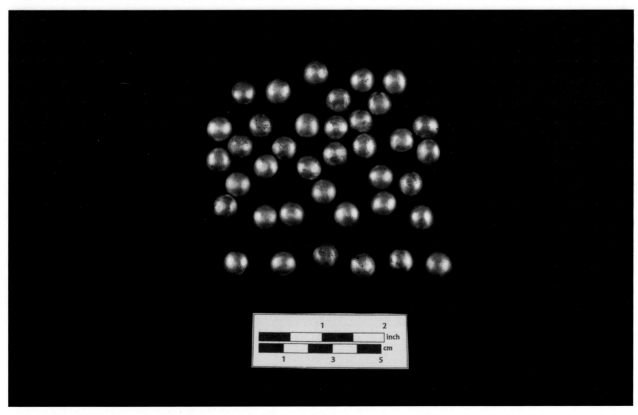

Brass "bullet" buttons found in Kiowa village campsite. Photograph by Wyman Meinzer, 2009.

Brass arrowpoint and cuttings found on Cannon Hill. Photograph by Wyman Meinzer, 2009.

Large brass key found in Kiowa village campsite. Photograph by Wyman Meinzer, 2009.

anxious to fight, their priorities surfaced upon spotting the remuda, and they gathered their bounty before they fought the battle.[12]

The Comanches likely kept their horses near their villages, which were seven or eight miles east of Dohäsan's village, and they did not join the Kiowas in battle until Carson's troops reached Adobe Walls. Just beyond the grassy area, a ridge ran from the base of a bluff to the edge of the river channel blocking Carson's view to the east, but as Carson and his men reached the crest, they could see for two miles across a flat plain. There stood tall, white tents. Pettis and his men, having never before seen Plains Indian tepees, took them to be Sibley tents. However, Carson assured them that the dwellings were tepees and not Sibley tents.[13]

And, tepees they were. Indeed, two miles in front of them was the winter village of old Chief Dohäsan. Dohäsan had been principal chief of the Kiowas since 1833, a position he held until his death in 1866.[14] Both Indians and white men held him in high esteem, and two separate artists preserved his image for posterity.

Fig. 60. Sibley military tent. From *The Prairie Traveler, A Handbook for Overland Expeditions,* by Randolph B. Marcy, 1859.

Fig. 59. Ridge from where Carson spotted Dohäsan's Kiowa village on November 25, 1864. *Orientation*: looking east. Photograph by Wyman Meinzer, 2009.

George Catlin (1796–1872), with the 1834 Colonel Henry Dodge Expedition, painted a portrait of Chief Dohäsan and described him as a gentleman and a high-minded man who treated the dragoons and officers with great kindness while in his country. Dohäsan wore his hair long, extending down to his knees. He fashioned it in several large clubs, ornamented with a great many silver brooches.[15]

Eleven years after Catlin's painting, Abert met Dohäsan, while passing through the Texas Panhandle, and made a watercolor of him. Abert depicted Dohäsan as having succumbed to a sedentary life and a healthy appetite—a man of middling stature, quite fat, with a wide mouth upon which played a constant smile. His whole face showed an intriguing character. Abert found him to be very intelligent.[16]

Chief Dohäsan had chosen his winter camp well. The tall Plains tepees nestled in a flat area surrounded by sand hills on the west, north, and east, with the south side opened toward the river. Just north of the village, a clear, running stream flowed around the base of a red bluff. This bluff, along with the other red bluffs Carson had passed near Mustang Creek earlier in the morning,

Fig. 61. A Kiowa tepee, detail from photograph. #1974-186/91a. Courtesy of Panhandle Plains Historical Museum.

Fig. 62. Chief Dohäsan's Kiowa village site. *Orientation*: looking north. Photograph by author, 2011.

were significant to the Kiowas for winter encampments and sun dances.

The Kiowa Calendar, a history of Kiowa activities, contains two accounts of this area. In the summer of 1840, the Kiowas held the *Guadal Doha Kado* (red-bluff sun dance), on the north side of the South Canadian near the mouth of Mustang Creek.[17] The area was still in use almost a quarter of a century later when the Kiowas, Apaches, and part of the Comanches made their 1864 winter camp at *Guadal Doha*, between Adobe Walls and Mustang Creek.[18]

In December 2004, at sunup on a clear, frosty morning, I stood alone on the same ridge where Carson and his men viewed the Kiowa village. From my vantage point, the bluffs behind me reflected a brilliant, red-orange color as the sun rose a few degrees in the eastern sky. Coyotes, scattered along the river, howled in unison as if sounding reveille to bid the night farewell and to wake the world. I envisioned the white Kiowa tepees as they stood nearly 150 years ago, scattered near the red bluff two miles to the east.

On the morning of November 25, 1864, the initial clash between McCleave's troops and the Indians was fierce and brief. When the cavalry stormed the village (of mostly Kiowas with a few Comanches and Apaches), McCleave was unaware that most of the Indian men were away on the warpath. His battle was to be with an old chief leading a small mix of seasoned and young warriors who had stayed in camp to protect their lodges and inhabitants.[19]

The attack was a surprise to the Indians. A few of the young warriors had left the village early in the morning to gather their horses when one of the Indians spotted the vanguard of Carson's troops advancing down the river. The Indians made haste back to camp with their string of mounts to warn of the impending danger and to clear the camp of women, children, and captives.[20]

Captives in Dohäsan's Kiowa Village

Among the Indian's captives were the widow and two children of a sergeant from the Colorado Volunteers who had been killed a month earlier in Kansas.[21] When Carson's soldiers burned the Kiowa village later in the day, they found accoutrements of the Colorado volunteer sergeant[22] along with women and children's clothing that would have belonged to non-Indian captives.

Of the two to four remaining captives, one of the children, an infant only eighteen months of age, was Millie Durgan. Two families, the Durgans and the Johnsons, were captured by a Kiowa-Comanche raiding party led by Comanche chief Little Buffalo, during the Elm Creek, Texas, raid of October 1864. Britt Johnson, the father of one family, trailed the Indians and helped bring back his family and all of the Durgan family except Millie.[23] A Kiowa couple, Gray Mare and his wife, Cry Woman, had adopted Millie, and they refused to trade her or to accept money for her. They gave her the name *Say-haye-do-hole* (Killed-with-blunt-arrow) and raised her as their daughter. Millie's Kiowa parents treated her well, and she loved them and their way of life and never considered going back to live with whites.[24]

Millie married a young warrior, *Tape-tsio*, and when he died, she became the wife of a prominent Kiowa warrior named *Goombi*. Millie Durgan, *Say-haye-do-hole Goombi*, died in 1934 at the age of seventy at Mountain View, Oklahoma.[25]

Fig. 63. Millie Durgan Goombi (1859–1934), *circa* 1931. #PL844. Fort Sill National Historic Landmark and Museum, Fort Sill, Oklahoma. Courtesy Towana Spivey.

In her later years, while living in Mountain View, Mrs. Goombi related the following account of the day in 1864 that Kit Carson raided Dohäsan's Kiowa camp. "Once when I was a child, our Kiowa camp was raided by the Ute Indians who were led by the white scout, Kit Carson. My parents hid me safely in the brush next to the camp, and I escaped any harm."[26]

A few historians do not accept that Mrs. Goombi was the same person as Millie Durgan, even though Mrs. Goombi, herself, said she was. One bit of evidence that supports their being the same, comes from a portion of a letter from C. T. Johnson, son of Britt Johnson, written in 1933 to Mrs. Millie Durgan Goombi:

> Mrs Millie Durgan Dear friend it a fords much pleasure to write you and family You was took By the Indians the same time my mother was you was about 18 months old at that time in 1864

i brought back memery your mother was name Susie Durgan She was killed in the Reid also my Brother Jimmy Johnson was killed i would like to see you Britt Johnson is my father i am the Baby Boy Born 1871 at the time 62 about 9 years younger than you or.[27]

Back to Carson's Attack on the Kiowa Village

When Carson, Pettis, and the artillery battery reached the Kiowa camp, following McCleave's attack, the village was vacant. Army records are silent on the skirmish, except for one account. Dr. Courtright, who was with McCleave during the initial charge, made one brief statement: "In the fight at the Indian village I saw the arrows flying in all directions, and could scarcely distinguish our own Indians from those of the enemy."[28]

Fig. 64. Brushy area north of Kiowa village where women, children, and captives hid during the First Battle of Adobe Walls, 1864. Photograph by author, 2011.

It is from the Kiowas' version that we get a description of the attack. The young Kiowa warriors were in the horse camp when they and McCleave's troops caught sight of each other. Carson's Ute scouts advanced, in Indian fashion, riding about and whooping, keeping up a constant yell to stampede the other Indians' ponies. The soldiers followed quietly in regular order.[29]

With most of the Kiowa men away on the warpath, the village was under the charge of Chief Dohäsan. The warriors who had remained in the village held the soldiers off long enough for the Indian women and children, along with the captives, to escape into the sand hills north of the camp, west of the red bluff where they hid themselves in the sumac, hackberry trees, and plum bushes.[30]

At the time of the attack, the aged Chief Dohäsan was yet a warrior. When he saw Carson's troops arriving, his military instinct spurred him to action. He raced ahead to warn the Kiowa and Comanche villages downstream. With wives and children safely hidden, the Kiowa warriors moved, with haste, across the four-mile stretch down the Canadian River toward Adobe Walls. McCleave and the cavalry were on their tail. The Indians, well acquainted with the area, played it to their advantage, taking protection behind the sandy, gravelly hills that veered toward the river bottom from the north. The battle was hot—each side contested for every foot of ground.[31]

Stumbling Bear's Magpie Magic

During the skirmish at Dohäsan's village, two Kiowas distinguished themselves. Stumbling Bear, one of the leading warriors, killed a soldier and a Ute and wounded a soldier who fell from his horse. Kiowa tradition relates that Stumbling Bear received personal power from a magpie. He attached the body of a magpie to his warbonnet inside the circle of eagle feathers. The story goes that, during the battle at the Kiowa village, soldiers shot away most of the eagle feathers, exposing the magpie on the crown of the bonnet. As Stumbling Bear was riding, the magpie's wings opened and flapped, making the bird seem to come alive and fly. The Kiowa women observed the strange sight from their hiding places and cheered Stumbling Bear as he fought bravely against the soldiers.[32]

Another Kiowa warrior, Lean Bear, distinguished himself by his bravery in singing the war song of his order, the Tönkönke, as he advanced to the charge, fulfill-

Fig. 65. Stumbling Bear, Kiowa warrior, with bow and arrows, *circa* 1872. Stumbling Bear participated in the 1864 Adobe Walls battle. Fort Sill National Historic Landmark and Museum, Fort Sill, Oklahoma. Courtesy Towana Spivey.

ing his military obligation. The Tönkönke, further, forbade Lean Bear from saving himself until he had killed an enemy.[33]

By the time the running skirmish reached Adobe Walls, Dohäsan had alerted the other villages. There the Indians made their stand and positioned themselves to meet the charging troops.

Carson heard the shooting between McCleave's troops and the Indians and saw the smoke of battle as it moved swiftly downstream. Not knowing the enormous number of Indians gathering from several villages, Carson was confident that the battle would be short, perhaps even finished by the time the howitzers reached the arena of action. Pitching his greatcoat onto a bush beside the road, Carson told Pettis that he would retrieve it after the battle, when they returned to burn the village. Carson encouraged Pettis and his men to do the same with their coats, but Pettis refused.[34] Pettis later wrote, "for once my judgment was better than Carson's for he never saw that coat of his again, while my own and those of my men did good service afterwards."[35]

About a mile and a half west of Adobe Walls, the men of the howitzer battery topped a high, gravel ridge. From it, they had a good view of the battle site. They saw the fire and accompanying smoke in front of the crumbling walls of the old adobe fort built by William Bent. The walls stood on a low promontory, just east of a running creek and about a hundred yards southwest of a saddleback ridge.

Bent's Fort: Adobe Walls

Today, ranch corrals spread across the knoll where the fort once stood, and there is no visible evidence of the walls. In October 2005, I scraped back dry manure in the largest pen of the corrals, which now occupy the site. I found three flat rocks lying in a north-south orientation in a bed of charcoal-tinged adobe, which I believe to be the remnant of an adobe wall.

There is some question as to when Bent erected the structure, but most evidence points to 1845.[36] Bent had made an excursion into the area about two years earlier and had built a wooden fort for trading with the Indians near the red bluffs at Mustang Creek, about nine miles west of the Adobe Walls. According to the Kiowa Winter Calendar of 1843–1844, Bent built another wooden fort just west of present-day Horse Creek near Canadian, Texas.[37]

On an expedition to Adobe Walls in 1860, Major Ruff reported that the remains of another fort or trading post, sometimes called Wooden Fort, existed nine miles west of Adobe Walls.[38] In 1874, Lieutenant H. J. Farnsworth, with Major William Redwood Price's command, spent the night at the fort on Mustang Creek and called it *Fuerte de Palo* (Fort of Wood).[39]

Bent knew that wooden forts offered little protection from fiery arrows. Concerned for his goods, and his life, he soon left the area and moved back to his main trading post on the Arkansas River in Colorado. There, he and his business partner, Ceran St. Vrain, hired Mexican adobe brick makers and headed back to the Canadian River. Bent chose to construct a stout, adobe fort near a creek that subsequently carried his name. He described the fort as eighty feet by eighty feet with nine-foot high walls.[40] Ruff, in 1860, recorded the fort as being much larger—the west wall was 100 feet long and the north wall 180 feet.[41] It appears that Bent added rooms to the original structure.

According to George Bent, William Bent's son,

Carson, in 1848, took a small expedition to Adobe Walls to open trade with the Indians, to no avail. Jicarilla Apaches killed Carson's herdsman and ran off all of the horses except two pack mules, forcing Carson and his partners to bury their trade wares, pack all the goods the two mules could carry, and return to Bent's Trading Post in Colorado. The return trip was unhappy; Indians attacked them, and cactus thorns and sharp rocks penetrated their moccasins on the long trek, inflaming their feet. They ended their trip footsore, weary, and feverish.[42]

In late 1848, after William Bent had made two more attempts to open trade at Adobe Walls, the Indians became so resistant that Bent, reportedly, blew up the interior of the building and returned to Colorado.[43] The explosion must have been small, because Ruff, in 1860, reported that a major part of the fort was in good condition.[44]

When Carson topped the ridge at Adobe Walls in 1864, chances are he recognized the old fort and the surrounding terrain from having been there in 1848, but he had no time for nostalgia. Surveying the scene before him, his quick eye noted Dr. Courtright setting up a medical station inside the walls of the old trading post, where the cavalry had corralled their horses. Looking farther, Carson saw hundreds of Indians charging the troops stationed as skirmishers in the high grass around the fort.[45]

As Carson, Pettis, and the howitzer battery reached a sandy rise, about a half-mile west of the battle site, the proximity to battle ignited the colonel. Jabbing the flanks of his mount and ignoring his physical ailments, the seasoned warrior advanced headlong into the battle with his mounted men close behind. Carson joined McCleave on a knoll at the west end of a ridge about a hundred yards northeast of the adobe fort. The high point afforded an unobstructed view south to the Canadian River and to the east for several miles, broken only by a few trees along Adobe Creek.[46]

Pettis and his foot soldiers, the last and slowest of the detail, proceeded forward with the two howitzers. Pettis said his men seemed to get new life and forget all their fatigue at the prospect of going into action. Only a few minutes elapsed before the mounted officers reached the center of the field at a gallop.[47] As soon as Pettis's detail reached the ridge northeast of the adobe fort, Carson yelled, "Pettis, throw a few shell into that crowd over thar," and Pettis responded, "Battery, halt! Section right—load with shell—LOAD!"[48]

Fig. 66. Cannon Hill, where Lt. George Pettis placed the two howitzers for the Adobe Walls battle. Photograph by author, 2010.

When Carson yelled, "that crowd over thar," he pointed to about two hundred yelling Kiowas and Comanches who were riding back and forth and firing under the necks of their horses at the soldiers. Behind the Indians was a line of twelve hundred to fourteen hundred additional warriors with several chiefs riding up and down the line urging them on.[49]

Pettis, observing from the ridge, spoke as a true soldier when he said, "A finer sight I never saw before and probably shall never see again."[50]

It took only a short time to load and sight the cannons; and then the command came, "Number one—FIRE!" followed quickly by, "Number two—FIRE!" The two howitzers belched smoke as their twelve-pound, cast-iron balls whistled across the plain toward the mounted warriors. The Indians, not familiar with the big guns, stood high in their stirrups and pondered the firing. As the shells began to explode around them, they headed their mounts, in a dead run, toward their villages

down river. By the time the artillerymen fired another volley, the Indians were totally out of range of the cannons.[51]

Pettis's order, "Section right," implied that most of the Indians were south and southeast of the hill. Fragments of exploded cannon balls buried under a foot of soil, four-tenths of a mile southeast of the howitzers confirmed the direction of fire.

The mountain howitzer could fire three types of ammunition: spherical shell, spherical cased shot, and canister. Spherical shells were powder-filled, hollow balls with a wall thickness averaging seven-tenths of an inch. The cast-iron cases served as shrapnel upon explosion. At five degrees elevation, the spherical shell had a 1,005-yard range.[52] Spherical cased shot had a round, cast-iron wall averaging one-half inch in thickness. The inside of the shell contained .69-caliber lead balls packed in sulfur. The spherical cased shot had an eight hundred yard range at five degrees elevation.[53] Canister ordnance was

Fig. 67. Lieutenant George Henry Pettis, First Regiment, New Mexico Volunteers. #246375. Meketa Collection. At U.S. Army Military Institute, Carlisle, PA.

a large tinned can filled with .69-caliber lead balls used for close range. Canisters had an effective range of 200 to 250 yards.[54]

The cannon ball fragments that I found averaged one-half inch in thickness, which is the average measurement for the wall of spherical case shot. I also found a .69-caliber lead ball in the vicinity of the fragments. Even though Pettis commanded, "load with shell," I believe the soldiers also fired spherical cased shot.

I found, on the ridge, five friction primers of the kind used to fire the howitzers. This helped me identify the spot where Pettis had placed the cannons.

When the Indians fled after the howitzer shells exploded, Carson thought the battle was over. He called for the cavalrymen to unsaddle their mounts, unhitch, and water the teams at a clear stream west of Adobe Walls. The horses drank their fill, and then the soldiers picketed them in the lush grass along the creek. Carson felt confident that the Indians had quit, so he called in his skir-

Fig. 68. *Indians Surprised by Firing of Howitzers,* oil on canvas, by Richard Hogue, 1977. Courtesy of Richard Hogue.

Fig. 69. Cannon ball fragment. 1864 Adobe Walls battlefield, southeast of Cannon Hill. Photograph by author, 2010.

Fig. 70. Lead ball, .69 caliber, found near a cannon ball fragment. May have been from spherical case shot. 1864 Adobe Walls battlefield. Photograph by author, 2010.

Fig. 71. Artillery friction primers found on Cannon Hill near where Pettis fired the howitzers. Photograph by Wyman Meinzer, 2009.

mishers. The troops filled their canteens and searched their haversacks for whatever they could find to eat. They had not eaten since the previous evening at Mule Creek before the night march and morning battle. As the troops took their respite in the early afternoon, Carson, ever on the lookout, noticed through his glass a large force of Indians approaching from downriver.[55]

To the Indians, the fight was not over; they had not quit, nor were they finished with the white intruders who were invading their winter camps.

Responding to Carson's commands, the officers quickly mounted. Pettis's men hitched the teams to the artillery pieces and pulled them back to the ridge. The troopers returned their horses to the protection of the adobe fort before they spread out again as skirmishers.[56]

It was only a few minutes before a fusillade of rifle balls flecked the ground around the soldiers. Carson's troops returned fire, producing a veil of acrid smoke that hovered above them as they crouched in the grass. Pettis's artillery battery returned to action but was not as effective as it had been in the morning, for the Indians had learned that they were a more difficult target if they spread out. Still, the mighty fire of the howitzers prevented the huge number of Indians from amassing and overrunning the troops.

One warrior, however, did not escape the fury of the big guns; a shell passed all the way through his horse and traveled some distance before exploding. As the horse stumbled forward in his death fall, the Indian flew high into the air. As soon as he hit the ground, two brave warriors rode alongside him, grabbed his arms, and dragged him from the battlefield.[57]

As the battle raged, an odd thing occurred that amused even the hardened soldiers. One lone Indian, a bugler, stationed himself behind the charging warriors and blew calls in opposition to the bugler with Carson's skirmishers. When the military bugler sounded *advance*, the Indian sounded *retreat*, and vice versa.[58]

"The Indian bugler answered our signals each time they were blown, to the infinite merriment of our men, who responded with shouts of laughter each time he sounded his horn," Pettis said.[59]

The Indian bugler was probably Satanta, a noted Kiowa warrior with a dry wit who, when younger, had stolen a bugle along with other goods, from a military post. It wasn't long before he learned to play the *charge* and *retreat* calls used by the U.S. Cavalry. On a later

Fig. 72. Satanta (1820–1874). Kiowa bugler during 1864 Adobe Walls battle. #1510/121b. Courtesy of the Panhandle Plains Historical Museum.

occasion, when Satanta returned to his village from searching for soldiers, he blew the cavalry charge to announce his arrival. The Kiowas thought the U.S. military was attacking, and they fled for several miles before learning the truth. This event occurred in the winter of 1869, and the Kiowas recorded it on their calendar as the *Year of the Bugle Scare*.[60]

Another curious incident occurred during the morning battle. A rattlesnake bit a Mexican soldier who

was about eighteen or nineteen years old, one of the New Mexico Volunteers. On that warm Friday, in late November, the snake had moved to the top of its den, perhaps a gopher hole, to bask in the sun. As the young soldier crawled through the grass, he placed his hand on top of the rattler, and it bit him. He ran, in frantic excitement, hand in the air, to Dr. Courtright's medical station inside the adobe corral. The doctor dressed the wound and gave him a stiff shot of whiskey. The young soldier said the medicine made him *very bold,* and soon, he was back in the skirmish line.[61]

By mid-afternoon, Carson realized the gravity of their situation. As he looked downriver, he saw Indian warriors, ten to twelve miles away, rushing toward battle. The number of Indians had been increasing throughout the day, soon dwarfing Carson's command of little more than three hundred. Carson estimated that a thousand Indians were charging upriver, many of them from a group of 350 tepees standing three miles to the east.[62] Pettis's approximation, on the other hand, was that by mid-afternoon, three thousand Indians had joined the battle from several villages downstream.[63] By either count, the odds greatly favored the Indians.

This heavily unbalanced battle gave Carson cause for concern. Several Indians passed around the troops riding west toward the Kiowa village that McCleave had ambushed earlier in the day—the village Carson intended to burn before the warriors could recover their livestock and goods. Carson also felt an urgency to locate Lieutenant Colonel Francisco Abreu and the seventy-five soldiers protecting the wagon train and supplies.

Most of the officers wanted to advance down river and destroy the large Indian village. Carson, however, considered the wounded men, and, after listening to the advice of his scouts, decided to retreat.[64]

Chapter 14
Hot Retreat

At about half-past three on the afternoon of November 25, 1864, Carson ordered the command to move out. With calm reserve, gained from more than thirty years of fighting Indians and surviving desperate situations, Carson stationed his troops in strategic positions for retreat back to the Kiowa village. Carson's forces, with the Indians in pursuit, moved out in columns of four. The number four man led the horses while the other three soldiers spread out as skirmishers. Captain Fritz, Company B, First Cavalry, California Volunteers, protected the right flank. Captain Gilbert Tapley Witham, Company M, First California Cavalry, and part of Captain Charles Deus's company were on the left flank. Protecting the rear were Captain Joseph Berney, Company D, First New Mexico Cavalry; Lieutenant Sullivan Heath, Company K, California Cavalry; and the remainder of Captain Deus's company. Pettis's howitzers brought up the last of the column, while McCleave was in the vanguard with Carson.[1] Dr. Courtright described the formation as a hollow square with his wounded men in the center.[2]

The command crossed Bent's Creek and marched directly up the grassy river valley toward the ridges to the west. When the Indians saw the soldiers heading in the direction of the Kiowa camp, which had been the site of the morning skirmish, they correctly surmised that Carson was on his way to destroy it. The Indians knew that if the troops reached the village first, it would be torched, leaving them without shelter and supplies for the winter. This stirred the warriors into a frenzy and they attacked Carson's troops with death-defying determination.

Carson's seasoned soldiers had been fighting since early morning, but the fight for their life was before

Fig. 73. Carson's route of retreat from the Adobe Walls battlefield. *View*: Photographer was standing midway between the battlefield and Dohäsan's Kiowa village, looking east. Photograph by author, 2010.

Fig. 74. Metal Indian utility knife found on the route of retreat. 1864 Adobe Walls battlefield. Scan by Lisa Jackson, 2011.

them. Carson commented that the most severe fighting of the day occurred during the retreat toward the Kiowa village. The Indians charged so repeatedly, and with such desperation, that for some time, Carson had serious doubts for the safety of the rear guard. But the steady and constant fire they poured into the Indians caused them to retire on every occasion with great slaughter.[3]

My search for relics turned up only one probable Indian knife and no military artifacts along the retreat route. An irrigated hay meadow now covers a portion of the area, and testing for gravel has laid bare the surface of some ridges west of the field, which may account for finding so few artifacts in the vicinity.

The Indians soon learned that direct charges against Carson's moving skirmishers were devastating their own ranks, so they devised a scheme to set fire to the weeds and grass behind the soldiers. The dry vegetation burned with intensity, and the east wind pushed the flames dangerously close to the rear of the column. Dense smoke created a screen, allowing the warriors to advance within a few yards of the troops.[4]

During one of the charges, the wind blew the smoke to the side, and for a moment, exposed one of the Comanche warriors a few feet from a young Mexican soldier—the same soldier bitten by a rattlesnake earlier in the day. Spotting each other at the same moment, they both raised their rifles to fire. The Comanche shot first and missed. The youthful trooper returned fire; his aim was true, and the Indian fell from his horse.[5] Several warriors attempted to pick up the Comanche and re-

move him from the battlefield, but the continuous gunfire from the New Mexico volunteers drove them back, while the soldier, who had defied death twice that day, scalped the fallen warrior. It was the only scalp taken during the battle.

Carson, sensing the gravity of the situation, lit the grass in front of the troops, allowing them to move across the charred ground toward the short-grass ridges to the right. Once on high ground and out of the smoke, Pettis made good use of the howitzers by firing a few shells into the hundreds of warriors attacking from the rear. The exploding rounds deterred the closest, charging Indians, but the resolute warriors continued to dog the troops as they advanced toward the Kiowa village. Near an elongated hill, about five hundred yards east of the village, the Indians left Carson's troops behind and raced ahead to their camp. A line of sand hills north and east of the encampment shielded the Kiowas from Carson's troops long enough for the Indians to rescue some of their goods from the tepees.[6]

Fig. 75. Prairie grass fire. Kiowas set fire to grass behind Carson's command during retreat, November 27, 1864. Photograph by Wyman Meinzer, 2009.

Fig. 76. Sand hills where Pettis placed howitzers north of Kiowa village. *Orientation*: looking south. Photograph by Wyman Meinzer, 2009.

Shortly, Carson's command passed below the red bluff north of Dohäsan's camp. It was nearly sundown, and the bluff glowed crimson as the column veered south and crossed a narrow, flowing creek. Near the Kiowa village, the troopers dismounted at the base of the sand hills and worked their way through sumac bushes to the top of the sand ridges. Using the embankments for protection, the soldiers commenced firing into the Indians who were scrambling to salvage their belongings. The Indians had plenty of fight left, returning fire from all segments of the village.[7]

Pettis's battery, out of sight of the Indians, unlimbered the two howitzers at the foot of the hill. When the order came, "By hand to the front," the firing unit shoved the five-hundred-pound cannon to the top of the hill where the gunner aimed the piece. When No. 4 heard, "Ready," he inserted the friction primer, dropped to the ground and lay prone with no part of his body exposed until the cannon fired. Upon firing, the piece recoiled violently, either tumbling or rolling on its wheels before

coming to rest at the bottom of the hill, whereupon, the artillerymen reloaded and again pushed it to the top.[8]

After a fierce exchange of fire, and with the aid of the howitzers, the soldiers drove the Indians to the lower end of the camp. Half of the troops set about destroying lodges and property, while the remaining soldiers provided protection with constant fire toward the Indians.[9] Carson estimated 150 lodges were demolished, while Pettis reported 176. Along with the tepees, the troops burned large stores of dried meat, berries, buffalo robes, powder, and cooking utensils, as well as Chief Dohäsan's buggy and spring wagon. Pettis reported that the troops found several hundred tanned buffalo hides stored in the lodges, and each man took one before destroying the village.[10]

Days later, when Carson returned to Fort Union, he bitterly reported to General Carlton that many of the supplies his men destroyed were trade items. Carson further stated that these trade items—the powder, lead, and caps used to kill and wound his men—were, undoubtedly, of the same store the Indians bought, illegally, from the *Comancheros* not more than ten days before the battle.[11]

As the sun dropped from the horizon, flames and billowing smoke rose high into the sky, revealing the destruction of the "lodges of the best manufacture."[12] The glow from the fire illuminated the haggard faces of the spent soldiers as they finished the task before them. A last, parting blast from one of the howitzers propelled a shell toward a group of Indians as they fled toward the river from the south end of the village.[13]

Today, almost a century and a half later, the village lies covered by a mantle of sand blown in from the Canadian River and the surrounding sand hills, burying evidence of the Kiowa winter camp and the artifacts of battle. Cattle now graze among the hackberry trees, sumac, and plum bushes where once stood majestic Plains Indian tepees.

The artifacts I uncovered helped me unravel some of the mysteries hidden beneath the sandy blanket and partially reconstruct what took place at the village on that fateful November day in 1864. Two hundred broken and charred metal relics that, for nearly one hundred fifty years, had rested in a layer of burned soil twelve to sixteen inches below the surface, attest to the fiery destruction of the village.

The soldiers dragged tepees and their contents into five or six large piles to burn them. This practice was common with the army and was probably similar to the scene three years later when General George Armstrong Custer and General Winfield Scott Hancock burned 251 tepees in a Sioux-Cheyenne village near Fort Larned, Kansas. A journalist with the Hancock and Custer expedition, Henry Morton Stanley (1841–1904), distinguished for his "Doctor Livingston, I presume?" inquiry, recorded the spectacular event: "Six different stacks were made of the effects taken from the village; everything was promiscuously thrown in, and fire set to them all at the same moment. The dry poles of the wigwams caught fire like tinder, and so many burning hides made the sky black with smoke. Flakes of fire were borne on the breeze to different parts of the prairie, setting the prairie grass on fire. With lightning speed the fire rolled on, and consumed an immense area of grass, while the black smoke slowly sailed skyward."[14]

Two items Carson's cavalry burned in the Kiowa village were Chief Dohäsan's buggy and spring wagon, given to him a few years earlier by a military unit in

Kansas.[15] Yet the only evidences I found of a wagon were two wagon bolts, near the south end of the camp, and a few rusted wagon pieces in a historic site near a spring about a mile northwest of the village. Ranchers who lived in the sparsely populated area in the late 1870s more than likely scavenged large metal pieces, including anything left of Dohäsan's wagon, for their own use.

By the time Carson finished burning the Kiowa village and accounting for all his troops, night had fallen. Fatigue and uneasiness overwhelmed the soldiers. They hadn't slept for two days, had eaten very little, and had been fighting since early morning. In addition, the Indians were still close by in the hills.

Carson turned his attention to locating Lt. Col. Abreu's detachment of infantry and the supply wagons. Able-bodied men helped Dr. Courtright move the more severely wounded soldiers onto the two gun carriages and the two ammunition carts.[16] Cavalrymen with less severe wounds mounted their horses for the return ride. The remaining soldiers, surely numb with fatigue, turned their mounts to the west and commenced the tedious march back, re-crossing the ground they had covered in the early hours of day. Every soldier and every beast needed rest, but they plodded on. Bedraggled and smoke-blackened, their dark silhouettes trekked westward, away from the flickering flames and smoldering embers of Dohäsan's camp.

The first two miles upriver crossed a sagebrush prairie that ended at the ridge where Carson and Pettis had gotten their first view of the Indian village. The column passed the meadow where the Ute and Jicarilla Apache scouts had gathered their bounty ponies, but Carson's report doesn't indicate whether the scouts, at that time, picked up the horses they had cut out for themselves.

Moving ever westward, the tired troopers marched over small, brush-covered sand hills on the east side of Mustang Creek, then dropped down to the tall clump-grass that had presented such a tricky crossing for the howitzer battery in the early hours of morning. The clumped grass again worked its evil, made audible by the moans and groans of the wounded soldiers, as the carts and carriages bumped along.

After marching for three hours, Carson still had not located Abreu's wagon train, but when the somber troops finally exited the dense vegetation of Mustang Creek, they spotted dim campfires far to the right. Wary that the fires might be from an Indian camp, the command moved cautiously until the men heard in good, clear,

Fig. 77. Lieutenant Colonel Francisco P. Abreu's wagon campsite. Photograph by author, 2010.

ringing Saxon, "Who comes there?" The men answered with cheers because they had found their wagons and knew food and sleep were not far away.[17]

The weary soldiers, with one last surge of adrenalin, marched into Abreu's camp. Doctor Courtright immediately set about unloading the wounded men and making them as comfortable as possible, while the rest of the troops unsaddled their horses, unhitched the teams from the howitzers, and picketed their animals.[18] After swapping battle stories and a good smoke, the men, at the end of a long and difficult day, succumbed to weariness, choosing sleep over food, and rolled up in their blankets on the ground.

Colonel Abreu had chosen a good, defensive site for his camp: a rounded ridge a little over three hundred yards long and about fifty yards wide. He situated his pickets on a rock-capped hill at the southwest end of the rise. There the guards had a good view of the confluence of Mustang Creek with the Canadian River, and they had an unobstructed view of the Fort Bascom–Adobe Walls Road both up and down river. The red bluffs half mile to

the west were too far away for the Indians to successfully fire on the soldiers. Pettis acknowledged that Abreu had selected an excellent site for defense.[19]

In January 2005, I unearthed an abundance of artifacts scattered about the site: eating utensils, harness buckles, buttons, horseshoe nails, cut nails, leaded cans—items common to a military camp. Along with these, I dug up a number of unfired rifle and pistol percussion bullets of the same calibers and types as those dropped by soldiers near the cannon positions at Adobe Walls. About a foot deep, in the blackened soil of an old fire pit, I found rusted, cut nails that had likely held together wooden supply boxes discarded by the soldiers and used for fuel. From this pit, perhaps, glowed one of the dim fires spotted by Carson as his troops marched upriver in search of their supply wagons.

A drawback to this camp was the scarcity of grass for livestock, so the next morning Carson moved his troops to a better grazing site.[20] Though Carson did not say which direction they moved, evidence points to the south where, today, tall grass grows along the river bottom. A small ridge extends into the low land from the north. I believe Carson used the small rise for a picket station at the new camp, because I found unfired bullets, percussion caps, a gun wrench, nipples from a percussion rifles, and a military button.

The abundance of water, wood, and winter protection made the mouth of Mustang Creek a popular spot—Indians had frequented it for years to hold sun dances; buffalo hunters and traders followed the trail from North Palo Duro Creek to here and set up camp; and William

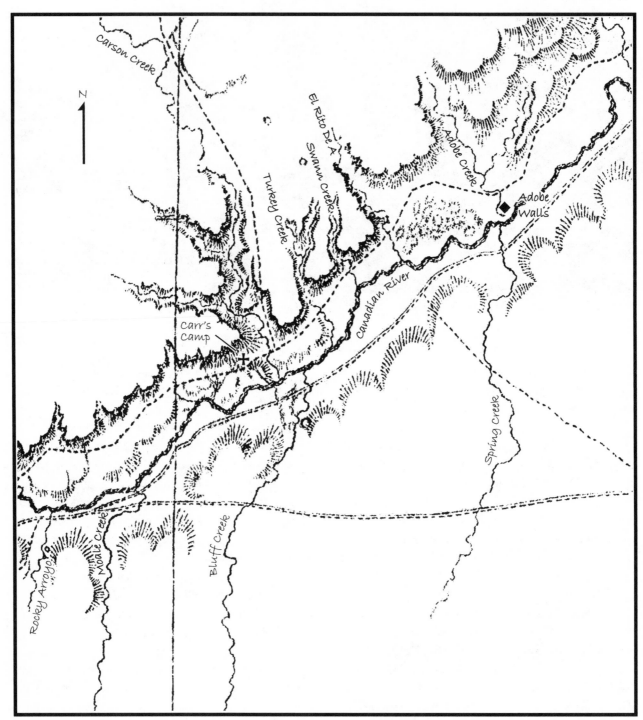

Map 14.1. Carr's Camp on Moore Creek. From manuscript map with no title by A. Hunnius, 1871. Courtesy of The National Archives, Washington, DC.

Bent established one of his wooden trading forts on this creek in the early 1840s.

Carson's command was not the only military unit to use this area. During General Phillip Sheridan's 1868 Winter Indian Campaign, Generals Eugene Asa Carr and William Henry Penrose from Fort Lyon, Colorado, spent time there during a blizzard.[21] On this expedition were two famous scouts, Wild Bill Hickok and Buffalo Bill Cody. The scouts learned that Mexicans were transporting, by bull train, a load of beer to Colonel Evans's depot twenty miles farther down river. Cody and Hickok decided the thing to do was hijack the wagon and buy the beer for their command's benefit.[22] Says Cody: "It was sold to our boys in pint cups, and as the weather was very cold we warmed the beer by putting the ends of our picket-pins heated red-hot into the cups. The result was one of the biggest beer jollifications I ever had the misfortune to attend."[23]

Chapter 15
The Aftermath

November 26, 1864: The Day After Battle

The trumpeter sounded reveille earlier than usual on November 26, 1864, as a safeguard against a predawn Indian attack. As darkness slipped away, Carson's eyes searched the surrounding area; he did not know what strategy the Indians might employ. Daylight passed; the sun rose; and to the relief of Carson and his men, they saw no Indians silhouetted against the horizon.

Carson, seeing that an attack was not imminent, focused on his troops and livestock. Taking note of his own aching muscles, he perceived the stiff gaits of both men and animals as they stirred about. The long, sleepless march followed by hours of fighting had taken its toll. Carson decided to lay over a day.[1]

Satisfied that a temporary safety prevailed, the soldiers, who had chosen sleep over victuals the night before, found that rest had awakened their ravenous appetites. They gulped down all the remaining food. The troopers devoured all of the wild game on hand, making it necessary to call the hunters to duty again.[2]

As the sun chased away the early morning chill, a party of Kiowas and Comanches appeared on a butte two miles east of the military camp. Having learned of the power of the howitzers on the previous day, the Indians stayed well out of range of fire. Their appearance set the troops on the alert, and a few of Carson's Ute and Jicarilla Apache scouts rode out of camp toward the butte. A small number of the Kiowas and Comanches answered the challenge, scrambling down the hill to meet the scouts on the plain near Mustang Creek.[3] The size of the two groups increased as Indians from each camp joined their comrades. Both sides fired a few shots, then as suddenly as they had appeared, the Kiowa and

Comanche warriors fled eastward. The scouts pursued only a short distance before turning their mounts back toward camp.[4]

With the combatant Indians again out of sight, troopers set to work repairing equipment and tending their mounts. Rest came only after they had cleaned and oiled their weapons, watered and fed their horses, and made sure the horse tack was in good repair. The soldiers welcomed Carson's day of rest and recuperation.

Indians required less upkeep than regular troops, and as the soldiers busied themselves with chores, some of the Indian scouts bartered for the Comanche scalp from the young soldier who had taken it during the retreat from Adobe Walls. That trophy became a bane to the troops, for just as the Indians had performed a war dance every night on the march to Adobe Walls, they celebrated victory with a *scalp dance* nightly on their return to Fort Bascom. Regardless of the purpose of the raucous dances, they annoyed the soldiers.[5]

On the morning of November 27, Carson ordered his command to saddle up and embark on the long trip back to Fort Bascom. The decision, however, displeased Carson's officers. Not having the experience or responsibility of Carson, they thought the command should head back downriver, attack the Comanche camp they had spotted east of Adobe Walls during the battle, and put an end to the Indians.[6]

Carson did not make the decision rashly. He decided that, due to the circumstances, it was impossible for him to punish the Indians further at that time. He considered the broken-down condition of his horses compared with the quality steeds of the Indians, who had fled in all directions. He didn't know whether the Comanches downriver had also taken flight or whether

Fig. 78. Looking upriver along return route to New Mexico. Photograph by Wyman Meinzer, 2009.

they were still nearby with reinforcement recruits joining them. What he did know, however, was that the number of his troops compared unfavorably with the superior number of Indians they had met in battle. The Indians, also, had learned the location of the army supply wagon train, making it vulnerable. Carson knew that if he chose to attack, it would open his command to disaster.[7]

Lieutenant Pettis, in his memoir, stated that he learned some years later that Carson had not consulted his officers, but had relied on the advice of his scouts, in determining not to attack the Comanche camp.[8] Carson's experience in the military and fighting Indians had taught him to respect the insight of Indian scouts in matters of battling other Indians. The veteran colonel knew that being cautious was prudent.

Back to Bascom

The column of men, horses, and wagons stretched along the north side of the river as they moved westward back to Fort Bascom. The trail of freshly trampled grass and newly cut wagon tracks they had created on the way to Adobe Walls was easy to follow.

The trip back to Bascom was uneventful, for neither Carson nor Pettis said much about it in their reports. Pettis did mention the nightly scalp dance, writing, "As we had been entertained every night until the fight by their 'war dance,' so for twenty-one days after, or as long as they remained with us, the monotony of the march was diversified by their own peculiar 'scalp dance,' and that with only one scalp."[9]

Carson, in his report, written from (what he supposed to be) Rita Blanca, penned a benedictory note concerning the return trip, "I have arrived at this point without any incident worthy of note."[10] He was silent concerning his wounded men, but mentioned the animals, saying that they traveled by easy marches so as to take all of the animals back to the fort, if possible.

The expedition spanned twenty-nine days. The command departed Fort Bascom in the early hours of November 12, and in spite of losing two days to a snowstorm, arrived in sight of Adobe Walls in the morning of November 25—a trip of fourteen days. Following the battle on November 25 and a day of recuperation on November 26, the column set its return course from Mustang Creek near Adobe Walls on November 27 and reached Fort Bascom on December 10—fifteen days later. The weary command rejoiced to be back at the fort, though they did not, yet, enter it. They instead set up camp along the Canadian River where there was good grazing for the animals.[11]

Carson received orders from Carleton for the different detachments to return to their various posts in the Territory. With the animals situated, Carson then turned his attention to quartering his men, as many had deployed from other forts, and their enlistment had expired.[12]

The soldiers stationed at Fort Bascom were not eager to return to their miserable bunks, which were only slightly better than their recent "beds" on the grass. Bascom was widely known as a substandard fort. From the time of construction, in 1863, until the military vacated it in 1870, it provided only minimal accommodations. Inhabitants complained to one another and to their higher-ups, but it always remained in the same state of disrepair—cold, crude, and leaky.[13] When Captain John Van Deusen Du Bois took command of Fort Bascom, in 1867, he disliked the post and wrote to his superiors that he would rather be anywhere else than Fort Bascom. He called Bascom "the most abandoned and forgotten post in the West."[14]

After a week of camping near Fort Bascom, Carson relocated twelve miles upriver, again, in search of grass for his horses. Healthy animals were necessary for a victory in battle. *An army with no horses was no army.* Carson wrote to General Carleton that his animals would not be fit for use for at least six weeks. Nurturing the horses back to health was a top concern for both Carson and Carleton.[15]

Subsequent to taking care of the horses, Carson's next task was to take an account of ordnances retuned from the Battle of Adobe Walls. In early October, Captain Edward H. Bergmann, Post Commander, Fort Bascom, issued to Carson six thousand rounds of .58-caliber elongated ball cartridges for the Kiowa and Comanche expedition.[16] On December 12, two days after returning from the battle Carson checked in two thousand rounds of .58-caliber cartridges to Bergmann.[17] I have no record that indicates whether the troops expended all of the four thousand rounds not returned.

Carson received orders on December 26 to go to Fort Union and turn in the rifles and ammunition that he had checked out for the Ute and Jicarilla Apache scouts who accompanied him to Adobe Walls.[18] The list of stores show that, of the one hundred guns checked out to Carson, he returned only ninety-two. Carson explained that five of the Indian scouts deserted the first day of the expedition and took with them five rifles.[19] Three more rifles were lost in battle: Carson's command, engaged with a very large number of Kiowas and Comanches, was in retreat when the Comanches wounded two and killed one, and in so doing captured three .58-caliber rifles.[20] Carson accounted for all one hundred rifles checked out to him.

After turning in the arms, Carson had the authority to go to Taos and, then, on to Ojo Caliente, to wait for further orders.[21] He no doubt visited his wife Josefa and their children in Taos before continuing on to Ojo Caliente to soak in the famous hot springs and sooth his ailing body.

Carson's Evaluation of the Expedition

Upon Carson's return to Fort Bascom, he had time to reflect on his campaign into the Texas Panhandle. Though he did not have the advantage of foreseeing the future, his expedition's penetration deep into the Kiowa and Comanche homeland near Adobe Walls was similar in effect to Lieutenant Colonel James Harold "Jimmy" Doolittle's raid into Japan in April 1942, seventy-eight years after the First Battle of Adobe Walls. In both cases, the physical damage was modest in relation to the overall picture, but the psychological impact was significant. Both surprised the adversary. In each instance, the enemy's aura of safety vanished when fire pierced their quarters. Additionally, the stations the foe thought secure, proved vulnerable.

When Carson considered his command's narrow escape at Adobe Walls, he factored in the sheer number of Kiowas and Comanches when developing his plan for a second campaign. He suggested to Carleton that, as soon as the horses were back in good condition, Carson would establish a military depot at Adobe Walls, stocked with four months of supplies, occupied by at least one thousand mounted men and foot soldiers, and protected with four artillery pieces.[22] Carson knew strong horses and a larger militia would be necessary to subdue the Indians.

Carson was infuriated to learn, upon returning from his campaign, that Mexican traders had sold munitions to Indians for use against him at Adobe Walls. But, what enraged him even more was the action of the United States Superintendent of Indian Affairs in Santa Fe, New Mexico, Doctor Michael Steck. A month before the Adobe Walls campaign, General Carleton requested that Steck stop giving out permits to trade with the Indians. Steck, however, ignored Carleton's petition and issued passes to two groups of *Comancheros* in October 1864. These traders preceded Carson's command to Adobe Walls, warned the Indians of the impending attack, and delivered to them a quantity of arms and ammunition.[23]

Following Carson's report to Carleton informing him that *Comancheros* had been near Adobe Walls during the battle, Carleton fired off letters to the Adjutant General U.S.A. in Washington, D.C. Carleton strongly condemned Steck's action of giving passports to *Comancheros* to trade with the Kiowas and Comanches, when he knew, full well, that they—the *Comancheros*—would give information concerning the movement of U.S. troops to the Indians.[24] Carleton's petition proved convincing, because in a few months, Steck received a letter calling for his resignation.[25]

Who Won the Battle?

The question of who won the Battle of Adobe Walls, Carson or the Indians, still resounds. Many times in the annals of history, the side accorded victory flows from the bias of the chronicler holding the pen.

Carson wrote from his camp, which he thought to be on Rita Blanca Creek, commending his troopers for their coolness and bravery during the Adobe Walls battle. He went on to say, "I flatter myself that I have taught these Indians a severe lesson, and hereafter they will be more cautious about how they engage a force of civilized troops."[26] His cautious statement had the ring of victory.

Carleton added his optimistic view of the campaign when he wrote to Carson, "This brilliant affair adds another green leaf to the laurel wreath which you have so nobly won in the service to your country."[27]

A more accurate assessment of the battle came from the testimony of Brigadier General James H. Ford, Commander, Second Colorado Cavalry at Fort Larned, Kansas, on May 31, 1865, "I understand Kit Carson last winter destroyed an Indian village. He had about four hundred men with him, but the Indians attacked him as bravely as any men in the world, charging up to his lines, and he withdrew his command . . . Carson said if it had

not been for his howitzers, few would have been left to tell the tale. This I learned from an officer who was in the fight."[28]

Two Mexicans who were in one of the Indian camps near Adobe Walls told Pettis, three years after the battle that, "if the whites had not had with them the two 'guns that shot twice,' referring to the shells of the mountain howitzers, they would never have allowed a single white man to escape out of the valley of the Canadian." Pettis added, "I may say, with becoming modesty, that this was also the often-expressed opinion of Col. Carson."[29]

These appraisals suggest that Carson was, perhaps, more straightforward in conversation with his contemporaries than he was in official reports. A true assessment of the Battle of Adobe Walls must consider the number of casualties, the economic loss, and the later effects of the encounter. Of the losses, which Carson's command accrued at that daylong battle on the twenty-fifth day of November, were two soldiers killed, ten

Fig. 79. Private Theodore Briggs (1836–1897). Wounded at the First Battle of Adobe Walls, 1864. He survived and became a productive citizen at Tascosa, Texas. Courtesy of Amarillo Public Library.

wounded; one Indian scout killed, five wounded; and a large number of horses wounded.[30] I was able to trace a few of these unfortunate men after they mustered out of the army.

Theodore Briggs, one of the ten wounded, received a shot through the right shoulder and lung from an Indian, who then lanced him under the right arm.[31] Another account of the injury, which ran in the *Santa Fe Weekly Gazette*, reported that Briggs's injuries were from two lead balls rather than a lance.[32] Time, however, was not up for Private Briggs. In 1870, he settled in Las Vegas, New Mexico, where he worked as a carpenter.[33] In the late 1870s, Briggs, his wife Ignacio (Yñesa), and their daughter Perfillia moved from Las Vegas, New Mexico, to Tascosa in the Texas Panhandle. He was a productive citizen in the thriving little settlement on the north bank of the Canadian.[34] When Yñesa died in 1897, Briggs interred her in the Tascosa Cemetery in Oldham County, Texas. In 1903, at the age of sixty-five, Theodore Briggs died. His family buried him in Garrett Cemetery northwest of Boise City, Cameron County, Oklahoma.

Another combatant, Patrick Brady, escaped harm during the battle but sustained an injury when he fell into a prairie dog hole.[35]

Yet another soldier, Samuel Eckstein, received a severe wound during the heated retreat from Adobe Walls to the Kiowa village, when a gun carriage ran over him. Eckstein recovered, and, in the 1870s, was one of Silver City, New Mexico's "most hospitable saloon keepers."[36]

Losing their life in the engagement were two privates serving with the California Volunteers, John H.

Fig. 80. Theodore Briggs's grave site, Garrett Cemetery, northwest of Boise City, Oklahoma. Photograph by author, 2009.

O'Donnell and John Sullivan.[37] In 1884, Theodore Briggs relayed to Marion Armstrong, an early settler in the Texas Panhandle, that in the 1864 battle, Colonel Carson buried the slain soldiers inside the old trading fort at Adobe Walls.[38]

From what Carson saw on the battlefield, he estimated that the Kiowa and Comanche losses were greater than sixty killed and wounded.[39] Carson was modest in his estimation, according to two Mexicans who were in the Comanche village during the battle. They told Pettis that the Indians sustained a loss of nearly one hundred warriors killed and one hundred fifty wounded.[40]

Even though Carson did not destroy the Comanche camp east of Adobe Walls, the total loss of the entire Kiowa village was devastating. With no shelter, no food, and no clothing, Dohäsan's people were destitute.[41] Winter was approaching, and winters on the Great Plains are often bitter with wind, snow, and subzero temperatures. To gain a perspective of the magnitude of the loss to the Kiowas, consider the arduous task of replacement—the expenditure in time, labor, and skill was enormous. It took twelve to fourteen finished buffalo hides to cover an average Kiowa lodge. To replace 150 tepees, Kiowa warriors would have to kill between 1,800 and 2,100 buffalo. At twenty lodge poles per dwelling, the villagers needed three thousand new poles, cut and dressed, to erect the tepee frames over which to stretch the hides.[42]

Henry M. Stanley, a reporter with generals Custer and Hancock, in 1867, when they burned a large Sioux and Cheyenne village near Fort Larned, Kansas, declared that the whole outfit of an entire wigwam costs, on an average, one hundred dollars.[43] If the Kiowa tepees were comparable in size to those in Fort Larned, the cost to replace the lodges in Dohäsan's village would have been fifteen thousand dollars.

Besides the obvious items needed to reconstruct dwellings (tepee poles and skins), the Indians needed tools and implements for daily use. When I located Dohäsan's camp in 2004, one hundred forty years after the battle, I found burned metal tools—some were unusable, but a large number of chisels and cutting tools were in good condition, scorched but serviceable.

After Carson and his troops moved upstream, the Indians more than likely returned to their camp to salvage what the soldiers had not destroyed. Think of the sadness the villagers felt as they foraged through the remains of their dwellings—acrid smoke filled their lungs and ashes darkened their clothing and skin. Items that could still be of service carried the indelible odor of fire that would forever be a reminder of that day.

The economic loss to the military from the battle was minor compared to that of the Indians. Dohäsan's people were destitute, but the soldiers had homes waiting for them. The main loss to the military was two soldiers and the death and weakening of horses.

The worn-out condition of the horses used by Carson's men concerned Carleton. He needed horses for the cavalry to use while patrolling the region and protecting settlers and travelers against Indian attacks in eastern New Mexico. Carleton reported the worrisome situation in a letter he sent to Bergmann, commander at Fort Bascom, reminding him that the cavalry horses Carson used on his recent expedition needed hay. As long as Bergmann had any hay at his post, he was to send it to Fort Bascom for Carson's horses, particularly when there was snow on the ground.[44]

Losing horses and having them wear out was not unique to Carson's Adobe Walls campaign. It was a widespread problem for the entire U.S. military. Many cavalrymen, when their mounts perished or were too lame to ride, became infantrymen. As foot soldiers, they wore out the soles of their boots. Beyond the individual soldier's discomfort of losing his animal, the dilemma spiraled up to the officers in charge of planning military operations.

When there are no horses, there are no campaigns.

Major Evans reported that he lost 172 horses and 64 mules to starvation during General Philip Henry Sheridan's winter campaign in 1868.[45] In 1874, Lieutenant Frank D. Baldwin, Fifth Infantry, and recipient of two medals of honor, complained about the condition of his soldiers' mounts while they were pursuing Grey Beard's Cheyenne warriors during the Red River War. He opined that if he only had a well-mounted company of cavalry, it would be but a short run to go right to the warrior's families who were in plain sight, not more than two and one-half miles distant. His success would be most complete, except for the cursed crime of the government's neglect to furnish his expedition with grain, which showed itself in his horses that were not at all fit for riding—in a word, he had no available mounted troops.[46]

Due to the broken-down condition of the army horses and the lack of soldiers, Carleton planned no other major expeditions into the Texas Panhandle. He lamented his dilemma in a letter on July 30, 1865, to Brigadier General Ford, Commander, Fort Larned, Kansas, stating that for lack of troops, it would be entirely impossible for him to help anyone outside of New Mexico Territory. Carleton said he could not cooperate in General Ford's contemplated movements, and added that Indians within the Territory required the attention of every man who was able to take to the field.[47]

Morrison's Search for Captive Women

The second campaign to Adobe Walls that Carson envisioned never materialized. In March 1865, however, retired Major Arthur Morrison, First Regiment, New Mexico Volunteer Infantry, of Las Vegas—Carleton's former military aide—obtained permission to go down the Canadian River toward Adobe Walls. Morrison left Fort Bascom, traveling Carson's route with the purpose of buying back the women Carson had heard were held captive by the Comanches and Kiowas.[48]

Accompanying Morrison was a small group of Mexicans led by a man named Jesus Añaya. They took a wagonload of trade items to barter for the captives. Carleton allowed the party to take only enough arms and ammunition for personal protection and none for trade.[49] Morrison found no Indians between New Mexico and Adobe Walls, so he bivouacked and sent out two of the Mexican party to search for an Indian camp. They were out eight days and found no village, but they encountered a band of Comanches who robbed them of everything, including their horses. When they returned to camp, they told Morrison that the Comanches were still sulking over the attack by Carson. The Comanches advised the Mexicans of a treaty the Kiowas and Comanches had formed with the Texans, who were furnishing the Indians arms and munitions to attack New Mexico. They further informed the two scouts that the Comanches had turned over the captive women to the Texans. After learning this, Morrison marched back to Fort Bascom without further incident.[50]

Carson's Last Years

To use the military more efficiently, Carleton decided to build an outpost on the Santa Fe Trail in Oklahoma Territory, midway between Fort Union, New Mexico, and Fort Dodge, Kansas, to quarter troops while they guarded the road to the States. Carleton gave the assignment to Carson. On May 4, 1865, Carleton wrote in a

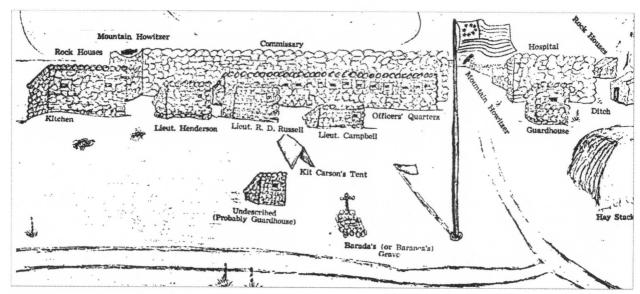

Fig. 81. *Camp Nichols,* pencil drawing, by Bucky Walters. *The Boise City News-*Historical Edition-Summer, 1968. Courtesy of Cimarron Heritage Center, Boise City, Oklahoma.

Fig. 82. Camp Nichols (established 1865), as it looked in 2009. Photograph by author, 2009.

Fig. 83. Christopher "Kit" and Josefa Carson's original gravesite at Boggsville, Colorado. Photograph by author, 2007.

Fig. 84. Christopher "Kit" and Josefa Carson's gravesites at Taos, New Mexico. Courtesy of the Jess Carson family.

communiqué that after the fifteenth of May, no more companies could be spared to escort trains and this would remain in effect until some of the units out on patrol returned. He offered encouragement with word that Colonel Carson would establish, at or near Cedar Bluffs or Cold Springs, a camp of three companies for the summer. This would afford all possible protection to trains passing through the dangerous neighborhood on the Cimarron route.[51]

Carson began construction of Camp Nichols, in June 1865, at which time, Carleton called him back to Santa Fe to serve in a variety of positions related to Indian and military affairs. In December 1865, Carson became commander of Fort Union. He remained there only a few months before receiving news of his appoint-

ment as brigadier general of the New Mexico Volunteers. In the spring of 1866, he transferred to Fort Garland, Colorado, where he served until he mustered out in the fall of 1867, ending his army career, which included six years as commander of the New Mexico Volunteer Army that had battled Confederates, Apaches, Navajos, Comanches, and Kiowas during his tenure.[52]

Christopher Houston "Kit" Carson died of an abdominal aortic aneurysm in the military hospital at Fort Lyon, Colorado, on May 23, 1868, not quite a month after his wife, Josefa, had died of complications following childbirth. Friends and family buried them both at Boggsville, Colorado. In response to one of Carson's last requests, the family moved them both to the cemetery near their home in Taos, New Mexico.[53]

Part II

Archeological Methods, Sites, and Artifacts

Chapter 16
Introduction to Part II

This section offers, in essence, an armchair tour of discoveries documenting Colonel Carson's 1864 Adobe Walls campaign. No telling of his and my intertwined journeys could be complete without it. It is my intent that these pages serve to guide readers along Carson's trail through artifact maps, site descriptions, descriptive tables, and selected images of the objects I unearthed. I hope that the archeological field and laboratory methodology applied in this section will enable all interested readers, not just archeologist and historians, to enjoy a deeper understanding of the artifacts recovered and the story they tell of the first Adobe Walls campaign.

From an archeological perspective, recovering the story of Carson's trail and the battle site was an intriguing challenge. My objectives were to locate camps and battle sites; gather, record, and analyze artifacts; and use artifact positions to interpret movements of the participants during the battle. At the beginning of the project, I was one man, with limited resources, searching for archeological sites that dotted a two-hundred-mile stretch of rough country from Fort Bascom, New Mexico, to Adobe Walls in the present Texas Panhandle. Wholly dependent on the kindness of private landowners and anticipating that a high percentage of the artifacts found would be metal, I set aside traditional excavation methods, opting instead for a metal-detector survey of Bascom Road, Carson's camps, Dohäsan's Kiowa village, and the Adobe Walls battle site.

After locating a site, I began sweeping my Garrett metal detector in a random pattern until I located an artifact. Then I used pin flags to set up a grid pattern. Each swipe of the detector took in four to five feet. If dense vegetation covered the site, I worked from two or three directions to get complete coverage.

Fig. 85. Alvin Lynn, author, searching for trail along north side of Canadian River. Photograph by Wyman Meinzer, 2009.

When I located an artifact, I dug it up using a trowel or shovel, then marked the location with a flag, and took a global positioning system (GPS) reading of the relic's coordinates. Before leaving the site, I retrieved the pin flags and placed the artifacts in plastic bags with labels. I gave each site a name and, when the landowner allowed it, a unique trinomial number designated by the Texas Archeological Research Laboratory. For example: [41HT60] "41" is the state number for Texas; "HT" is a county abbreviation, in this case "Hartley"; and "60" is a sequential number for a site in that county. When it was not possible to use a trinomial number, I substituted my personal numbering system: [HLOL5] "H" for historical site; "L" for Lynn (my name); "OL" for a county abbreviation, in this case "Oldham"; and "5" as my sequential number for a site in that county.

After arriving home in the evenings, I downloaded the GPS coordinates to my computer using "All Topo Maps," a map-generating program. Artifact placement on the resulting maps revealed areas of concentrated activity at the site.

Lab Work

Processing artifacts is a multi-step procedure that involves cleaning; identification, analysis, and recording; and photography.

Cleaning

First, I washed the relics in soapy water, then rinsed and dried them. Next, I placed the iron pieces in an electrolytic bath of sodium carbonate (washing soda) and water. The metal artifacts were the anode, and a sheet-metal box served as the cathode. A trickle charger furnished less than one ampere of current to operate the electroly-

Fig. 87. Uncleaned and cleaned mule shoe. Photograph by author, 2007.

sis unit. The size of the artifact determined processing time, usually just a few days for even the largest pieces.

At the end of the electrolysis process, I finished cleaning the iron specimens with a soft, metal wheel-brush; rinsed and dried them; and sprayed them with a coating of Teflon silicone.

To clean copper and brass, I used the electrolysis process for a short time before rinsing and brushing. To clean lead bullets I used a diluted vinegar solution but did not use a wheel brush.

After the pieces dried, I placed them in individual plastic bags with paper labels containing site number, site, field number, date, and artifact name. I then sorted specimens into lots of like types—cartridges, bullets, horse gear, buttons, and so on.

Identification, Analysis, and Recording

Identification and analysis of artifacts are the means by which we interpret historical events. Finding artifacts *in situ* is key to putting them in proper context within the overall scheme of an incident. For example, the unfired percussion rifle and pistol bullets scattered around the two cannons at Adobe Walls indicated where Carson stationed some of his troops. Moreover, rifle balls and bullets fired into the east and south sides of the hill near the cannon placements showed the direction from which the Indians fired their rifles.

Doctor Doug Scott at the Midwest Archeological Center of the National Park Service did a comparative analysis of the unfired bullets from the Adobe Walls battle site and bullets found in multi-component camps along the Bascom Road. His findings helped confirm my hypothesis that Carson's men had bivouacked in most of these campsites.

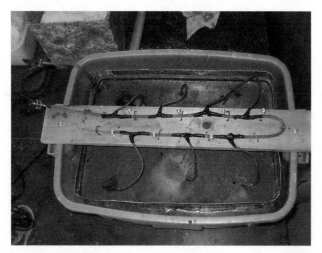

Fig. 86. Electrolysis unit used for cleaning iron artifacts. Photograph by author, 2007.

Metal and ceramic pieces often have a maker's mark imprinted on them. Such an identifying mark is an added benefit in analysis. Rust and corrosion often coat metal objects, but as soon as I took military buttons and other metal artifacts out of the cleaning solution, I searched for a mark. If I found one, I went to my reference books to find the maker and establish the production date of the piece. Knowing the year of manufacture of the artifacts was helpful in determining whether the items were contemporary with the period of Carson's campaign or whether travelers lost them at another time. For example, a soldier in Carson's command could not have lost a button manufactured after 1864 since the Adobe Walls battle occurred in 1864.

Photographic Record

The final laboratory procedure was to create a pictorial record of the artifacts. To do this, I scanned small specimens into my computer. Larger pieces, with considerable depth, I photographed with a digital camera and uploaded the images to my computer. After entering the images, I integrated them, along with their site and field numbers, into my field notes; printed a hard copy; and made a disk.

Overview

In contrast to the appeal of field and lab work, compiling my research was time-consuming, tedious, and difficult. I wrestled with how to set down the technical archeological data in a readable form and how to share this segment of Texas Panhandle history. The data I collected fell into four parts: Fort Bascom–Adobe Walls Road; campsites along the Bascom Road; Chief Dohäsan's Kiowa village; and the battlefield at Adobe Walls. I further divided each of the four components into site description and artifact analysis. Beyond what the artifacts tell of the first battle of Adobe Walls, I hope they reveal how every recovered object carries in it at least a piece of some larger story, waiting only to be read.

Chapter 17
Fort Bascom–Adobe Walls Road

A key part of my study of Carson's campaign was locating his route from New Mexico to Adobe Walls. The only previously recorded information was that he "traveled by easy stages on a practicable wagon road along the north bank of the Canadian River."[1]

Finding the Bascom Road, where the old trail passed near water sources, was the first step in locating Carson's campsites. Using aerial photographs and early surveyors' reports, I mapped segments of the road beginning with the known camps, such as Red River Springs, Nara Visa, and Blue Creek. After depleting my research sources, it was time for me to go to the field and walk the trail to fill in the missing sections.

Since the old Bascom Road is now on private land, a primary hurdle was to get permission from landowners to search for the trail. Next, I looked for someone familiar with regional history who might know about the old road. The ranchers were agreeable to the task I was undertaking and were helpful in showing me ranch roads and giving me combinations to gate locks.

Duane Moore of Tucumcari, New Mexico, a historian, has a wealth of knowledge about the history of the Canadian River from Fort Bascom to Red River Springs. His family has lived in the area since the turn of the twentieth century, and he was a valuable resource in helping me obtain permission from New Mexico landowners. Duane made several trips with me, walking the old trail. Lewis James and Bill Bell, of Nara Visa, were instrumental in my finding the old road through the sand hills northeast of Red River Springs, near Nara Visa Springs, and on to the Texas boundary.

When I began my quest for the Bascom Road in the Texas Panhandle, I needed to find someone from the Texas side who was fond of history and had knowledge of the local terrain. One day I stopped for lunch at the Cowboy Café in Channing, Texas, where I ate with local historian and artist Don Ray. He was interested in my project and told me that Red Skelton was a retired cowboy who knew the history of this area better than any other man around. That was just the information I needed.

On a hot day in September 1994, I set out to meet Red. The sun had reached the western sky when I pulled into Channing. As I drove up to Red's house, he and his wife Alice were sitting on the front porch enjoying the cool shade. I studied Red before leaving my pickup. He was in his eighties—tall and lean. His ruddy face, lined from years of working in the burning, Texas sun, reminded me of the western Panhandle—a land battered by harsh elements. I liked what I saw.

I figured Red was studying me, too. I gathered my maps and notes, walked to the porch, and introduced myself. Red offered me a seat in a spring-back, metal lawn chair. When he asked what he could do for me, I explained my research on the Bascom Road and told him that Don Ray said I should meet him. Red told me he had seen parts of the old road on Los Redos Creek. In his West Texas drawl, he told stories he had heard about the trail, which signaled to me that he was a genuine find. I was greatly pleased when Red agreed to help me search for the road.

For the next year, Red and I were a common sight driving across the large ranches in my white Chevrolet pickup, bouncing over yucca and sagebrush, in pursuit of Carson's route to Adobe Walls. Red became a good friend of mine. An added benefit was that he was a walking encyclopedia of history. My pickup cab was the classroom; Red, the teacher; and I, the student. I tried to absorb everything he said. Red added to his character a great sense of humor. While going through a metal gate one day, Red noted that it was a good gate—not like some, where the fence falls down for a quarter of a mile when you open the gate.

Another time, we were on a high hill overlooking the Canadian River. From there, we could see the caprock of the Llano Estacado, about twenty miles to the south, across the rugged Canadian River Valley. To the west, we could see an equal distance—to where the earth met the sky.

I said, "Red, this is all new country to me."

Red replied, "Naw, Alvin, this isn't new country, it's always been here. You're just seeing it for the first time."

Red was right. I *was* seeing it for the first time, and it is big country.

Todd Browning, another cowboy from Channing, helped me search the country along Punta de Agua Creek. I have two images etched in my mind of Todd walking the old Bascom Road—he wore his spurs even though we were afoot, and he could roll a cigarette in the wind and never lose a grain of tobacco.

Red, Todd, and I located the Bascom Road in the western section of the Panhandle, and, then, I continued searching eastward toward Adobe Walls until I was satisfied that I had found most of the trail. One of the rules for trail verification is having sufficient geomorphic and artifact evidence to identify an area as an authentic trail.[2] *How well did the places I thought could be a trail fit the criteria?* Geomorphically, there was a swale. Looking across the country, I saw the indelible depression, formed decades earlier when animal hooves pounded the sod and wagon wheels rolled over the prairie grasses cutting through the roots until only bare land remained. Rains came and winds blew, carrying off the loosened soil. *The landform passed the test for being a trail; it was visible to*

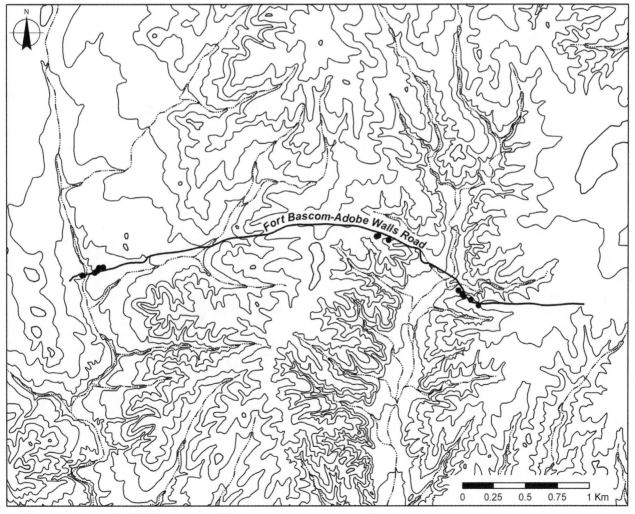

Map 17.1. Fort Bascom–Adobe Walls Road. Illustration by Luis Alvarado, 2011.

eyes trained to see—even if more noticeable in some places than others.

Were there enough period artifacts to conclude that I had located a trail? The objects that early travelers had lost or discarded had now lain exposed to sun and rain for upwards of two centuries. Sand had sifted over them; grass had sprouted and encased them in their roots. *Would I find artifacts?* The answer proved to be an emphatic *Yes.*

Studying the trail, I considered the areas where activity may have been concentrated, the places where wagons endured strain to the point of breakage, and men and animals stressed to exhaustion. I looked for creeks, rough roads, slopes, and hilltops, for it would have been in those places that wagons creaked, groaned, and broke, and harnesses and straps snapped as teamsters and animals struggled up difficult inclines. Bouncing over rocky roads loosened wagon bolts, wore out horseshoes, and jarred the innards of creatures. Captain Marcy wrote in his book, *The Prairie Traveler,* that one of the chief causes of accidents to carriages upon the plains arises from nuts coming off the bolts that secure the running gear. Marcy suggested that to prevent this, the ends of all bolts should be riveted.[3]

Relief came for travelers when they reached the top of the hill, the other side of a steep embankment, or a smooth stretch in a rocky road. There they paused: teamsters and riders to make repairs; travelers to rest; and animals to regain strength. As I collected the broken pieces left by those early sojourners, I took GPS readings

Fig. 89. Spencer 56-50-caliber cartridge, unfired. Scan by Lisa Jackson, 2011.

and bagged them for processing. In the lab, I sorted them according to function or type. With each trip to the trail, I returned home with relics that helped identify those who traveled the old road. The story of the Fort Bascom–Adobe Walls Trail began to take shape.

Fig. 88. Three *GENERAL SERVICE* military buttons. Scan by Lisa Jackson, 2011.

Fig. 90. Bottle shards from Fort Bascom–Adobe Walls Road. Scan by Lisa Jackson, 2011.

Table 17.1 Fort Bascom–Adobe Walls Road Artifact Descriptions

Artifact Categories	Quantity	Description
Arms and Ammunition		
Cartridge Cases		
.44 caliber	1	Head stamp. none. Base dia .46-in/1.17-cm. Lgth 1.27-in/3.23-cm. These dimensions are the same as the Russian manufactured Smith & Wesson that was in production from 1870 to 1875.[4]
.44-40 caliber	2	Head stamp. none. Ave base dia .47-in/1.19-cm. Ave lgth 1.31-in/3.33-cm.
.45 caliber	8	Head stamp. none. Ave base dia .48-in/1.22-cm. Ave lgth 1.27-in/3.23-cm.
.45 caliber	2	Head stamp. none. Ave base dia .48-in/1.22-cm. Ave lgth 1.30-in/3.30-cm.
.45 caliber	5	Head stamp. *.45 COLT WRA CO.* Ave base dia .48-in/1.22-cm. Ave lgth 1.27-in/3.23-cm.
.45 caliber	1	Head stamp. *.45 COLT UMC.* Base dia .48-in/1.22-cm. Lgth 1.27-in/3.23-cm.
56-50 caliber	1	Head stamp. *SAW.* RF. No measurement because of damage to the case.
Unfired Cartridges		
56-50 caliber	3	Head stamp. *SAW.* RF. Ave base dia .56-in/1.42-cm.
Bullets		
.00 shot	1	Fired. Dia .315-in/.80-cm. Wt 51.6 gr. Consistent with .00 buckshot.*[5]
.38 caliber	1	Fired. Dia .347-in/.88-cm. Wt 152.7 gr. Consistent with Smith & Wesson revolver.*
.44 caliber	1	Fired. Dia .426-in/1.08-cm. Wt 195 gr. Consistent with Colt .44-caliber revolver.*
.45 caliber	3	Fired. Ave dia .45-in/1.14-cm. Ave wt 239.6 gr. Consistent with post-1875 Colt revolver.*
.45 caliber	2	Fired. Ave dia .464-in/1.18-cm. Ave wt 235.2 gr. Consistent with M1873 .45-Colt.*
.50 caliber ball	1	Fired. Dia undetermined. Wt 219.4 gr.*
.50 caliber	1	Fired. Dia .484-in/1.23-cm. Wt 424.3 gr.*
Primers		
Percussion cap	1	Fired. Dia .241-in/.61-cm. Height .237-in/.60-cm. Hat-type with four-flanged base.

Table 17.1 Fort Bascom–Adobe Walls Road Artifact Descriptions (*cont.*)

Artifact Categories	Quantity	Description
Personal Items		
Buttons		
Four-hole metal button	1	Dia .75-in/1.9-cm. Has depressed center. Common pant or suspender button.
Metal utility button	1	Dia .69-in/1.75-cm. Has depressed center with hashed design on front. There is a brass rivet type of attachment on the back.
Brass button	1	Dia 1.0-in/2.54-cm. Two-piece, convex style brass button with a horseshoe design stamped on the front. The back plate is missing.
Army general service button	1	Dia .75-in/1.9-cm. A two- piece brass button. Maker's mark. *SCOVILL MFG CO. WATERBURY* as a rmdc. The manufacture date is between 1855 and 1860. The shank is slightly bent.[6]
Army general service button	1	Dia .88-in/2.2-cm. This flattened specimen is a two-piece brass button. Maker's mark. ****EXTRA***QUALITY* as a dm. between two rows of dots. This back-mark dates the button to the early 1860s.[7]
Army general service button	1	Dia .75-in/1.9-cm. A two-piece brass button. Maker's mark. none. There is some damage to the front of the button, and the shank is bent.
Army general service button	1	Dia .81-in/2.05-cm. A two-piece brass button. Maker's mark. none. There is some damage to the front of the button, and the shank is bent.
Army general service button	1	Dia .75-in/1.9-cm. A two-piece brass button. Maker's mark. none. There is some damage to the front of the button.
Coins		
Penny	1	The one coin found on the trail is an 1879 copper, Indian-head penny.
Miscellaneous		
Hairpin	1	Lgth 2.39-in/6.1-cm. Wdth .35-in/.89-cm. Wire stock dia .06-in/.15-cm. The hairpin is not crimped but is straight wire in the standard long "U" shape.
Fasteners		
Nails		
Machine-cut nail	22	Lgth 1.5/in/3.81 to 3.0-in/7.6-cm. Tapered on two sides. Gripping marks on some of the faces date them to after 1835.[8]

Nails (cont.)		
Hand-forged square nails	3	Lgth 1.75-in/4.45-cm. to 2.0-in/5.1-cm. All sides tapered. All are hand-forged with rose-heads.
Flat-backed staples (Steeples)	2	Lgth 1.75-in/4.45-cm. Wdth .88-in/2.24-cm.
Bird's-eye galvanized steeple	1	Broken. Lgth 1.88-in/2.24-cm. Galvanized. The type of steeple used on the XIT ribbon wire and the drift fence of the 1880s.
Other Fasteners		
Square nuts	5	Dia .5-in/1.27-cm. to 2.0-in/5.08-cm.
Carriage bolts	5	Various sizes and conditions.
Washers	2	Dia .5-in/1.27-cm. to 1.0-in/2.54-cm.
Round pins	6	Various sizes and conditions.
Horse Tack and Wagon Hardware		
Horseshoes		
Complete shoes	3	Lgth 5.0-in/12.7-cm. to 5.5-in/13.97-cm. Ave wdth 4.75-in/12.1-cm. All shoes have worn toes and heel calks.
Broken shoes	8	Ave lgth 4.4-in/11.2-cm. All shoes are broken at the toe. Five have heel calks.
Mule Shoes		
Complete shoes	3	Ave lgth 4.9-in/12.4-cm. Ave wdth 3.7-in/9.40-cm. All three shoes have heel calks.
Broken shoes	3	Ave lgth 5.0-in/12.7-cm. All three of the broken shoes have heel calks.
Horseshoe Nails		
Unused nails	10	Lgth 1.75-in/4.45-cm. to 2.25-in/5.7-cm.
Used nails	3	Lgths Vary. All have tips broken.
Buckles		
Sunk-bar buckle	1	Lgth 1.5-in/3.8-cm. Wdth 1.0-in/2.54-cm. The tongue is attached to the center bar.
Elongated buckle	1	Lgth 1.75-in/4.45-cm. Wdth 1.0-in/2.54-cm. The tongue is attached to a center-bar. The front of the buckle is flat and wider than the base that has a guide for a .75-in/1.9-cm.-wide leather strap.
Brass buckle	1	Lgth 1.38-in/3.50-cm. Wdth 1.44-in/3.66-cm. This buckle could be from a bridle or personal accoutrement. The tongue normally fastened to the back end, but it is broken from this specimen.

Table 17.1 Fort Bascom–Adobe Walls Road Artifact Descriptions (*cont.*)		
Artifact Categories	**Quantity**	**Description**
Horse Tack and Wagon Hardware		
Wagon Hardware		
Broken wagon rod	1	Lgth 6.88-in/17.5-cm. Rod dia .38-in/.97-cm. One end of the rod is looped.
Broken whiffletree center clip	1	Lgth 3.25-in/8.26-cm. Flat metal from around whiffletree broken away.
Broken wagon tug	1	Lgth 4.5-in/11.43-cm. Wdth across curved hook 3.5-in/8.89-cm. Greatest thk. .88-in/2.23-cm. The tug is hand forged.
Broken wagon tug	1	Lgth 4.0-in/10.16-cm. Greatest thk. .75-in/1.9-cm. The tug is hand forged.
Hame ring with broken stud	1	Outside dia 2.0-in/5.08-cm. Broken stud lgth 1.25-in/3.20-cm.
Camp Utensils		
Containers and Lids		
Bottle shards	5	Base dia 3.0-in/7.72-cm. Base thk. .40-in/1.02-cm. Wall thk. .28-in/.71-cm. The oxidized bottle has an amber color. The concave base has a ring circling a maker's mark, mostly missing, over *"MG Co."* Under this is the number 10.
Bottle shards	9	Base dia 2.6-in/6.6-cm. Greatest base thk. .29-in/.74-cm. The oxidized bottle has an amber color. The concave base has a ring circling a maker's mark made up of a cross over *"MG Co."* Under this is the number 2.
Pewter lid	1	Lid dia 1.0-in/2.54-cm. The lid has no maker's mark but has inscribed *"Pat. Mch. 30-58 Exp. Mch. 30-72."*
Miscellaneous Metal Pieces		
Unidentified objects	13	Most of these objects are broken pieces of flat metal, some with holes.

Chapter 18
Red River Springs Site and Artifacts

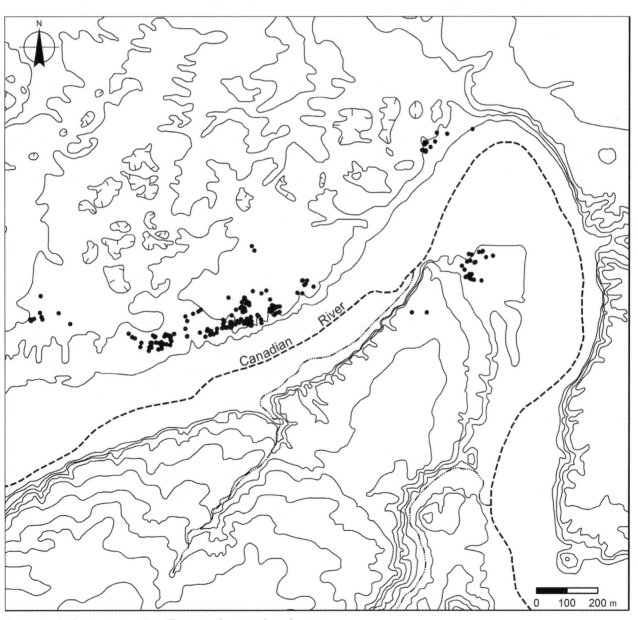

Map 18.1. Red River Springs Site. Illustration by Luis Alvarado, 2011.

The first night out from Fort Bascom, Colonel Carson and his troops camped at Ute Creek. This camp now rests beneath the waters of Ute Lake. The second night out, Carson encamped on a flat between two springs on the northwest side of the Canadian River, where it makes a large loop to the northeast. The soldiers set up camp near a river crossing where a northeasterly-bound wagon road became one with the Bascom Road. Though Carson did not give a name to this site, cartographers of the late nineteenth century showed it as Red River Springs, and current locals call it Ritter Springs. Sand hills encroaching from the north have covered much of the area and choked out one of the original springs. Ritter Springs continues to flow a few hundred yards to the east, as does Beaver Dam Springs less than a mile to the west.

Three sub-sites comprise the Red River Springs camp. The site numbers assigned them are HLQ3, HLQ4, and HLQ6.

HLQ3 stretches, lengthwise, from just west of Beaver Dam Springs to the northeast, where it ends at the base of sand hills. The width of the site extends approximately one hundred yards from the gravel ridges near the river, northwestward, to a modern, ranch road paralleling the river. Sand has covered the site beyond the ranch road.

HLQ4 is about three hundred yards northeast of HLQ3. It is in a sandy valley near the river crossing. The small camp spreads over an acre. A mott of cottonwood and black locust trees covers most of the valley, and a large sand hill borders the valley on the north. At a nearby camp, François des Montaignes, while traveling with James Abert in 1845, described this as a beautiful spring, bursting from a bed of snow-white sand.[1] The sand hill has long since choked the spring. Not far away, hidden among large trees, a crumbling rock structure is the last vestige of early occupants. An 1881 surveyor's map shows this to be Lackey's Ranch.[2]

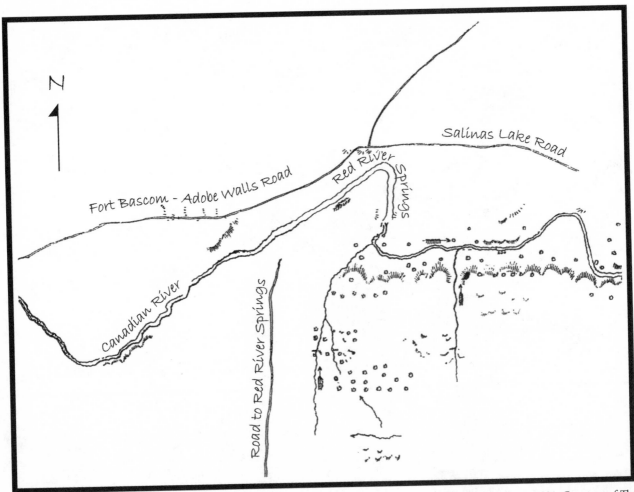

Map 18.2. Red River Springs Area. From Survey General Office, Santa Fe, New Mexico. Township Range map. 1881. Courtesy of The Bureau of Land Management.

HLQ6, a military camp, is across the river on a low, rounded hill that spreads over approximately two acres. A wagon road, bearing from the southwest, passes through the site and continues across the river to the north.

Fig. 91. Post–Civil War Colt ejector rod and housing. Photograph by Wyman Meinzer, 2009.

Fig. 92. Pre-1830s hand-wrought, square nails. Photograph by Wyman Meinzer, 2009.

Fig. 93. Fired lead ball and various-caliber (cal.) unfired bullets. *Left to right*: .45-cal. fired lead ball, .36-cal. unfired Colt bullet, .44-cal. unfired Colt bullet, .52-cal. Sharps unfired bullet with flat base and small cone, .52-cal. unfired Sharps bullet with ringtail on base. Photograph by Wyman Meinzer, 2009.

Table 18.1 Red River Springs Artifact Descriptions. HLQ3, HLQ4, HLQ6		
Artifact Category	**Quantity**	**Description**
Arms and Ammunition		
Cartridge Cases		
.38 caliber	9	Head stamp. none. EP. CF. Ave base dia .385-in/.98-cm. Ave Lgth .77-in/1.96-cm.
.38 caliber	1	Head stamp. *UMC S-H 38*. EP. CF. Bottle-neck case. Measurements show this to be a .38-40 case.
.41 caliber	4	Head stamp. none. EP. CF. Ave base dia .407-in/1.03-cm. Ave Lgth .94-in/2.38-cm. The 1877 double action Colt Lightning used this type of cartridge.[3]
.44 caliber	2	Henry RF with double firing pins. Ave base dia .445-in/1.12-cm. Ave lgth 1.31-in/3.32-cm. One case has 3 sets of RF marks and one CF indention indicating it misfired three times in two different rifles.
.44 caliber	3	RF. Single firing pin. Ave base dia .45-in/1.14-cm. Ave lgth .915-in/2.32-cm. One case has a RF mark and a CF indention caused from being fired in two different rifles.
.44-40 caliber	20	Head stamp. none. EP. Ave base dia .47-in/1.20-cm. Ave lgth 1.32-in/3.3-cm.
.44-40 caliber	6	Head stamp. *WRA Co .44 WCF*. EP. Ave base dia .47-in/1.20-cm. Ave lgth 1.32-in/3.3-cm.
.45 caliber	90	Head stamp. none. EP. Ave base dia .48-in/1.22-cm. Ave lgth 1.27-in/3.22-cm.
.45 caliber	4	Head stamp. *WRA Co .45 Colt*. EP. Ave base dia .48-in/1.22-cm. Ave lgth 1.27-in/3.22-cm.
.45/60 caliber	1	Head stamp. *UMC Co. 45-60*. EP. CF. Base dia .50-in/1.27-cm. Lgth 1.86-in/4.72-cm.
.45/60 caliber	1	Head stamp. *UMC Co. 45-60*. EP. CF. Base dia .50-in/1.27-cm. Lgth 1.88-in/4.7-cm. In late 1879 or early 1880, Winchester developed the 45/60 cartridge for the Winchester Centennial model rifle; production continued until 1935.[4]
.45/70	1	IP. CF. Base dia .51-in/1.30-cm. Lgth unknown Broken case.
.45/70 caliber	1	Head stamp. none. EP. CF. Base dia .505.-in/1.27-cm. Lgth 2.1-in/5.37-cm.
.50 caliber	1	Maynard. Base disk missing. Fired by a percussion cap.[5]
.50/70 caliber	4	Head stamp. none. IP. CF. Base dia .57-in/1.7-cm. Ave lgth 1.77-in/4.50-cm.

Cartridge Cases (cont.)		
.50/70 caliber	3	EP. Head stamp. none. CF. Base dia .57-in/1.7-cm. Ave lgth 1.77-in/4.50-cm.
Unfired Cartridges		
.44 caliber	1	EP. Head stamp. none. CF.
.45/60 caliber	1	EP. Head stamp. *UMC Co.* CF.
.50/70 caliber	1	IP. Head stamp. none. CF.
56-50 caliber	1	Spencer. IP. Head stamp. *SAW.* RF
Bullets		
.32 caliber	1	Fired. Dia .352-in/.92-cm. This is a modern bullet with a low-velocity impact.*6
.36 caliber	1	Unfired. Dia .379-in/.96-cm. Wt 139.4 gr. In 1855, the St. Louis Arsenal began manufacturing this type of bullet for the Navy Colt revolver.*
.38 caliber	3	Fired. Dia one bullet is .365-in/.93-cm. The diameter of the other 2 could not be determined. Wt varies from 184 gr. to 193.7 gr.*
.38 caliber	1	Unfired. Dia .385-in/.98-cm. Wt 190.4 gr.*
.40 caliber	1	Fired. Dia .403-in/1.02-cm. Wt 247.3 gr. The properties of this bullet are consistent with the Sharps Meecham, post-1875.*
.44 caliber	10	Unfired. Percussion pistol bullets. Ave dia .454-in/1.15-cm. Ave wt 230.8 gr. Two of the bullets have twisted and torn noses.
.45 caliber	9	Fired. From post-1875 Colt revolvers. Dia vary from .442-in/1.12-cm. to .454-in/1.15-cm. Wt vary from 137.5 gr. to 249.5 gr.*
.45 caliber	2	Fired. Dia one is .461-in/1.17-cm. The other dia could not be determined. The wt of one bullet is 230.8 gr. and the other is 244 gr.*
.45 caliber	1	Fired ball. Dia .445-in/1.14-cm. Wt 143.2 gr. The ball is faceted with a ramrod impression and low impact marks.*
.50 caliber	1	Fired. Dia not determined. High-velocity impact. Wt 324 gr.*
.52 caliber	2	Unfired. Sharps bullets with two rings and small cones in flat bases. Ave dia .55-in/1.40-cm. Wt of one bullet is 466.8 gr. The other weighs 435 gr.
.52 caliber	1	Unfired. Sharps bullet with two rings and a pigtail for attaching powder sack. The bullet base is flat. Dia .557-in/1.41-cm. Wt 448 gr.

Table 18.1 Red River Springs Artifact Descriptions. HLQ3, HLQ4, HLQ6 (*cont.*)

Artifact Category	Quantity	Description
Arms and Ammunition		
Primers		
Ext. primer	1	Fired. Dia .25-in/.635-cm. This primer is from a brass case.
Gun Parts and Tools		
Colt Ejector rod and housing	1	Total lgth of the rod and housing 4.63-in/11.77-cm. A tempered spring is intact around the ejector rod. A rounded channel runs the length of the housing where it fits against the pistol barrel. A broken screw in front of the housing indicates its breakage was the cause of the separation of the ejector rod from the pistol. According to gunsmith Paul McFadden, this came from a Colt pistol dating to the late 1880s.[7]
Combination L-type gun screwdriver	1	Long blade lgth 3.13-in/7.94-cm. Short blade lgth 1.06-in/2.69-cm. The dimensions and shape of this screwdriver indicate it is a Colt model.
Personal Items		
Buttons		
Towers wire fastened	5	Dia from .91-in/2.31-cm. to .98-in/2.49-cm. The buttons have "Towers Wire Fastened" stamped on them. All have a recessed center with two holes for wire fasteners. Two of the buttons still have a wire that passes through the buttonholes and a small disk showing their method of attachment. The buttons were originally plated, but due to damage, some have lost their plating.
Four-hole metal buttons	3	Dia from .55-in/1.44-cm. to .65-in/1.65-cm. These metal buttons have recessed centers with four holes. This was a popular style for use on pants and shirts.
Small brass buttons	2	Dia .503-in/1.27-cm. and .52-in/1.33-cm. Both buttons have a convex face and swiveling brass tabs on the back.
Small brass buttons	2	Dia Ave .87-in/2.21-cm. These two brass buttons have iron backs and shanks.
Pewter button	1	Dia .83-in/2.1-cm. The button has a horseshoe design on the convex front and a small brass disk attached to the back.
Army general service buttons	2	Small button dia .57-in/1.46-cm. Large button dia .75-in/1.9-cm. Small button maker's mark. none. Large button maker's mark. *SCOVILL-MFG Co. WATERBURY*, which dates the manufacture of the button to around 1860.[8]

Buttons (cont.)		
Texas Dragoon button	1	The most notable button from the Red River Springs camp is a Texas Dragoon button. Dia .763-in/1.94-cm. This is a two-piece, brass button with an omega-style shank. Scovill Manufacturing Co. produced these rare buttons to fill an order from the Republic of Texas in 1837. Maker's mark. *SCOVILLS-WATERBURY* as rmdc. On the front is a large star on a plain field inscribed with D at the center and *TEXAS* above the star.[9]
Suspender Fasteners		
Iron latches	2	Lgth 2.13-in/5.4-cm. Greatest wdth 1.4-in/3.5-cm. The two iron-wire latches are a matched pair. They have elongated loops to fit over a button or other style of catch.
Brass latch with clip	1	Lgth 1.5-in/3.75-cm. Wdth 1.9-in/4.82-cm. This specimen has a three-pronged suspender clip with a latch hook. One prong of the clip is missing. There is a floral design stamped around the latch-hook.
Brass latch with take-up slide	1	Lgth 1.19-in/3.02-cm. Wdth 1.25-in/3.18-cm. An incised scroll and floral design is on front of the latch.
Iron clip	1	Lgth .88-in/2.22-cm. Wdth 1.5-in/3.81-cm. This a two-pronged clip.
Thimble		
Tailor's thimble	1	Base dia .75-in/1.89-cm. Ht .58-in/1.47-cm. The thimble is brass with a rough tin coating around the body. The top of the thimble is open.
Knives		
Pocket knife	1	Lgth 3.75-in./9.50-cm. The knife is three-bladed with brass ends. A bone handle is intact on one side, but is missing from the opposite side. There is a small brass shield on the side without the bone. One blade is missing, and the other two are corroded to the extent that it is not possible to find a maker's mark.
Tobacco Tag		
Tin tag	1	Dia .503-in/1.28-cm. The tin tobacco tag is a pronged piece of metal that processors stuck into a plug of chewing tobacco to identify the brand. This specimen is a round, two-pronged tag with one prong missing. The painted company logo has long since corroded and disappeared.[10]

Table 18.1 Red River Springs Artifact Descriptions. HLQ3, HLQ4, HLQ6 (*cont.*)		
Artifact Category	**Quantity**	**Description**
Personal Items		
Smoking Pipe Lids		
Brass frames for lids	2	These two specimens are brass frames for lids to smoking pipes. They have two small holes in the top for attachment to the pipe bowl and a small hinge where the lid fastened to the frame. The larger frame has a small line of decorations around the side. Dia 1.31-in/3.33-cm. The smaller frame has no decorations. Dia 1.24-in/3.15-cm.
Military Paraphernalia		
Scabbard Tip		
Brass scabbard tip	1	Lgth 2.5-in/6.35-cm. Greatest wdth 1.5-in/3.8-cm. This brass tip appears to be from a Bowie knife scabbard. Four stamped symmetrical rings decorate the piece, which has a small, ball-shaped finial.[11]
Military Insignia		
Shoulder-belt plate	1	Dia 2.5-in/6.36-cm. This insignia is a U.S. regulation shoulder-belt plate. It is stamped brass with solder filled back. It normally has two iron wire loops on the back, but they are missing from this specimen. Stamped on the front is an eagle facing left toward the olive branch in his talons; his right talons grasp three arrows.[12]
Fasteners		
Nails		
Machine-cut nail	33	Lgth from 1.5-in/3.81-cm. to a large broken spike. Twenty-four of the nails are intact; nine are broken. All exhibit two tapered sides and two sides that are parallel.
Hand-forged square nails	2	Lgth 2.19-in/5.5-cm. One nail is straight while the other one is bent. Both nails are hand-wrought with all sides tapered. Both have irregular heads-one the classic rose-head and the other beaten flat.
Screws		
Wood screws	2	Large screw head dia .38-in/.97-cm. Screw lgth 2.81-in/7.13-cm. Threads 10. Small screw head dia .41-in/1.05-cm. Screw lgth 1.25-in/3.18-cm. Threads 8. Both screws have flat heads.

Bolts and Pins		
Square-headed bolt	1	Lgth 4.5-in/11.43-cm. Dia .31-in/.79-cm.
Round pin	1	Lgth 2.22-in/5.64-cm. Dia .25-in/.64-cm. The pin has a round, flattened head.
Washers		
Flat washer	1	Outside dia 1.75-in/4.45-cm. Thk .15-in/.38-cm.
Horse Tack and Wagon Hardware		
Horseshoes		
Complete shoes	8	Lgth 4.5-in/12.1-cm. to 5.5-in/13.97-cm. Wdth same variation as lgth. Two shoes are bent, and all show considerable wear. Four have heel calks; one has a toe protector.
Broken shoes	3	Lgth 5.0-in/12.7-cm. to 5.5-in/13.9-cm.
Horseshoe Nails		
Unused nails	21	Lgth 2.0-in/5.1-cm. to 2.25-in/5.5-cm.
Used nails	8	The broken nails are of various lgths.
Buckles		
Sunk-bar buckles	4	Two buckles lgth 1.5-in/3.81-cm. Wdth 1.0-in/2.54-cm. Two other buckles lgth 1.9-in/4.83-cm. Wdth .75-in/1.91-cm. All of the buckles have recessed middle bars on which the tongues pivot.
Roller buckles	3	Lgth .88-in/2.2-cm. to 2.0-in/5.1-cm. Wdth .75-in/1.9-cm. to 1.5-in/3.8-cm. The tongues are fastened on one end, and the roller is on the other end.
Metal Stakes		
Tent or picket line stake	1	Lgth 15.5-in/39.37-cm. Dia 1.0-in/2.54-cm. The metal stake is straight, has a pointed end, and a beaten top.
Picket pin	1	Lgth 18-in/45.7-cm. Dia .5-in/1.27-cm. This homemade picket pin is constructed from a wagon rod. One end is bent into an oval for tying the horse. I found this rod *in situ*, upright in position, and 15 inches below ground surface.
Bridle Bits		
Broken bit with mouthpiece	1	Lgth 4.75-in/12.06-cm. Wdth 5.0-in/12.7-cm. One side is missing on this bit, but the entire mouthpiece bar is intact with a brass, ridged roller in the port.
Bit shank	1	Lgth 4.5-in/11.4-cm. All that remains of this bit is a broken shank from one side.

Table 18.1   Red River Springs Artifact Descriptions. HLQ3, HLQ4, HLQ6 (*cont.*)

Artifact Category	Quantity	Description
Horse Tack and Wagon Hardware		
Harness Snaps		
Snap Formed from small twisted rod	1	Lgth 2.75-in/6.7-cm. The snap will accommodate a one-inch wide leather strip.
Harness Couplers		
Quick coupler	1	Lgth 4.0-in/10.2-cm. This type of coupler attaches to a chain at its center point and passes through a harness ring. To make the closure secure, the action is reversed and the coupler is pulled back against the ring.
Harness Decorations		
Brass concha	1	Dia 1.0-in/2.54-cm. This convex, brass concha appears to be a harness decoration. It had two prongs to fasten it to leather, though one prong is now missing.
Harness Rings		
Iron ring	1	Outside dia 2.13-in/5.4-cm. Inside dia 1.56-in/3.97-cm. Ave metal dia .19-in/.48-cm.
Leather and Canvas Fasteners		
Grommets	2	Ave outside dia .56-in/1.43-cm. Ave inside dia .25-in/.64-cm.
Rivets	2	Head dia .5-in/1.27-cm. The other specimen is damaged and no measurement could be taken.
Camp Utensils		
Flatware		
Spoons	5	This assemblage includes two spoon bowls; one large spoon handle; one broken spoon with both pieces; and one complete spoon with *Rogers Nickel Silver* imprinted on the handle. Ave lgth 7.25-in/18.42-cm.
Forks	3	Two metal forks have channel handles while a third fork has a flat metal handle, which at one time had bone or wood coverings held in place by five pins. All three forks are missing some tines.
Handcrafted S-hooks		
Flat metal hook	1	Lgth 6.0-in/15.2-cm. Wdth .7-in/1.78-cm. Thk .11-in/.26-cm. There is a rounded hook on each end.
Iron rod hook	1	Lgth 4.5-in/11.4-cm. Dia .15-in/.38-cm. The rod has a rounded hook on each end.

Metal Cup Handle		
Handle fragment	1	The handle fragment has rolled edges wrapped around a wire for added strength. Widest point where it joins the cup 1.19-in/3.02-cm.
Metal Lid		
Solid lid	1	Dia 1.92-in/4.88-cm. This lid has a solid top with slash marks around the edge. Two soldered spots are visible inside the lid.
Indian Tools		
Stone Tools		
Scraper	1	Lgth 2.0-in/5.1-cm. Maximum wdth 1.5-in/3.81-cm. This tool is a chert, uniface end-scraper.
Dart point	1	Lgth 1.5-in/3.81-cm. Shoulder wdth 1.0-in/2.54-cm. Stem lgth .38-in/.95-cm. Stem wdth .63-in/1.59-cm. This is a late archaic dart point chipped from tan quartzite. It is corner-notched with one barb broken.
Metal Tools		
Awl	1	Lgth 5.0-in/12.75-cm. The awl has one sharpened end.
Miscellaneous Metal Pieces		
Unidentified objects	9	These 9 unidentified metal artifacts vary from broken rods to small, complete objects. Although they had a purpose at one time, they are not significant artifacts for dating.

Chapter 19
Nara Visa Springs Site and Artifacts

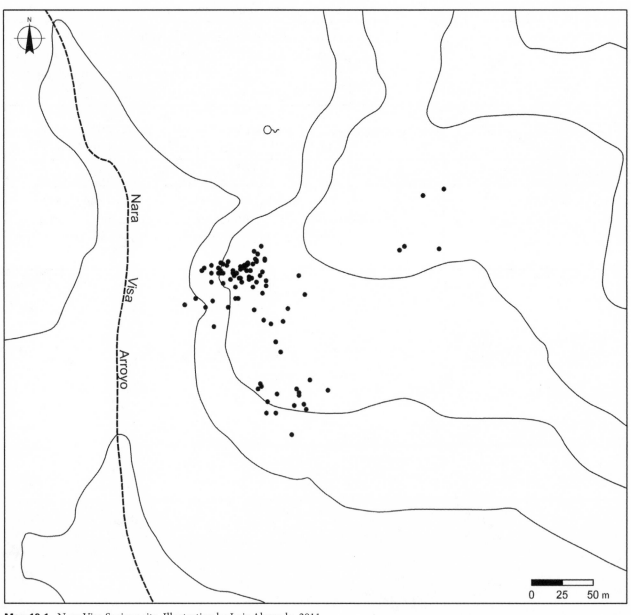

Map 19.1. Nara Visa Springs site. Illustration by Luis Alvarado, 2011.

The Nara Visa Springs camp extends over five acres, more or less, with the Fort Bascom–Adobe Walls Road bisecting it in a northeasterly direction. The site is on a high terrace northeast of the confluence of East Nara Visa and West Nara Visa creeks. The site overlooks a spring flowing into East Nara Visa Creek. The spring, today, flows mostly in the winter months, but the landowner told me it once flowed throughout the year. The gravel hill northwest of the old road exhibits little vegetation, mainly little bluestem and sideoats grama grass, while the terrain southeast of the road is sandier with a scattered growth of skunk berry sumac.

Lieutenant Pettis, traveling with Colonel Carson, in 1864, named the camp Cañada de Los Ruedos (Canyon of the Wheels).[1] Present day maps show it as Nara Visa Springs, and its site number is HLQ5.

Archeological evidence indicates that HLQ5 is a multi-component site dating from early Native Americans (prehistoric) to late nineteenth century occupation.

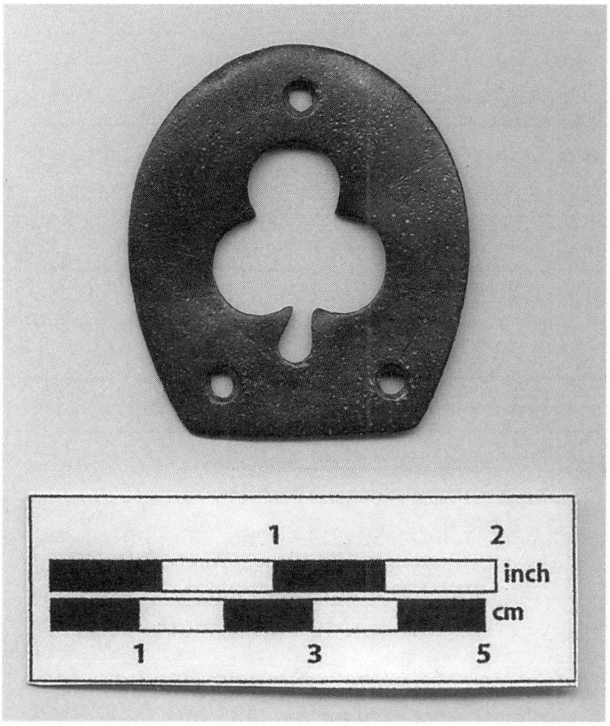

Fig. 95. Cut copper-alloy bucket with bail socket. Photograph by Wyman Meinzer, 2009.

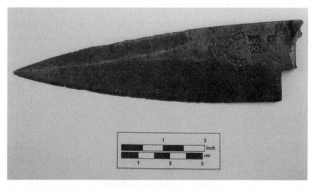

Fig. 96. Broken shears blade. Maker's mark: Crown over arc with *CAST STEEL* stamped in the arc. The numeral *38* is stamped below the arc. Photograph by Wyman Meinzer, 2009.

Fig. 94. Copper alloy boot-heel plate with trefoil cut-out symbol for the Second Corps. Scan by Lisa Jackson, 2011.

Table 19.1 Nara Visa Springs Artifact Descriptions. HLQ5		
Artifact Category	**Quantity**	**Description**
Arms and Ammunition		
Cartridge Cases		
.38 caliber	3	Head stamp. *US-38 S&W.* EP. Ave base dia .38-in/.97-cm. Ave lgth .75-in/1.92-cm.
.44 caliber	1	Head stamp. none. RF. Damaged.
.44-40 caliber	8	Head stamp. none. EP. Ave base dia .47-in/1.19-cm. Ave lgth 1.31-in/3.31-cm.
.44-40 caliber	1	Head stamp. *WRA Co.* EP. .44 WCF. Base dia .47-in/1.19-cm. Lgth 1.31-in/3.31-cm.
.44-40 caliber	1	Head stamp. *.44 CFW.* EP. Base dia .47-in/1.19-cm. Lgth 1.31-in/3.31-cm.
.45 caliber	26	Head stamp. none. EP. Ave base dia .48-in/1.22-cm. Ave lgth 1.27-in/3.22-cm.
.50/70 caliber	1	Head stamp. none. EP. Base dia .57-in/1.45-cm. Lgth 1.76-in/4.47-cm. Case flattened except at base.
Unfired Cartridges		
.44 or 45 caliber	1	Head stamp. none. EP. Damaged cartridge.
56-52 caliber	1	Head stamp. *SAW.* Spencer RF. Cartridge is broken.
Bullets		
.44 caliber	2	Unfired. Percussion pistol bullets. Ave dia .452-in/1.15-cm. Wt varies from 207.1 gr. to 227.8 gr. Both bullets have a flat base and a reduced diameter at the rear.
.44 caliber	1	Fired. High-velocity impact. Base dia .431-in/1.09-cm. Wt 191.1 gr. Post-1875 bullet.*[2]
.44 caliber	1	Fired. Low-velocity impact. Base dia .431-in/1.09-cm. Wt 197.8 gr. Post-1875 Smith and Wesson bullet.*
.45 caliber	1	Fired. Low-velocity impact. Base dia .446-in/1.13-cm. Wt 236.6 gr. Colt revolver.*
.52 caliber	4	Unfired. Percussion rifle bullets. Ave dia .55-in/1.4-cm. Wt varies from 437.3 gr. to 446.3 gr. Sharps bullets with two rings and small cones in flat bases.
Undetermined caliber	1	Fired. Medium-velocity impact. Base dia undetermined. Wt 189.5 gr.*
Undetermined caliber	1	Fired. Medium-velocity impact. Base dia undetermined. Wt 187.8 gr.*

Bullets (cont.)		
Lead ball	1	Fired. Flattened on one side. Dia .50-in/1.28-cm. Wt 148.0 gr.
Damaged bullets	4	No measurements.
Gun Parts		
Musket-top barrel band	1	The barrel band has a thimble for the ramrod attached to the base. Overall lgth of band and thimble. 4.1-in/10.43-cm. The thimble sets back 1.86-in/4.72-cm. from the forward end of the band. The top front of the band is open to allow the musket barrel to pass through it.
Personal Items		
Buttons		
Four-hole metal button	1	Dia .66-in/1.68-cm. The button is two-piece with a recessed center.
Stud fastener or collar stud	1	Dia of convex, hollow front .40-in/1.02-cm. Dia of solid brass back-piece .3-in/.77-cm. The back-piece is flexible.
Broken concha	1	Dia .6-in/1.5-cm. Ht .26-in/.67-cm. Hat shaped with the wire attachment missing from the back.
Suspender Fastener		
Brass fastener	1	Overall lgth 2.2-in/5.66-cm. Greatest wdth 1.1-in/2.8-cm. The fastener has a two-prong gripper with an oval brass ring attached to a hook on the bottom. There is a floral design stamped on the front side of the fastener.
Locks		
Inset trunk lock	1	Overall lgth 3.75-in/9.5-cm. Greatest wdth 3.0-in/7.7-cm. The lock has an iron back-plate with brass key slot and dust cover. Cover lgth 2.2-in/5.6-cm. Wdth 1.1-in/2.8-cm. There is an insignia on the dust cover of a crown with an F imprinted below it. Collectors sometimes call this type of lock a "Mickey Mouse" lock because the top round pieces on the back-plate resembles mouse ears.
Military Paraphernalia		
Military Insignias		
Company D letter	1	Lgth 1.0-in/2.54-cm. Wdth 1.0-in/2.54-cm. Pin fastener missing. Uniform regulations of the U.S. Army in 1861 prescribed for enlisted men to wear on their hats a one-inch letter to designate their company.[3]

Table 19.1 Nara Visa Springs Artifact Descriptions. HLQ5 (*cont.*)		
Artifact Category	**Quantity**	**Description**
Military Paraphernalia		
Military Insignias (cont.)		
Trefoil cut in copper alloy	1	Lgth 1.74-in/4.43-cm. Greatest wdth 1.56-in/4.0-cm. The insignia is oval with one straight edge. Two holes are at each end of the straight edge and one at the extreme end of the oval. The trefoil is the insignia for the 2nd Corp. and this particular type of specimen served as a boot heel guard.[4]
Fasteners		
Nails		
Machine-cut nail	6	Length varies from 2.5-in./6.37-cm. to 3.75-in./9.52-cm. Five nails are complete and one is broken. All have two tapered sides.
Bolts and Pins		
Rounded pin	1	Lgth 1.55-in/3.95-cm. Pin dia .24-in/.62-cm. The pin has a forged flat head.
Broken square-headed bolt	1	Lgth 2.3-in/3.9-cm. Bolt dia .5-in/1.33-cm. Head. 1.0-in/2.54-cm. square. The bolt is broken.
Broken carriage bolt	1	Lgth 2.0-in/5.7-cm. Bolt dia .25-in/.64-cm. Round head with square shoulders beneath the head.
Horse Tack and Wagon Hardware		
Horseshoes		
Complete shoes	1	Lgth 4.5-in/11.4-cm. Wdth 5.0-in/12.7-cm. Worn toe. No calks.
Broken shoes	3	Lgth varies from 4.25-in/10.8-cm. to 6.0-in/15.2-cm. All have calks.
Horseshoe Nails		
Unused nails	7	Lgth 1.9-in/4.79-cm. to 2.5-in/6.2-cm.
Used nails	2	Lgth varies.
Picket Pins or Metal Stakes		
Broken end of metal stake	1	Lgth 2.1-in/5.2-cm. Dia .66-in/1.67-cm.
Harness Hardware		
Harness clip cockeye	1	Lgth 2.94-in/7.47-cm. Greatest wdth 1.78-in/4.5-cm. Strap roller is nearly worn out.

Harness Hardware (cont.)		
Brass harness brad	1	Lgth .52-in/1.34-cm. Washer dia .5-in/1.28-cm. The other end of brad is irregular shaped.
Broken bit chain	1	Lgth 6.0-in/15.2-cm. Six one-inch twisted links. Metal dia .12-in/.31-cm.
Wagon Hardware		
Wagon bow staple	1	Overall lgth 2.3-in/5.9-cm. Prong lgth 1.2-in/3.1-cm. One prong broken.
Chain link	1	Lgth 2.8-in/7.1-cm. Wdth 1.95-in/4.95-cm. Metal dia .4-in/1.0-cm. Link shows wear.
Broken chain link	1	Lgth 2.0-in/5.1-cm. Wdth ?. Metal dia .32-in/.82-cm. Link pulled apart at one end.
Wagon rim band	1	Inside dia 3-in/7.62-cm. Depth. 1.25-in/3.18-cm. There are two small holes in one side. The metal is polished, malleable iron.
Broken flat bar	1	Lgth 4.5-in/11.4-cm. Wdth 1.1-in/2.8-cm. Thk .22-in/.56-cm. Small hole near one end.
Camp Utensils		
Flatware		
Metal fork handle core	1	Lgth 3.6-in/9.1-cm. Greatest wdth .68-in/1.7-cm. This handle core has two pins to hold wooden or bone handle.
Cookware		
Broken cast iron skillet handle	1	Lgth 4.1-in/10.4-cm. Greatest wdth 1.8-in/4.5-cm. Deep oval cut out in handle.
Containers		
Leaded can	1	Height. 4.5-in/11.4-cm. Approx. dia 3.5-in/8.9-cm. Flattened can with missing top.
Bottle neck	1	Outside mouth dia 1.2-in/3.1-cm. Ht 1.5-in/3.8-cm. Amber color with heavy oxidation.
Broken metal cup handle	1	Lgth 2.3-in/5.9-cm. Greatest wdth 1.1-in/2.85-cm. Rolled edges with wire inside the roll.
Copper alloy bucket fragment	1	Lgth 6.0-in/15.2-cm. Greatest wdth 3.25-in/8.26-cm. Thk .02-in/.052-cm. One solid copper bail-ear present.

Table 19.1 Nara Visa Springs Artifact Descriptions. HLQ5 (*cont.*)		
Artifact Category	**Quantity**	**Description**
Tools		
Cutting Tools		
Broken shears blade	1	Lgth 7.0-in/17.8-cm. Greatest wdth 1.84-in/4.68-cm. Maker's mark. Crown over arc with *CAST STEEL* stamped in the arc. The number 38 stamped on the blade is probably patent date. Crossed hammers are stamped at the base of the blade.
Files		
Broken flat file	1	Lgth 2.4-in/6.1-cm. Wdth 1.3-in/3.34-cm. Thk .29-in/.73-cm. 24 ridges/in
Mexican or Indian Artifacts		
Decorations		
Coscojo (Hispanic pendant)	1	Overall lgth 1.45-in/3.69-cm. Ovate shaped bowl with hanger. Bowl lgth .91-in/2.3-cm. Wdth .77-in/1.96-cm.
Cutting Tools		
Metal point cutting blade	1	Lgth 1.54-in/3.52-cm. Wdth at shoulder .51-in/1.3-cm. Small hole in base of tool.
Cut Metal		
Cut copper alloy	1	Lgth 2.65-in/6.72-cm. Triangular shape. Greatest wdth 1.1-in/2.85-cm. Thk .025-in/.062-cm. Probably cut from copper bucket.
Miscellaneous Pieces		
Metal Specimens		
Cut barrel band	1	Lgth 6.5-in/16.5-cm. Wdth 1.43-in/3.64-cm. Thk .041-in/.11-cm. Two rivets hold band together.
Box band	1	Lgth 3.74-in/9.5-cm. Wdth .75-in/1.9-cm. Thk .042-in/.12-cm. Broken at each end near nail holes.
Box or barrel band	1	Lgth 2.9-in/7.3-cm. Wdth .9-in/2.25-cm. Thk .036-in/.092-cm. Two rivets hold band together.
Broken metal pieces	3	Various shapes and sizes.
Nonmetal Pieces		
Small bone	1	Lgth 2.5-in/6-31-cm. Greatest wdth 1.44-in/3.65-cm. Found in hearth. Possible turtle bone.

Chapter 20
Hay Creek Site and Artifacts

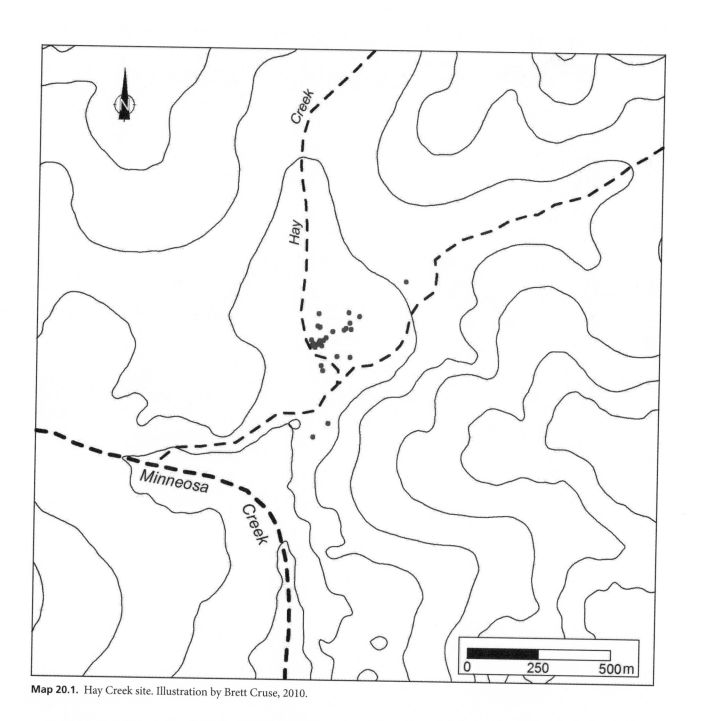

Map 20.1. Hay Creek site. Illustration by Brett Cruse, 2010.

The Fort Bascom–Adobe Walls Road crosses Hay Creek a little more than a mile south of its head-spring and about one hundred yards north of its confluence with a minor east-west oriented creek. At present, water flowing from the spring reaches the wagon road crossing only in the winter, but the creek (like many others in the area) probably flowed year-round before irrigation and overgrazing lowered the Ogallala Aquifer.

The site spreads over about two acres. Short grasses cover the low hill on the east side of the creek. The lower area, west of the creek, is sandier and has a dense growth of sagebrush. Except for a few scrawny willows, the creek is void of trees.

The thirty-one artifacts from this site, numbered HLOL5, came mostly from the east side of the creek along both sides of the trail. This could be because the ground was firmer and better for camping, or it could be that sand has covered the evidence of camping on the west side.

Fig. 97. Broken picket pin with loop missing. Photograph by Wyman Meinzer, 2009.

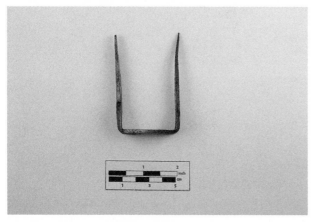

Fig. 98. Wagon bow staple. Photograph by Wyman Meinzer, 2009.

Fig. 99. Broken bi-face blade made from Alibates flint. Photograph by Wyman Meinzer, 2009.

Table 20.1 Hay Creek Artifact Descriptions. HLOL5		
Artifact Category	**Quantity**	**Description**
Arms and Ammunition		
Cartridge Cases		
.45 caliber	1	Head stamp. none. EP. Base dia ?. Lgth 1.07-in/2.72-cm.
Unfired Cartridges		
.44 caliber	1	Head stamp. *H.* Unfired Henry RF. Double firing pin. Misfired. Base dia .445-in/1.13-cm. Overall lgth 1.38-in/3.5-cm. Wt 205.3 gr.
Bullets		
.45 caliber	1	Fired. Low-velocity impact. Dia .458-in/1.16-cm. Wt 245.7 gr. Fired from Colt revolver.
.52 caliber	1	Unfired. Sharps bullet with two rings and a small cone in a flat base. Dia .539-in/1.37-cm. Lgth .892-in/2.27-cm. Wt 434.9 gr.
Lead piece	1	Lgth, irregular shaped, .56-in/1.43-cm. Wdth .34-in/.85-cm. Wt 28 gr.
Cut lead piece	1	Lgth .44-in/1.12-cm. Wdth .33-in/.84-cm. Wt 63.1 gr.
Personal Items		
Buttons		
Metal button	1	Dia .69-in/1.75-cm. Four-hole, iron button with recessed center.
Fasteners		
Nails		
Complete machine-cut nail	5	Lgth varies from 1.5-in/4.0-cm. to 3.0-in/7.7-cm. All nails are tapered on two sides.
Broken machine-cut nail	4	Varied lgths.
Bolts and Pins		
Wagon bolt	1	Lgth 8.5-in/22.5-cm. Greatest thk .5-in/1.3-cm. Square carriage head. Shaft is square from head to threads. Extreme wear near head.
Screws		
Flat-head screw	1	Lgth 1.5-in/3.8-cm. Blade type screw.
Nuts		
Square nut	1	.71-in/1.8-cm. x .71-in/1.8-cm. Thk .33-in/.85-cm. Threaded hole dia .31-in/.79-cm.

Table 20.1 Hay Creek Artifact Descriptions. HLOL5 *(cont.)*		
Artifact Category	**Quantity**	**Description**
Horse Tack and Wagon Hardware		
Horseshoe Nails		
Used nail	1	Lgth 2.13-in/5.5-cm. Broken in two pieces.
Buckles		
Roller buckle	1	Lgth 1.13-in/3.0-cm. Wdth 1.0-in/2.54-cm. Tongue fastens on one side and roller is on the other side.
Roller buckle	1	Lgth 1.32-in/3.4-cm. Wdth 1.13-in/2.9-cm. Tongue fastens on one side and roller is on the other side.
Chain Links and Rings		
Broken harness ring	1	Ring dia ?. Stock metal dia .19-in/.48-cm.
Hame hook	1	Lgth 3.88-in/9.86-cm. Wdth 1.88-in/4.78-cm. The hook swivels on the hame.
Chain link	1	Lgth 3.0-in/7.7-cm. Wdth 1.75-in/4.5-cm. Link is forge welded.
Broken chain link	1	Lgth 3.0-in/7.7-cm. Wdth 1.88-in/4.8-cm. Link is badly worn.
Picket Pins or Metal Stakes		
Broken picket pin	1	Lgth 13.25-in/34.0-cm. Two pieces. Figure-8 tie loop missing. Appears to be 1859 model.
Wagon Parts		
Wagon bow staple	1	Wdth 3.0-in/7.7-cm. Prong lgth 1.88-in/4.77-cm.
Wagon bow or hame staple	1	Wdth 1.88-in/4.78-cm. Prong lgth 3.5-in/8.9-cm. Round stock material.
Broken wagon tug	1	Lgth 5.5-in/13.97-cm. Tug broke at pulling point.
Mexican or Indian Artifacts		
Metal		
Coscojo (Hispanic charm)	1	Overall lgth 1.19-in/3.0-cm. Plain rectangular blade. lgth .56-in/1.4-cm. Wdth .31-in/.80-cm. Small hook attached to blade.
Nonmetal		
Tip of Harahey knife	1	Lgth 2.5-in/6.5-cm. Greatest thk .31-in/8.0-cm. Grayish white Alibates flint with dull red spot.
Miscellaneous Pieces		
Broken metal strap	1	Lgth 3.63-in/9.3-cm. Wdth .5-in/1.227-cm. There are two holes in each end of the strap.

Chapter 21
Romero Creek Site and Artifacts

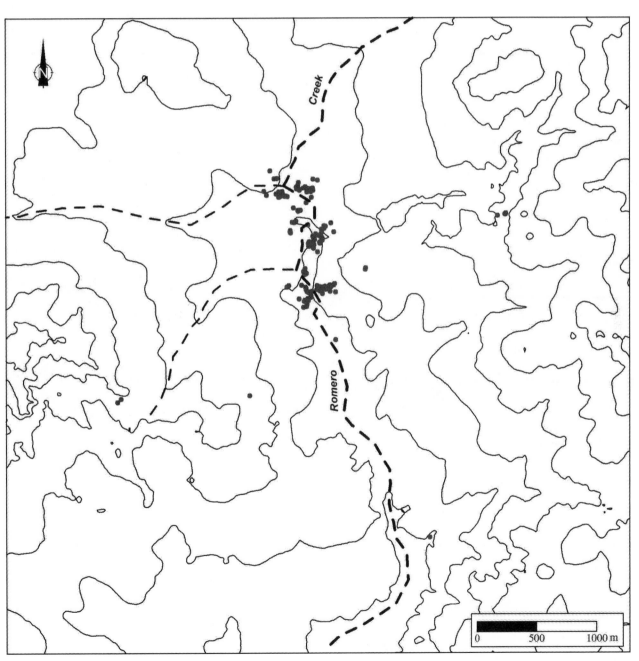

Map 21.1. Romero Creek site. Illustration by Brett Cruse, 2010.

The topography of Romero Creek varies from a wide valley with spring-filled tributaries at its head, to deep-cut canyons near its confluence with the Canadian River to the south. The Fort Bascom Adobe–Walls Road crosses about three and one-half miles below the springs and one and one-half miles above the canyons. The camp, which I've designated as HLHT4, extends almost a mile along the creek, mostly north of the road in an area that is barren of trees except for a few small mesquites scattered on the hills.

During wet years, and winter of normal years, the springs flow as far down as the camp. In drier times, the creek does not run, though water is usually present in deep holes.

This must have been a favorite camping place for a long time because the site produced 229 artifacts dating from early Native American (prehistoric) to late nineteenth century occupation.

Carson's camp began about three-quarters of a mile north of the road where West Romero Creek runs into Romero Creek. From there, the camp extends south along the east side of the creek for a few hundred yards. Artifacts include Mexican items, as well as military buttons, horseshoes, horseshoe nails, gun wrenches, and percussion bullets of the calibers found at the Adobe Walls battle site.

Fig. 100. Oval fire steel similar to one found in an 1840 campsite in Nebraska. Fire steels (strikers) used to strike on flint and start a fire were prized items, usually obtained from white traders. Photograph by Wyman Meinzer, 2009.

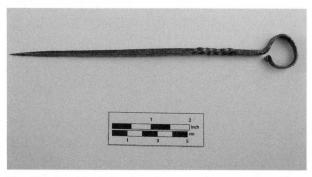

Fig. 101. Spanish Colonial–style iron awl, *circa* 1860s. Photograph by Wyman Meinzer, 2009.

Fig. 102. U.S. Springfield combination gun tool, *circa* 1841–1842. Photograph by Wyman Meinzer, 2009.

Table 21.1 Romero Creek Artifact Descriptions. HLHT4		
Artifact Category	**Quantity**	**Description**
Arms and Ammunition		
Cartridge Cases		
.38 caliber	2	Head stamp. *UMC 38 Long S-H.* EP. Ave base dia .378-in/.96-cm. Ave lgth 1.27-in/3.23-cm.
.38 caliber	2	Head stamp. none. RF. Ave base dia .38-in/.97-cm. Ave lgth .88-in/2.24-cm. The firing pin struck twice on one case.
.41 caliber	1	Head stamp. none. EP. Base dia .41-in/1.04-cm. Lgth .95-in/2.41-cm.
.44 caliber, short	1	Head stamp. none. EP. Base dia .44-in/1.12-cm. Lgth .91-in/2.3-cm.
.44 caliber	1	Head stamp. none. EP. Base dia .445-in/1.13-cm. Lgth .999-in/2.54-cm. Split on one side.
.44-40 caliber	2	Head stamp. *WRA Co. 44 WCF.* EP. Ave base dia .47-in/1.19-cm. Ave lgth 1.33-in/3.38-cm.
.44-40 caliber	5	Head stamp. none. EP. Ave base dia .47-in/1.20-cm. Ave lgth 1.32-in/3.3-cm.
.45 caliber	3	Head stamp. *US .45 Cal. Colt.* EP. Ave base dia .485-in/1.23-cm. Lgth 1.25-in/3.18-cm.
.45 caliber	1	Head stamp. *WRA Co. .45 Colt.* EP. Base dia .485-in/1.23-cm. Lgth 1.25-in/3.18-cm.
.45 caliber	38	Head stamp. none. EP. Ave base dia .48-in/1.22-cm. Ave lgth 1.27-in/3.22-cm.
.45 caliber, short	1	Head stamp. none. EP. Base dia ? Lgth .93-in/2.36-cm.
.50/70 caliber	3	Head stamp. none. EP. Ave base dia .57-in/1.45-cm. Ave lgth 1.77-in/4.50-cm.
Unfired Cartridges		
.38 caliber	1	Head stamp. none. EP. Unfired. Base dia .385-in/.98-cm. Overall lgth 1.15-in/2.92-cm.
.45 caliber	1	Head stamp. none. EP. Unfired. Base dia .48-in/1.22-cm. Overall lgth 1.60-in/4.06-cm.
Unfired Bullets		
.44 caliber	2	Unfired. Percussion bullets with small ringtails. Ave dia .455-in/1.16-cm. Ave wt 229.35 gr.

Artifact Category	Quantity	Description
Table 21.1 Romero Creek Artifact Descriptions. HLHT4 (*cont.*)		
Arms and Ammunition		
Unfired Bullets (cont.)		
.52 caliber	12	Unfired. Sharps percussion bullets with two rings and small cones in flat bases. Ave dia .546-in/1.39-cm. Ave wt 440.0 gr.
Lead ball	1	Slightly flattened. Dia .433-in/1.10-cm. Wt 133.4 gr.
Fired Bullets		
Undetermined caliber	1	High-velocity impact. Wt 120.2 gr.*[1]
.38 caliber	1	Medium-velocity impact. Dia .383-in/.97-cm. Wt 180 gr.
.41 or .42 caliber	1	Low-velocity impact. Slightly dished base. Dia .42-in/1.07-cm. Wt 213.7 gr.
.42 caliber	1	High-velocity impact. Post-1875. Dia .429-in/1.09-cm. Wt 193.4 gr.*
.42 caliber	1	Low-velocity impact. Dia .401-in/1.02-cm. Wt 193.7 gr.*
.44 caliber	1	Fired by Smith and Wesson. Medium-velocity impact. Dia .447-in/1.14-cm. Wt 223.6 gr.*
.44 caliber ball	1	Medium-velocity impact. Ramrod impression, consistent with Colt M1860 Army revolver. Dia .440-in/1.12-cm. Wt 133.5 gr.*
.45 caliber	1	Colt. Medium-velocity impact. Dia .452-in/1.15-cm. Wt 239.4 gr.*
.50 caliber	1	Medium-velocity impact. Wt 404.3 gr.*
.50 caliber ?	1	Cut bullet. Base missing. Wt 233.4 gr.
Waste Lead		
Lead piece	1	Irregular shape. Size 1.62-in/4.1-cm. x .69-in/1.75-cm. Wt 229.0 gr.
Broken spring ?	1	Lgth 1.09-in/2.78-cm. Wdth .22-in/.57-cm. The piece has a channel running lengthwise and a small extension on the side.
Broken spring	1	Lgth 1.1-in/2.8-cm. Wdth .075-in/.19-cm. Thk .065-in/.167-cm. Small round extension with catch on one end.
Combination tool	1	1841 Springfield rifle/1842 Springfield musket combination tool. Lgth 3.56-in/9.1-cm. Head wdth .56-in/1.42-cm. Two blades.[2]

Waste Lead (cont.)		
Combination tool	1	Very rusty. Appears to be 1841 Springfield rifle/1842 Springfield musket combination tool. Lgth 3.48-in/8.84-cm. Head wdth .52-in/1.32-cm. Two blades.[3]
Combination tool	1	Very rusty with one blade broken. Appears to be 1841 Springfield rifle/1842 Springfield musket combination tool. Lgth 3.55-in/9.02-cm. Head wdth .53-in/1.35-cm. Two blades.
Personal Items		
Buttons		
Towers wire fastened	1	Dia 1.0-in/2.54-cm. *"Towers Wire Fastened"* stamped around face. Recessed center with two holes for wire fastener. Wire with metal disk on back.
Four-hole metal buttons	4	Dia ranges from .66-in/1.68-cm. to .675-in/1.71-cm. All have recessed centers and one has a stippling design on the front.
Army general service button	1	Dia .56-in/1.42-cm. Two-piece button with bent shank. Maker's mark. *SCOVILLS & Co. * EXTRA.* dm. Manufactured about 1840.[4]
Army general service button	2	Ave dia .57-in/1.45-cm. Two-piece button. Shanks good. Maker's mark. none.
Army general service button	1	Dia .614-in/1.56-cm. Two-piece button. Shank good. *HORSTMANN* button, but maker's mark is incomplete so manufacture date not determined. dm.
Army general service button	1	Dia .78-in/1.98-cm. Two-piece button with missing shank. Maker's mark. *WATERBURY BUTTON CO*.* rmdc. Manufacture dates from early 1860s to 1870s.[5]
Army general service button	1	Dia .79-in/1.98-cm. Two-piece with missing shank. Maker's mark. none. Slightly flattened.
Smooth brass button	1	Dia. 72-in/1.83-cm. One piece with soldered Omega-style shank on back. Maker's mark. none.
Smooth brass button	1	Dia .95-in/2.41-cm. One piece with soldered Omega-style shank on back. Maker's mark *? COLOUR ****.
Brass button face	1	Dia .89-in/2.26-cm. Horse-head design on front. Bent wire attachment on back. Concave shape.
Copper concha	1	Dia 1.33-in/3.37-cm. No design. .28-in/.71-cm. slots for leather strings. Maker's mark. none.
Copper button	1	Dia .64-in/1.63-cm. Stippling design on front. Appears to be suspender latch button.

Table 21.1 Romero Creek Artifact Descriptions. HLHT4 (*cont.*)

Artifact Category	Quantity	Description
Personal Items		
Buttons (cont.)		
Iron button with brass disk on back	1	Dia .55-in/1.40-cm. Depressed ring on front. Appears to be suspender latch button.
Brass spool fastener	1	Spool head dia .62-in/1.57-cm. Spool wdth .58-in/1.47-cm. Used to fasten various leather belts, pouches, etc.
Pocket Knives		
Two-blade pocket knife	1	Lgth 4.1-in/19.4-cm. Maximum wdth 1.0-in/2.54-cm. Small blade broken. Brass end caps at hinge end of knife. Handle coverings missing.
Broken pocket knife side plate	1	Lgth 1.75-in/4.45-cm. Maximum wdth .49-in/1.24-cm. One broken side of core with end cap. Brass metal.
Pocket knife core fragment	1	Lgth 3.5-in/8.89-cm. Maximum wdth .74-in/1.88-cm. Rusted iron rim with two pins.
Jewelry		
Brass crucifix	1	Lgth 1.5-in/3.81-cm. Wdth .80-in/2.03-cm. Christ's figure is loose and right arm is broken. Something missing from pin above Christ's figure. Chain loop broken.
Coins		
1882 penny	1	Dia .78-in/1.98-cm. *United States of America* and Indian Head on front. *One Cent* and laurel leaf on back. Copper metal.
Fasteners		
Nails		
Complete machine-cut nail	44	Lgth varies from 1.25-in/3.18-cm. to 3.5-in/8.89-cm. All are tapered on two sides.
Broken machine-cut nail	20	Lgth varies. All tapered on two sides.
Hand-forged square nails	1	Lgth 1.68-in/4.27-cm. Tip missing. Hand-forged with rosette head. All sides tapered.
Screws		
Small wood screw	1	Lgth .75-in/1.91-cm. Head dia .25-in/.64-cm. Straight slot.
Wood screw	1	Lgth 1.25-in/3.18-cm. Head dia .42-in/1.08-cm. Straight slot.

Washers		
Flat washer	1	Outside dia 3.13-in./7.95-cm. Inside dia 1.76-in/4.47-cm. Thk .24-in/.61-cm.
Horse Tack and Wagon Hardware		
Horseshoes		
Complete shoes	5	Lgth 4.4-in/11.12-cm. to 5.62-in/13.20-cm. Wdth 4.25-in/10.80-cm. to 5.0-in/12.70-cm. Two shoes have calks and two have toe plates. All are worn.
Broken shoe	1	Lgth 4.25-in/10.80-cm. Wdth 4.34-in/11.02-cm. Calk present on one heel. The other heel is broken. Heavy wear on toe.
One-half shoe	3	Lgth 3.75-in/9.53-cm. to 4.86-in/12.37-cm. Two shoes have calks on heels.
Mule Shoes		
Complete shoes	3	Lgth 4.75-in/12.1-cm. to 5.25-in/13.34-cm. Wdth 3.75-in/9.52-cm. to 4.6-in/11.68-cm. All shoes have calks on heels.
One-half shoe	1	Lgth 4.75-in/12.1-cm. Worn calk on heel.
Horseshoe Nails		
Complete nails	13	Lgth varies from 1.5-in/3.81-cm. to 2.5-in/6.35-cm.
Used and broken nails	19	Lgth varies.
Buckles		
Small roller buckle	2	Lgth of both buckles .88-in/2.24-cm. Wdth 1.13-in/2.87-cm. Tongue fastens on one end and the roller on the other.
Small roller buckle	1	Lgth .88-in/2.24-cm. Wdth .75-in/1.9-cm. Tongue fastens on one end and the roller on the other.
Large roller buckle	1	Lgth 1.5-in/3.81-cm. Wdth 2.1-in/5.33-cm. Tongue fastens on one end and the roller on the other.
Harness Rings		
Cinch ring	1	Outside dia 3.63-in/9.22-cm. Inside dia 3.37-in/.8.56-cm. Tongue lgth 3.75-in/9.53-cm.
Harness Fasteners		
Quick coupler	1	Lgth 3.5-in/8.89-cm. Metal thk .25-in/.64-cm. Curved ends on coupler. S-hook attached.
Harness snap	1	Lgth 6.0-in/15.24-cm. Snap opens on one end with chain hook on the other. Snap spring is bent outward. _UUO_ stamped on back of snap.

Table 21.1 Romero Creek Artifact Descriptions. HLHT4 (*cont.*)		
Artifact Category	**Quantity**	**Description**
Horse Tack and Wagon Hardware		
Chains		
Broken chain links	2	Large bent link. Lgth 2.5-in/6.35-cm. Small twisted link. Lgth 1.25-in/3.18-cm. Stock dia .19-in/.48-cm. Both links are worn and broken.
Broken chain link	1	Lgth 2.75-in/6.99-cm. Stock dia .25-in/.64-cm.
Short chain	1	Total lgth 6.5-in/16.5-cm. Three links. Lgth of links varies from 2.60-in/6.6-cm. to 2.70-in/6.86-cm. Stock dia .28-in/.71-cm.
Broken chain link	1	Lgth .89-in/2.26-cm. Stock dia .12-in/.30-cm. Link is pulled apart on one end.
Small chain	1	Lgth 8.5-in/21.59-cm. Made up of small S-shaped links .61-in/1.55-cm. long. Appears to be a canteen stopper chain.
Small chain hook	1	Lgth 1.76-in/4.47-cm. Hook on each end. Bent to right angle. Stock ave thk .25-in/.64-cm.
Metal Stakes		
Picket pin or tent stake	1	Lgth 14-in/35.56-cm. Dia .75-in/1.9-cm. Hand-forged from large bolt. Beaten to a point on threaded end.
Bridle Bits		
Broken bit	1	Side plate. Lgth 4.25-in/10.80-cm. Maximum wdth 1.75-in/4.45-cm. Metal thk .29-in/.74-cm. D-shaped opening on one end and a round opening on the other.
Curb bit chain	1	Total lgth 7.5-in/19.0-cm. Chain links are interwoven.
Leather and Canvas Fasteners		
Copper rivet	1	Head dia .5-in/1.27-cm. Lgth .48-in/1.22-cm. Spool bent.
Copper rivet	1	Head dia .43-in/1.09-cm. Lgth .35-in/.89-cm. One end is missing.
Small copper rivet	1	Head dia .30-in/.76-cm. Lgth .27-in/.69-cm.
Wagon Hardware		
Wagon bow staple	1	Wdth 2.5-in/6.35-cm. Staple lgths 2.5-in/6.35-cm. Tips of staples broken.
Wagon part	1	Lgth 7.5-in/19.1-cm. Wdth 1.25-in/3.18-cm. Thk .19-in/.48-cm. Metal is offset in two places. Could be wagon standard. There is .80-in/2.03-cm. dia hole in one end and a broken bolt in the other end.

Wagon Hardware (cont.)		
Metal plate	1	Lgth and wdth 3.0-in/7.62-cm. There is a 1.1-in/2.79-cm. hole in the center of the plate. There are four small holes at each corner. Two 2.25-in/5.72-cm. cut nails accompany the plate.
Strap hinge	1	Lgth 8.0-in/20.32-cm. Maximum wdth 1.5-in/3.81-cm. Thk .25-in/.64-cm. Hinge is tapered with four holes while the base strap is rectangular with three holes.
Metal straps	2	One has a lgth of 8.0-in/20.32-cm. and the other is 7.5-in/19.1-cm. long. Both have a wdth of 1.5-in/3.81-cm. Both straps have a .31-in/.79-cm. tapered hole at each end.
Unidentified wagon hardware	1	Lgth 9.0-in/22.86-cm. Maximum wdth 1.75-in/4.45-cm. Curved strap with a .95-in/2.41-cm. hole on one end and a .50-in/1.27-cm. hole on the other end.
Unidentified wagon hardware	1	Overall lgth 9.5-in/24.13-cm. The piece has a .75-in/1.9-cm.-wide square handle with a broken tug loop on the end. There is a rectangular hole cut through the handle.
Tools		
Drills		
Broken drill bit?	1	Lgth .88-in/2.24-cm. Broken at first twist. This piece could be twisted and broken stock metal and not a bit.
Hatchet or Ax		
Broken hatchet	1	Lgth 3.0-in/7.62-cm. Wdth 3.5-in/8.89-cm. Hatchet head is missing. Slot for nail pulling is present on side of blade. "1" stamped in blade.
Awl	1	Lgth 7.75-in/19.69-cm. There is a .75-in/1.90-cm. diameter loop at one end. The shaft has five twists approximately one-third distance between the loop and the point. The awl is of Spanish-Colonial style.
Camp Utensils		
Containers and Lids		
Leaded cans	2	Ht 4.5-in/11.43-cm. Dia 3.0-in/7.62-cm. Flattened.
Broken metal cup handle	1	Lgth 4.13-in/10.49-cm. Maximum wdth .94-in/2.39-cm. Rolled edges.
Striker		
Fire Steel	1	Lgth 3.63-in/9.22-cm. Wdth 1.5-in/3.81-cm. Thk .164-in/.42-cm. Oval shape.

Table 21.1 Romero Creek Artifact Descriptions. HLHT4 (*cont.*)		
Artifact Category	**Quantity**	**Description**
Mexican or Indian Artifacts		
Metal Artifacts		
Metal point	1	Lgth 2.30-in/5.84-cm. Shoulder wdth .67-in/.1.7-cm. Thk at shoulder .064-in/.16-cm. Triangular stem with serrations. Stem not symmetrical.
Metal point	1	Lgth 3.21-in/8.15-cm. Shoulder wdth ?. Thk at shoulders .067-in/.17-cm. Stem lgth .56-in/1.42-cm. Sloping shoulders. Sides of point rusted away.
Chisel-cut metal	8	Various shapes and sizes. Cut for metal point production.
Chisel-cut metal	1	Lgth 1.43-in/3.64-cm. Maximum wdth .83-in/2.12-cm. Ave thk .075-in/.19-cm. Irregular shape. Cut for metal point production.
Twisted chisel-cut metal	5	Varied lgths 1.5-in/3.81-cm. to 4.75-in/12.1-cm. Cut for metal point or coscojo production.
Chisel-cut metal	4	Various shapes and sizes. Cut box bands. One band has a hole and another has a rivet. Cut for metal point or coscojo production.
Lead beads	49	Varied sizes. Maximum dia .20-in/.64-cm. to .69-in/1.76-cm. Irregular shapes. Flat to concave on one side and convex on the other side. Individually poured.
Broken coscojo (Hispanic charm)	1	Lgth 1.33-in/3.38-cm. Blade wdth .35-in/.89-cm. Hook broken. Chisel-cut on end of blade.
Small S-hooks	2	Lgth varies. 1.32-in/3.35-cm. to 1.46-in/3.71-cm. Handmade. Bit chain or large coscojo hooks.
Non-Metal Artifacts		
Quartzite chopper	1	Lgth 3.73-in/9.48-cm. Max wdth 2.64-in/6.71-cm. Max thk 1.25-in/3.18-cm. Tan-colored Dakota quartzite.
Quartzite flakes	5	Various sizes. Colors: 3 tan, 1 brown, and 1 dark grey. Material Dakota quartzite.
Dart-point base	1	Stem wdth .657-in/1.67-cm. Stem lgth .45-in/1.14-cm. Thk at shoulder .22-in/.56-cm. Point is broken at shoulder. Alibates chert.
End scraper	1	Lgth 1.15-in/2.92-cm. Max wdth .88-in/2.24-cm. Max thk .23-in/.59-cm. Alibates chert.

Miscellaneous Metal Pieces		
Box band fragments	2	Lgth 2.25-in/5.72-cm. to 2.75-in/6.99-cm. Wdth .75-in/1.91-cm. Ave thk .0 35-in/.089-cm. Both pieces broken at nail holes.
Broken and bent metal strap	1	Lgth 2.75-in/6.99-cm. Wdth .75-in/1.91-cm. Ave thk .11-in/.28-cm. Large and small holes near beveled end.
Broken metal rod	1	Lgth 5-in/12.7-cm. Dia .259-in/.66-cm. One end smaller.
Metal piece	1	Lgth 3.61-in/9-16-cm. Maximum wdth 1.14-in/2.90-cm. Irregular shape with hole in each end.
Tapered metal strap	1	Lgth 3.25-in/8.26-cm. Maximum wdth .61-in/1.55-cm. Ave thk .10-in/.25-cm. Metal tapers to rounded end.
Broken metal strap	1	Lgth 3.25-in/8.26-cm. Wdth .41-in/1.03-cm. Thk .045-in/.11-cm.

Chapter 22
Playa Lake Site and Artifacts

The Playa Lake site, trinomial number of HLHT6, is on a tongue of the High Plains that extends between Punta de Agua Creek and the Canadian River Valley to the south. Blue grama and buffalo grass, with a scattering of cholla and yucca, are the prevalent vegetation in the area.

The camp covers almost ten acres along the south and southwest sides of the large playa lake. Although the site stretches about half a mile, the twenty-six artifacts from the site were concentrated at the southwest end. The likely reason for so few artifacts is that this camp is only five miles from the last encampment on Romero Creek.

The Bascom Road crosses Pedarosa Creek two-tenths of a mile south of the playa lake. A faint trail leads from the wagon road to the lake. Teamsters may have pulled off the main road and soaked wooden wagon spokes in the shallow lake to prevent shrinkage.

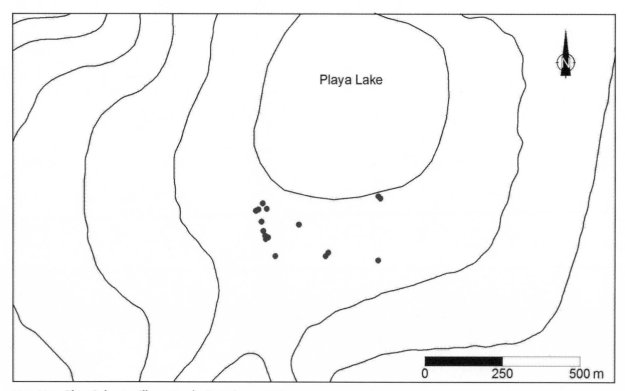

Map 22.1. Playa Lake site. Illustration by Brett Cruse, 2010.

Fig. 103. Grouping of unused horseshoe nails. Scan by Lisa Jackson, 2011.

Fig. 104. Copper shaker lid. Scan by Lisa Jackson, 2011.

Table 22.1 Playa Lake Artifact Descriptions. HLHT6		
Artifact Category	**Quantity**	**Description**
Arms and Ammunition		
Cartridge Cases		
.44 caliber	2	Head stamp. none. EP. Ave base dia .45-in/1.14-cm. Lgth .69-in/1.75-cm. Fired in a British Webley Royal Irish Constabulary model revolver. The British introduced the R.I.C. Webley into the American market in 1868.[1]
.44 caliber	1	Head stamp. *H. Henry RF.* Double firing pin. Base dia ?. Case is flattened. Lgth .93-in/2.36-cm.
.44-40 caliber	2	Head stamp. none. EP. Ave base dia .47-in/1.19-cm. Lgth 1.32-in/3.35-cm.
.44-77 caliber	2	Head stamp. none. EP. Necked case. Ave base dia .51-in/1.30-cm. Lgth 2.26-in/5.74-cm. Introduced in 1875 for the Sharps breech-loading sporting rifle.[2]
.45 caliber	4	Head stamp. none. EP. Ave base dia .48-in/1.22-cm. Lgth 1.26-in/3.2-cm.
.45 caliber	1	Head stamp. *U.M.C. .45 COLT.* EP. Base dia .48-in/1.22-cm. Lgth 1.26-in/3.2-cm.
Bullets		
.41 caliber	1	Flattened lead ball. High-velocity impact. Dia .41-in/1.04-cm.
.52 caliber	1	Fired. Low-velocity impact. Base dia .53-in/1.35-cm. Lgth .85-in/2.16/cm. Wt 385.4 gr. The bullet has 3 rings with a cone base.
Fasteners		
Nails		
Machine-cut nail	10	Lgth varies from 1.25-in/3.18-cm. to 2.5-in/6.35-cm. All nails have two tapered sides.
Horse Tack and Wagon Hardware		
Horseshoe Nails		
Unused nails	19	Lgth varies from 1.87-in/4.76-cm. to 2.1-in/5.3-cm.
Horse and Mule Shoes		
Complete mule shoe	1	Lgth 5.13-in/13.0-cm. Wdth. 4.0-in/10.16-cm. No calks. Shoe is worn through on right front side.

Saddle Hardware		
Iron saddle strap holder	1	Lgth 2.2-in/5.59-cm. Strap holder width .87-in/2.21-cm. Screw hole on each end.
Camp Supplies		
Lids		
Copper shaker lid	1	Flattened. Approximate dia 1.15-in/2.92-cm.

Chapter 23
Rita Blanca Creek Site and Artifacts

The Rita Blanca site rests on top of the east side of a long ridge northwest of the confluence of the Rita Blanca, Sand, and Punta de Agua creeks. Dense brush, mostly skunkberry sumac, covers the sandy ridge. Non-vegetated areas have blown out, leaving a deflated surface of burned rock, gravel, and flint.

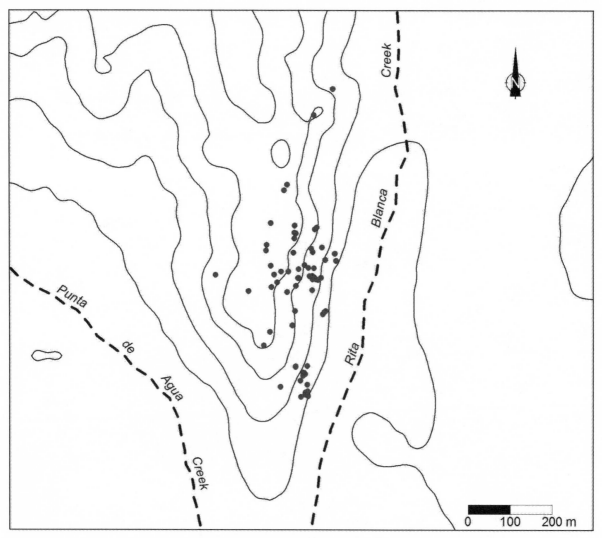

Map .23.1. Rita Blanca Creek site. Illustration by Brett Cruse, 2010.

Most of the artifacts came from the east side of the ridge, where the topography gradually slopes, leveling into a narrow terrace along the west side of Rita Blanca Creek. Small mesquite, skunkberry sumac, yucca, and various grasses grow all along the eastern slope.

The north branch of the Fort Bascom–Adobe Walls Road passes through the camp and rejoins the main road approximately one-half mile up Punta de Agua Creek.

Although, there is evidence that the military camped here, metal arrow points, awls, *coscojos* (Hispanic charms), and hand-made tools point to major activity from historic Indians and *Comancheros.* The location, in relation to the three creeks and Bascom Road, makes it a candidate for a *Comanchero* trading area.

Fig. 106. Indian tool made from flattened bolt. Photograph by Wyman Meinzer, 2009.

Fig. 105. Indian-made awls. *Top*: bell clapper awl. *Bottom*: straight awl. Photograph by Wyman Meinzer, 2009.

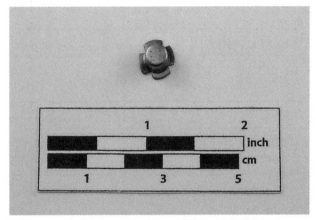

Fig. 107. Musket-size percussion cap. Photograph by Wyman Meinzer, 2009.

Table 23.1 Rita Blanca Artifact Descriptions. HLHT9		
Artifact Category	**Quantity**	**Description**
Arms and Ammunition		
Cartridge Cases		
.45 caliber	2	Head stamp. none. EP. Ave base dia .48-in/1.23-cm. Ave lgth 1.28-in/3.25-cm.
.50/70 caliber	2	Head stamp. none. IP. Ave base dia .555-in/1.40-cm. Ave lgth 1.75-in/4.55-cm. Both cases are flattened and both have extractor marks.
Unfired Bullets		
.44 caliber	3	Unfired percussion bullets with ringtails. Ave dia .452-in/1.15-cm. Ave lgth .74-in/1.88-cm. Ave wt 231.0 gr.
Fired Bullets		
.38 caliber	1	Dia .38-in/.98-cm. Wt 161.4 gr. Dished base. Medium-velocity impact.
.44 caliber	1	Dia undetermined. Wt 189.2 gr. High-velocity impact.*[1]
.44 caliber	1	Dia .431-in/1.09-cm. Wt 198.6 gr. Medium-velocity impact.
.44 caliber	1	Dia .446-in/1.13-cm. Wt 240.2 gr. Deep concave base. Medium-velocity impact.
.44 caliber	1	Dia .43-in/1.11-cm. Wt 201.1 gr. Medium-velocity impact.
.44 caliber	1	Dia undetermined. Wt 198.5 gr. High-velocity impact. Rifling consistent with post-1875 Henry or Winchester.*
.44 caliber	1	Dia undetermined. Wt 186.8 gr. High-velocity impact.*
.44 caliber	1	Dia .430-in/1.09-cm. Wt 226.2 gr. Low-velocity impact. Rifling is consistent with Frank Wesson gun.*
.45 caliber	1	Dia .446-in/1.13-cm. Wt 219.0 gr. Rifling consistent with post-1875 Colt revolver.*
.54 caliber	1	Dia .55-in/1.38-cm. Wt 467 gr. Three ring with deep concave base. Medium-velocity impact.
Lead Balls		
.45 caliber	1	Dia .447-in/1.14-cm. Wt 126.3 gr. Low-velocity impact.*
Undetermined caliber	1	Dia undetermined. Wt 223.8 gr. High-velocity impact.
.50 caliber	1	Dia .501-in/1.27-cm. Wt 200.4 gr. Medium-velocity impact.*

Lead Balls (cont.)		
.50 caliber	1	Dia .488-in/1.24-cm. Wt 177.3 gr. Low-velocity impact.*
.00 Buckshot	1	Dia .31-in/.79-cm. Wt 31.5 gr. Faceted.*
Percussion Caps		
Hat-type musket percussion cap	1	Head stamp. none. Fired. Ht .22-in/.55-cm. Dia .223-in/.569-cm. Four flared flanges.
Hat-type musket percussion cap	1	Head stamp. none. Fired. Ht .237-in/.602-cm. Dia .241-in/.615-cm. Four flared flanges.
Gun Parts		
Possible frontal barrel band	1	Lgth 2.43-in/6.16-cm. Elongated brass handle on bottom. Iron loop on upper side inside brass.
Personal Items		
Buttons		
Four-hole metal button	1	Dia .673-in/1.71-cm. Recessed center. No markings. Folded edges.
Military button	1	General service button. Dia .789-in/2.00-cm. Two piece with shank missing. Maker's mark. **Scovill MFG Co**Waterbury. rmdc. Date about 1860.[2]
Military button	1	General service button. Dia .539-in/1.34-cm. Two-piece with complete shank. No maker's mark but two concentric circles around shank.
Suspender Hardware		
Brass latch and slide	2	Elongated oval slide. Lgth 1.5-in/3.81-cm. Roller on one side. Strap guide. Lgth 1.5-in/3.81-cm. Pin missing.
Fasteners		
Nails		
Machine-cut square nails	11	All nails tapered on two sides. Lgth varies from .94-in/2.38-cm. to 2.5-in/6.35-cm.
Iron square tack	1	Lgth .64-in/1.62-cm. Round head.
Brads		
Iron brad or pin	1	Lgth 1.6-in/3.9-cm. Dia .25-in/.64-cm. One end expanded.
Horse Tack and Wagon Hardware		
Mule Shoes		
Heel fragment	1	Lgth 3.18-in/7.94-cm. Greatest wdth .643-in/1.63-cm. Shoe fragment has calk.

Table 23.1 Rita Blanca Artifact Descriptions. HLHT9 (*cont.*)		
Artifact Category	**Quantity**	**Description**
Horse Tack and Wagon Hardware		
Buckles		
Small iron buckle	1	Lgth .91-in/2.29-cm. Wdth 1.15-in/2.97-cm. Tongue fastens on one side.
Chains		
Bridle chain link	1	Lgth 1.75-in/4.44-cm. Wdth .55-in/1.4-cm. Dia of rod stock .16-in/.43-cm.
Wagon Hardware		
Broken tug	1	Lgth 4.75-in/11.5-cm. Dia at break .9-in/2.29-cm. Curved with pointed end.
Tools		
Shears		
Shears blade fragment	1	Blade mid-section lgth 3.13-in/7.95-cm. Max wdth 1.75-in/4.45-cm. Marks. *ATN 51 CAST STEEL.* Two crowns above *CAST STEEL.*
Shears blade	1	Blade lgth 6-in/15.24-cm. Overall lgth 12.5-in/31.75-cm. Maximum wdth 1.75-in/4.5-cm. Spring-loaded handle. Marks. *PATN 51 ? STEEL.*
Shears blade	1	Blade lgth 5.75-in/14.6-cm. Overall lgth 12-in/30-cm. Max wdth 1.5-in/4.0-cm. Marks. *PATN 51.* Crown stamped in blade. Probably the other half of previous blade.
Camp Utensils		
Containers and Lids		
Leaded can lid	1	Raised circle on lid. Air hole closed with lead. Lid cut to oblong shape with knife. Lgth 3.03-in/7.80-cm. Wdth 2.46-in/6.42-cm.
Knives		
Broken knife blade	1	Distal section of utility knife blade. Lgth 3.44-in/8.74-cm. Cutting edge rusted away.
Mexican or Indian Artifacts		
Metal Artifacts		
Iron metal point	1	Lgth 1.86-in/4.73-cm. Shoulder wdth .66-in/1.67-cm. Stem lgth .28-in/.71-cm. Stem wdth .21-in/.51-cm. Thk at shoulders .05-in/.14-cm. No serrations. Straight base. Rounded uneven shoulders.

Metal Artifacts (cont.)		
Brass metal point	1	Lgth 1.08-in/2.74-cm. Shoulder wdth .51-in/1.3-cm. Stem lgth .37-in/.94-cm. Stem wdth .22-in/.56-cm. Thk at shoulders. .03-in/.09-cm. No serrations. Slanted base. Sloping shoulders.
Coscojo (Hispanic charm) with hook	1	Overall lgth 3.0-in/7.62-cm. Blade lgth 1.25-in/3.18-cm. Blade wdth .31-in/.79-cm. Chisel-cut decorations on blade with typical *Fica* extension on one side.
Coscojo	1	Blade lgth 1.0-in/2.54-cm. Blade wdth .36-in/.91-cm. No decorations.
Coscojo, oval shape	1	Lgth 1.4-in/3.57-cm. Wdth .77-in/1.96-cm. Chisel-cut decorations around edges.
Awl	1	Lgth 2.89-in/7.33-cm. Double-pointed awl made from square stock. Maximum wdth of stock material .12-in/.31-cm.
Awl	1	Awl made from bell clapper and hook. Lgth 4.12-in/10-cm. Dia of clapper ball .96-in/2.44-cm.
Tool made from bolt	1	Hand-forged flesher or scraper made from threaded bolt. Lgth 6.25-in/15.9-cm. Max wdth of blade 1.1-in/2.79-cm.
Scraper	1	Scraping tool made from hoe blade. Lgth 4.21-in/10.7-cm. Wdth 2.94-in/ 7.5-cm. Thk .09-in/.23-cm. Rounded and sharpened on one corner.
Broken Hispanic ring bit	1	Lgth 4.25-in/10.8-cm. Wdth 4.0-in/10.16-cm. No decorations.
Broken S-hook	1	Spanish-Colonial style hook with curved eye on each end. Lgth 1.94-in/4.93-cm. Stock material dia .14-in/.36-cm.
Cut brass	1	Irregular shape. Lgth 1.8-in/4.57-cm. Wdth .94-in/2.39-cm. Thk .04-in/.10-cm. Chisel-cut edges.
Cut brass	1	Irregular shape. Lgth 1.38-in/3.5-cm. Max wdth .63-in/1.6-cm. Thk .027-in/.069-cm.
Cut brass	1	Rectangular shape. Lgth 2.19-in/5.56-cm. Wdth .63-in/1.6-cm. Thk .038-in/.097-cm. Chisel-cut.
Cut brass	1	Irregular shape. Lgth 4.1-in/10.27-cm. Wdth 1.36-in/3.45-cm. Thk .019-in/.048-cm. Chisel-cut.
Cut brass	1	Rectangular shape. Lgth 1.5-in/3.84-cm. Wdth .64-in/1.62-cm. Thk .035-in/.09-cm. Chisel-cut.
Brass bucket piece	1	Irregular shape. Lgth 5.0-in/12.7-cm. Wdth 4.25-in/10.8-cm. Thk .036-in/.09-cm. Chisel-cut. Two holes may be where rivets for bale holder were.

Table 23.1 Rita Blanca Artifact Descriptions. HLHT9 (*cont.*)		
Artifact Category	**Quantity**	**Description**
Mexican or Indian Artifacts		
Metal Artifacts (cont.)		
Cut tin	2	Irregular shapes. Lgth varies from 1.25-in/3.2-cm. to 1.6-in/4.2-cm. Wdth varies from .7-in/1.5-cm. to .74-in/1.9-cm. Chisel-cut.
Cut tin	1	Irregular shape. Lgth 1.75-in/4.5-cm. Wdth .76-in/1.96-cm. Thk .026-in/.066-cm. Chisel-cut.
Curved brass piece with hole	1	Possible pendant made from trigger guard. Hand-drilled hole in brass. Lgth 1.60-in/4.06-cm. Wdth .51-in/1.29-cm. One end polished, the other end broken.
Miscellaneous Metal Pieces		
Decorated pewter piece	1	Lgth 1.5-in/3.81-cm. Max wdth .44-in/1.12-cm. Floral design on curved surface.
Metal bracket	1	Lgth 4.0-in/10-0-cm. Max wdth 1.1-in/2.7-cm. Small hole in each end.
Broken metal band	1	Lgth 3.5-in/9.0-cm. Wdth .38-in/.96-cm. Thk .04-in/094-cm. Broken on one end. Three small holes drilled in band.
Flattened shears handle	1	Lgth 4.12-in/10.5-cm. Max wdth 1.59-in/4.05-cm. This handle fits the two shears blades found at the same site.
Threaded pewter piece	1	Possible lamp part. L-shaped and threaded on both ends. Lgth 1.79-in/4.57-cm. Wdth .96-in/2.43-cm.

Chapter 24
Sand Creek Site and Artifacts

Sand Creek site, a quarter-mile east of Rita Blanca site, encompasses about eight acres along the north side of Sand Creek. Skunkberry sumac, yucca, little bluestem grass, and other vegetation form a dense cover along the low hills.

Most of the fifteen artifacts recovered from Sand Creek were Mexican or Indian tools and ornaments, which indicate that the site was probably an extension of the Rita Blanca campsite—both having been *Comanchero* and Indian trade areas. Because of the distance

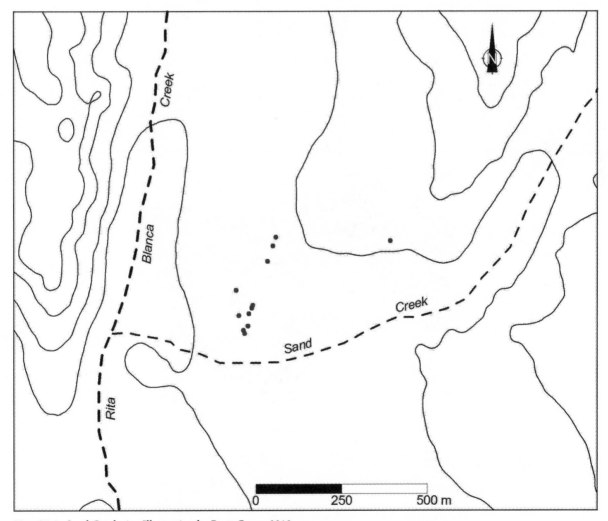

Map 24.1. Sand Creek site. Illustration by Brett Cruse, 2010.

between them, they warranted different site names and numbers.

The north branch of the Fort Bascom–Adobe Walls Road bears southeast a few hundred yards south of Sand Creek. In addition, an old XIT freight road runs north through the site and continues up Rita Blanca Creek toward Buffalo Springs. Indians and Mexicans probably used it before the establishment of the XIT Ranch.

Fig. 108. Bell clapper, large tinkler, and three *coscojos* (*coscojos* are Hispanic charms). Mexicans and Indians used all three of these trinkets to decorate their bridles, bits, and saddles. Photograph by Wyman Meinzer, 2009.

Fig. 109. Spoon bowl. Scan by Lisa Jackson, 2011.

Table 24.1   Sand Creek Artifact Descriptions. HLHT10

Artifact Category	Quantity	Description
Arms and Ammunition		
Bullets		
.44 caliber	1	Fired. Dia .44-in/1.12-cm. Lgth .647-in/1.64-cm. Wt 201.3 gr. One grease ring. Dished base.
.50 caliber	1	Fired. Dia .496-in/1.26-cm. Lgth .99-in/2.52-cm. Wt 428 gr. Three grease rings. Flat base.
Flattened lead ball	1	Fired. Dia ? Wt 404.2 gr.
Gun Parts		
Brass trigger guard base	1	Broken at tapered screw hole. Chisel-cut on the other end. Lgth 1.5-in/3.81-cm. Wdth 1.25-in/3.18-cm. Solid brass.
Fasteners		
Brads		
Small iron brads	2	Lgth varies from .46-in/ 1.17-cm. to .492-in/1.25-cm. Ave dia .185-in/.47-cm. One end has round head and the other end is braded.
Small iron brads	2	Lgth varies from .289-in/.73-cm. to .512-in/1.30-cm. Ave dia 186-in/.47-cm. One end has round head and the other end is braded.
Camp Utensils		
Flatware		
Spoon bowl	1	Lgth 3.0-in/7.63-cm. Max wdth 1.66-in/4.22-cm. Someone sharpened the point of the spoon, probably for pouring melted lead or gun powder.
Mexican or Indian Artifacts		
Coscojos (Hispanic Charms)		
Tear-shaped coscojo	1	The coscojo has two figure-8 shaped chain links fastened to it. Overall lgth 3.0-in/7.66-cm. Coscojo lgth 1.41-in/3.58-cm. Blade wdth .67-in/1.71-cm.
Bell-shaped coscojo	1	The coscojo has one figure-8 shaped chain link fastened to it. Overall lgth 2.23-in/5.66-cm. Coscojo lgth 1.37-in/3.47-cm. Blade wdth .53-in/1.35-cm.
Bell-shaped coscojo	1	The coscojo has one figure 8 shaped chain link fastened to it. Overall lgth 2.40-in/6.2-cm. Coscojo lgth 1.40-in/3.56-cm. Blade wdth .42-in/1.07-cm.

Table 24.1 Sand Creek Artifact Descriptions. HLHT10 (*cont.*)		
Artifact Category	**Quantity**	**Description**
Mexican or Indian Artifacts		
Tinkler		
Large tin tinkler	1	Lgth 1.97-in/5.0-cm. Max wdth 2.25-in/.89-cm. Probably made from a tin can.
Bell Clapper		
Iron bell clapper	1	Lgth 2.39-in/6.1-cm. Max dia .65-in/1.65-cm. Eye worn out.
Cut Metal		
Chisel-cut pieces from tin can	2	Max Lgth 1.83-in/4.65-cm. Max wdth 1.39-in/3.5-cm.
Miscellaneous Metal Pieces		
Curved flattened metal	1	Lgth 1.55-in/3.94-cm. Ave wdth .41-in/1.04-cm.
L-shaped metal	1	Lgth 1.92-in/4.88-cm. Wdth .75-in/1.91-cm. Thk .09-in/.23-cm.

Chapter 25
Los Redos Creek Site and Artifacts

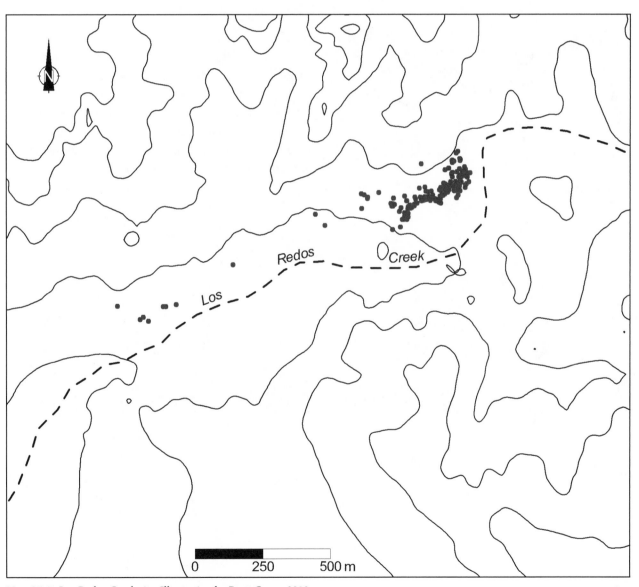

Map 25.1. Los Redos Creek site. Illustration by Brett Cruse, 2010.

os Redos Creek (41HT60) meanders southward out of caliche-capped canyons, across a wide valley, and into Punta de Agua Creek. The Fort Bascom Adobe–Walls Road crosses the creek at the point where it changes course from south to west, just below the canyons. Springs surface there and form small ponds on their path down the creek.

A low, flat terrace spreads over approximately thirty acres north and west of the creek. A ridge on the east, and rounded hills on the north, protect the campsite from north winds. Scrubby mesquite trees grow along the hills, while sage and grasses cover the lower terrace. Cottonwoods, plum thickets, and cattails flourish along the creek.

Weary travelers, including Colonel Carson and his troops, found it a suitable camping spot. Two hundred two artifacts recovered from Los Redos Creek indicate a long period of use. Early lithic tools and ceramics confirm that many different groups occupied the place hundreds of years before Carson's expedition. Some *Comanchero* trading probably occurred there, as evidenced by the metal points and Mexican paraphernalia found at the site.

Later relics also dot the landscape along the creek. Southwest of Carson's camp, the broken structure of Los Redos windmill lies in repose like a skeleton on the prairie of the XIT Ranch.

The remains of another old structure litter the ground north of the wagon road. Looming as a reminder of the past, the scattered rocks of a house beg passers-by to pause and wonder. Local lore has it that the house belonged to an old wolf hunter who died of a contagious disease, causing the men of the community to burn the wooden part of the edifice.

Fig. 110. Bridle chain chinstrap. Photograph by Wyman Meinzer, 2009.

Fig. 111. Four wood screws. Photograph by Wyman Meinzer, 2009.

Fig. 112. Rare Maynard cartridge case. Photograph by Wyman Meinzer, 2009.

Table 25.1 Los Redos Creek Artifact Descriptions. 41HT60		
Artifact Category	**Quantity**	**Description**
Arms and Ammunitions		
Cartridge Cases		
.32 caliber	2	Head stamp. *"U"*. RF. Ave base dia .321-in/.82-cm. Lgth .571-in/1.46-cm.
.32 caliber	1	Head stamp. *"H"*. RF. Base dia .33-in/.84-cm. Lgth .588-in/1.50-cm.
.32 caliber	1	Head stamp. none. RF. Base dia 3.17-in/.81-cm. Lgth .796-in/2.02-cm.
.38 caliber	1	Head stamp. none. EP. Base dia .386-in/.98-cm. Lgth .765-in/1.94-cm.
.44 caliber	1	Head stamp. *WRA Co. .44 WCF.* EP. Flattened. Base dia ? Lgth 1.29-in/3.28-cm.
.44-40 caliber	5	Head stamp. none. EP. Ave base dia .47-in/1.20-cm. Ave lgth 1.32-in/3.35-cm.
.44-40 caliber	1	Head stamp. *UMC .44 CFW.* EP. Base dia .467-in/1.19-cm. Lgth 1.30-in/3.3-cm.
.44-40 caliber	1	Head stamp. *U.S. 44 WCF.* EP. Base dia .47-in/1.19-cm. Lgth 1.31-in/3.33-cm.
.44-40 caliber	1	Head stamp. EP. Base dia .47-in/1.20-cm. Lgth 1.31-in/3.33-cm.
.45 caliber	3	Head stamp. none. EP. Ave Base dia .485-in/1.23-cm. Ave lgth. 1.264-in/3.22-cm.
.45 caliber	5	Head stamp. *WRA Co. .45 COLT.* EP. Ave base dia .48-in/1.22-cm. Ave lgth 1.27-in/3.22-cm.
.46 caliber	1	Head stamp. none. RF. Matches the .46 caliber short cartridge used in the Remington Arms single-action revolver. Base dia .455-in/1.16-cm. Lgth .82-in/2.09-cm.[1]
.50 caliber	1	Pin-fire Maynard. Head stamp. none. Base dia ?. Disk dia .77-in/1.96-cm. Lgth 1.228-in/3.12-cm. Case flattened. (Rare cartridge case).
56-50 caliber	4	Head stamp. *SAW.* RF. All cases flattened. Base dia ?. Ave lgth 1.15-in/2.90-cm.
Unfired Cartridge		
.56-50 Spencer	1	Head stamp. *SAW.* RF Base dia .564-in/1.43-cm. Lgth 1.547-in/1.43-cm.

Table 25.1 Los Redos Creek Artifact Descriptions. 41HT60

Artifact Category	Quantity	Description
Arms and Ammunitions		
Bullets		
.40 caliber	1	Fired. High-velocity impact. Dia ?. Wt 154.7 gr. Post-1875 bullet.*[2]
.44 caliber	1	Fired. High-velocity impact. Dia .435-in/1.11-cm. Wt 181.3 gr. Post-1875 bullet.*
.44 caliber	1	Fired. High-velocity impact. Dia .442-in/1.12-cm. Wt 155.9 gr. Post-1875 bullet.*
.44 caliber	9	Unfired. Percussion bullets. Ave dia .454-in/1.15-cm. Ave lgth .73-in/1.85-cm. Ave wt 228 gr.
.45 caliber	1	Fired. Medium-velocity impact. Concave base. Two ring. Dia .445-in/1.14-cm. Lgth .70-in/1.79-cm. Wt 251.1 gr.
.50 caliber	1	Fired. High-velocity impact. Dia .549-in/1.39-cm. Wt 397.8 gr. Possible Sharps bullet. Cone in flat base.*
.52 caliber	6	Unfired. Sharps bullets with two rings and small cones in flat bases. Ave dia .545-in/1.38-cm. Ave lgth .94-in/2.39-cm. Ave wt 433.6 gr.
Lead ball	1	Fired. Low-velocity impact. Dia .547-in/1.39-cm. Wt 226.0 gr. Cast ball. No rifling evident. Possible trade-gun ball.*
Lead ball	1	Fired. High-velocity impact. Dia ?. Wt 153.6 gr.
.36-caliber lead ball	1	Unfired. Dia .362-in/.92-cm. Wt 68.8 gr.
Lead piece	1	Oval shape. Lgth .46-in/1.17-cm. Wdth .36-in/.91-cm. Thk .25-in/.63-cm. Wt 89.4 gr.
Gun Parts and Tools		
Gun screw	1	Blade-type with raised head. Lgth .763-in/1.94-cm. Head dia .30-in/.76-cm.
Rifle bore brush	1	Male threaded end. Bristles missing. Lgth 5.11-in/12.98-cm. Max dia .31-in/.79-cm.
Rifle bore brush	1	Male threaded end. Bristles missing. Tip broken. Lgth 3.53-in/8.96-cm. Max dia .31-in/.79-cm.
Personal Items		
Buttons		
Metal button	1	Dia .675-in/1.72-cm. *"TOOTLE FACTORY"* with star on front. Deep-set center. Keeper on back.
Brass button base	1	Dia .55-in/1.40-cm. Dia of hole in center .25-in/.64-cm.

Buttons (cont.)		
Brass button with missing set	1	Dia .67-in/1.70-cm. Set dia .43-in/1.09-cm. Maker's mark not readable.
Military cavalry button	1	Dia .81-in/2.1-cm. "C" in shield. Maker's mark. none. Shank bent.
Small military buttons	6	Ave dia .57-in/1.45-cm. General Service. Five of the buttons have bent shanks and one has a dent on the face. Maker's mark •SCOVILLS & Co. •EXTRA. dm. Manufactured during 1840s.[3]
Military button	1	Dia .785-in/2.0-cm. General Service. Flattened with shank bent. Maker's mark •EXTRA•••QUALITY. dm. Manufactured about 1860.[4]
Military button	1	Dia .77-in/1.96-cm. General Service. Dent on face. Maker's mark. WATERBURY BUTTON Co. **. dmdc. In use from late 1850s to 1865.[5]
Military button	1	Dia .775-in/1.97-cm. General Service. Maker's mark. HORSTMAN & ALLIEN*N.Y. rmdc. Steele and Johnson produced these buttons for Horstman Bros. during the Civil War and early 1860s.[6]
Military button	1	Dia .794-in/2.02-cm. General Service. Flattened with shank missing. Maker's mark •SCOVILL MFG Co.•WATERBURY. rmdc Manufactured about 1855 to 1860.[7]
Small military buttons	4	Ave dia .577-in/1.47-cm. General Service. Maker's mark. none.
Pocket Knives		
Pearl-handle pocket knife	1	Lgth 3.62-in/9.19-cm. Wdth .65-in/1.65-cm. Brass shield on one side. Pearl cracked on both sides. Three blades.
Damaged pocket knife	1	Lgth 3.59-in/9.13-cm. Wdth .43-in/1.1-cm. Handle coverings missing. Chisel-cut on both sides. Two blades.
Garter Clips		
Decorated brass garter clip	1	Lgth .90-in/2.28-cm. Max wdth .52-in/1.33-cm. Stamped decorations on front and back. Spring loaded.
Decorated brass garter clip	1	Lgth 1.20-in/3.1-cm. Max wdth .64-in/11.63-cm. Stamped design. Spring loaded. LINDSAY PATENT. Nov-3-74 Apr. 29-78.
Jewelry		
Brass watch gear and spindle	1	Lgth .89-in/2.26-cm. Max dia .30-in/.76-cm.

Table 25.1   Los Redos Creek Artifact Descriptions. 41HT60 (*cont.*)

Artifact Category	Quantity	Description
Military Paraphernalia		
Hooks		
Knapsack hook	1	Lgth 1.99-in/5.1-cm. Two small brads in holes.
Metal Tent Stakes		
Metal tent stake	1	Lgth 14.0-in/35.56-cm. Hand-forged. Considerable corrosion.
Broken metal tent stake	1	Lgth 18.25-in/46.34-cm. Dia .50-in/1.27-cm. Hand-forged. Top missing.
Top to metal tent stake	1	Lgth 4.2-in/10.7-cm. .50-in/ 1.27-cm. diameter metal rod bent over to form top of stake and rope tie. Top for previous rod listed.
Broken metal tent stake	1	Lgth 21.0-in/53.34-cm. Dia .50-in/1.27-cm. Hand-forged. Top missing.
Broken metal tent stake	1	Lgth 6.88-in/15.24-cm. Dia .47-in/1.19-cm. Hand-forged. Top hammered.
Fasteners		
Cut Nails		
Complete machine-cut nails	15	Lgth varies from 1.0-in/2.54-cm. to 3.0-in/7.62-cm. All tapered on two sides. Most heads irregular.
Broken machine-cut nails	13	Lgth varies from .96-in/2.44-cm. to 2.13-in/5.4-cm. All tapered on two sides. Most heads irregular.
Tacks		
Square tack with raised head.	1	Lgth .694-in./1.76-cm.
Square tack with flat round head.	1	Lgth .895-in./2.28-cm.
Wood Screws		
Flat-head wood screws	7	Ave lgth 1.97-in/5.0-cm. Ave head dia .47-in/1.19-cm. One broken head. Blade-type screws.
Flat-head wood screw	1	Lgth 2.0-in/5.08-cm. Head dia .43-in/1.1-cm. Blade-type screw.
Broken screw	1	Lgth .83-in/2.1-cm.
Bolts, Pins, and Brads		
Broken metal pin	1	Lgth 1.83-in/4.65-cm. Dia .50-in/1.27-cm. One end beaten flat. Bent.

Bolts, Pins, and Brads (cont.)		
Broken pin	1	Lgth 1.09-in/2.77-cm. Dia .40-in/1.02-cm. Flattened on one end.
Iron brad	1	Lgth 1.45-in/3.69-cm. Max head dia .55-in/1.40-cm.
Washers		
Large metal washer	1	Max outside dia 3.4-in/8.64-cm. Max inside dia 1.97-in/5.0-cm. Max thk .28-in/7.13-cm. Hand-forged.
Oval metal washer	1	Lgth 1.43-in/3.62-cm. Wdth 1.05-in/2.66-cm. Center hole dia .24-in/.64-cm. Small hole at each end.
Nuts		
Split square nut	1	Square 1.26-in/3.2-cm. Thk .60-in/1.53-cm.
Horse Tack and Wagon Hardware		
Horseshoes		
Complete shoes	3	Lgth 4.5-in/11.43 to 5.49-in/13.94-cm. Wdth 4.3-in/10.90-cm. to 5.65-in/14.13-cm. Two shoes have calks; one has a toe guard. All show considerable wear.
Large draft horseshoe	1	Lgth 6.5-in/16.5-cm. Wdth 6.25-in/15.88-cm. Shoe is warped. Calks on heels.
Broken shoes	2	Lgth 4.75-in/12.1-cm. to 5.56-in/14.12-cm. No calks.
Mule Shoes		
Complete shoes	5	Lgth 4.5-in/11.43 to 5.92-in/15.0-cm. Wdth 3.46-in/8.79-cm. to 4.54-in/11.53-cm. Four shoes have calks on heels. The other shoe has a toe plate.
Broken shoes	2	Lgth 4.75-in/12.1-cm. to 5.0-in/12.72-cm. One shoe has a calk on heel.
Horseshoe Nails		
Complete nails	22	Lgth 1.70-in/4.75-cm. to 2.86-in/7.27-cm.
Broken nails	2	Lgth 1.36-in/3.46-cm. to 1.67-in/4.24-cm.
Bridle Bits		
One-half Hispanic ring bit	1	Lgth 5.61-in/14.26-cm. Wdth 2.86-in/7.26-cm. Broken at port. Ring and bridge missing.
Front of Hispanic ring bit shank	1	Lgth 2.33-in/5.92-cm. Max wdth .93-in/2.36-cm. Four holes for coscojos are worn through. Piece is chisel-cut from ring bit.
Front of Hispanic ring bit shank	1	Lgth 2.49-in/6.33-cm. Max wdth .92-in/2.33-cm. Three holes for coscojos are worn through. Piece is chisel-cut from ring bit.

Table 25.1 Los Redos Creek Artifact Descriptions. 41HT60 (*cont.*)

Artifact Category	Quantity	Description
Horse Tack and Wagon Hardware		
Bridle Bits (cont.)		
Curb bit chain	1	Lgth 9.0-in/22.86-cm. Links lgth .71-in/1.80-cm. to .98-in/2.49-cm. Three iron chains interwoven. Graduated in link size from center outward.
Picket Pins or Metal Stakes		
Broken metal stake	1	Lgth 2.11-in/5.36-cm. Dia .80-in/2.03-cm. Top flattened.
Figure-8 loop from top of picket pin	1	Lgth 2.98-in/7.58-cm. Max wdth 1.53-in/3.88-cm. Rod stock dia .25-in/.64-cm.
Buckles		
Sunk-bar type buckles	2	Lgth 1.56-in/3.93-cm. Wdth 1.02-in/2.58-cm. Tongue fastened in center on sunk bar.
Roller buckle	1	Lgth 1.0-in/2.54-cm. Wdth 1.36-in/3.44-cm. Tongue on one side; roller on the other side.
Roller buckle	1	Lgth .965-in/2.45-cm. Wdth 1.0-in/2.54-cm. Curved on one side with roller. Tongue on opposite straight side.
Rings		
Bent harness ring	1	Bent to oval shape. Lgth 1.86-in/4.72-cm. Wdth 1.30-in/3.30-cm.
Saddle skirt ring	1	Outside dia 1.64-in/4.17-cm. Stock dia .18-in/.46-cm.
Harness Snap		
Broken harness snap	1	Lgth 4.13-in/10.5-cm. Max wdth 1.53-in/3.88-cm. Brass spring loaded. Eye broken. Clip missing.
Chains		
Broken chain	1	Lgth 13.25-in/33.66-cm. Links lgth vary from 2.18-in/5.54-cm. to 2.25-in/5.97-cm. Seven links with half twists.
Broken chain link	1	Lgth .73-in/1.86-cm. Max wdth 1.02-in/2.59-cm. Stock dia .25-in/.64-cm.
Broken chain link	1	Lgth 1.21-in/3.08-cm. Stock dia .25-in/.64-cm.
Expanded chain link	1	Lgth 2.31-in/5.87-cm. Max wdth 1.54-in/3.91-cm. Stock dia .25-in/.64-cm.
Broken canteen or rein chain	1	Lgth 2.40-in/6.1-cm. Link lgth .71-in/1.80-cm.
Small, broken chain hook	1	Lgth 1.28-in/3.26-cm.

Chains (cont.)		
Broken metal hook	1	Lgth 3.24-in/8.2-cm. Max wdth 1.73-in/4.39-cm. Stock dia .25-in/.64-cm. Twisted S-shape.
Saddle Hardware		
Strap bracket	1	Lgth 2.0-in/5.08-cm. Max wdth .43-in/1.20-cm. Opening wdth for strap .69-in/1.75-cm. Brass screw in one end of bracket.
Leather and Canvas Hardware		
Copper rivet	1	Lgth .53-in/1.35-cm. Head dia .40-in/1.02-cm.
Brass grommet	1	Outside dia .56-in/1.443-cm. Hole dia .25-in/.64-cm.
Wagon Hardware		
Broken tug	1	Lgth 2.92-in/7.42-cm. Dia ?. Metal split.
Strap hinge with machine-cut square nails	1	Strap lgth 6.0-in/15.26-cm. Base ht 3.48-in/8.84-cm. Three holes in base; four holes in strap. Nails are all bent with irregular heads. Nail ave lgth 2.1-in/5.27-cm.
Tools		
Needles		
Canvas needle tip ?	1	Lgth 1.4-in/3.56-cm. Two sides tapered.
Proximal end of broken sewing needle	1	Lgth 1.57-in/4.0-cm. Needle is triangular in cross section at break.
Camp Utensils		
Containers and Lids		
Flattened leaded can	1	Dia 3.0-in/7.65-cm. Ht ?. Top missing.
Flattened leaded can	1	Dia ?. Ht 4.0-in/10.17-cm. Top missing.
Flattened leaded can	1	Dia ?. Ht 4.5-in/11.43-cm.
Leaded can lids	10	Dia varies from 2.53-in/6.43-cm. to 4.0-in/10.16-cm. All lids are knife-cut and irregular shaped.
Broken metal cup handles	6	Lgth varies from small fragment to 3.30-in/8.38-cm. Max wdth 1.23-in/3.12-cm. All handle fragments have rolled edges.
Dutch Oven		
Dutch oven piece	1	Max lgth 5.6-in/14.2-cm. Max wdth 3.86-in/9.81-cm. Thickness varies. Cast iron, irregular piece.
Lamp Parts		
Brass burner cap	1	Dia ?. Ht 1.43-in/3.64-cm. Slot in middle for wick.

Artifact Category	Quantity	Description
Table 25.1 Los Redos Creek Artifact Descriptions. 41HT60 (*cont.*)		
Mexican and Indian Artifacts		
Metal Arrow Points		
Broken metal point	1	Lgth 1.71-in/4.35-cm. Shoulder wdth .70-in/1.78-cm. Thk at shoulders .05-in/.13-cm. Stem missing. Small hole in point. Sloping shoulders.
Small metal point	1	Lgth 1.07-in/2.73-cm. Shoulder wdth .58-in/1.48-cm. Stem lgth .36-in/.92-cm. Stem wdth .20-in/.51-cm. Thk at shoulders .06-in/1.53-cm. Small hole in point. Sloping shoulders. Serrated stem.
Coscojos (Hispanic charms)		
Coscojo with link	1	Overall lgth 2.19-in/5.56-cm. Coscojo lgth 1.3-in/3.31-cm. Max coscojo wdth .527-in/1.34-cm. Bell-shaped.
Coscojos	3	Overall lgth 2.7-in/6.86-cm. Bottom coscojo lgth 1.0-in/2.54-cm. Bottom blade wdth .39-in/.99-cm. Two coscojos have holes in blades for attaching. Two attached and one broken.
Small coscojos	2	Ave lgth .92-in/2.32-cm. Ave blade wdth .30-in/.76-cm. Both are bell-shaped and have serrated blades.
Coscojo	1	Lgth 1.40-in/3.56-cm. Blade wdth .41-in/1.04-cm. Rectangular blade.
Chisel-cut iron metal	1	Lgth 1.52-in/3.88-cm. Max wdth .41-in/1.05-cm. Triangular-shaped.
Chisel-cut iron metal	4	Max lgth 1.42-in/3.61-cm. Max wdth .32-in/.81-cm.
Miscellaneous Pieces		
Box band	1	Lgth 7.25-in/18.42-cm. Wdth .75-in/1.91-cm. Thk .045-in/.12-cm. Three nail holes in box band.
Small pewter tube	1	Lgth 1.36-in/3.46-cm. Unthreaded end outside dia .61-in/1.56-cm. Threaded end outside dia .60-in/1.53-cm. Small ears on outside of tube.
Tapered brass ring	1	Large end dia .72-in/1.83-cm. Small end dia .66-in/1.68-cm. Ave ht .37-in/.94-cm.

Chapter 26
Rica Creek Site and Artifacts

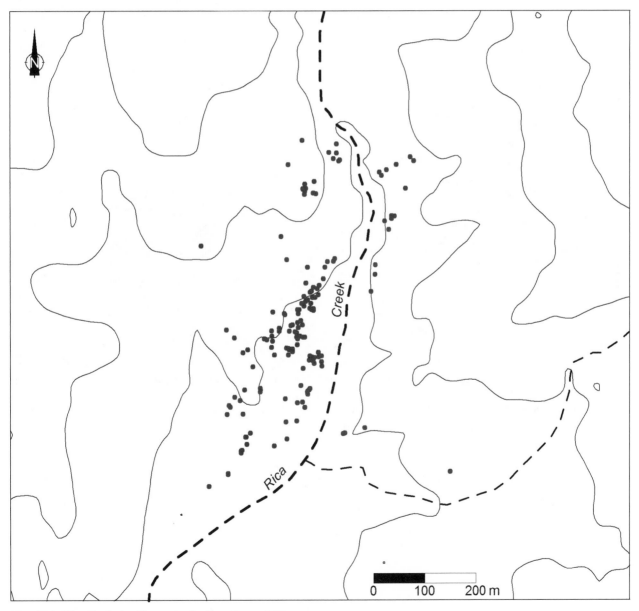

Map 26.1. Rica Creek site. Illustration by Brett Cruse, 2010.

Rica Creek Campsite (41HT61) covers approximately twenty-five acres of sagebrush flat west of Rica Creek, with a minor part of the camp extending to the east side. A small picket camp occupied the higher ground about one hundred fifty yards north of the main encampment.

The hill to the north, and a low-curved ridge that circled to the west and southwest, would have afforded protection to troops, but icy, winter winds from the northeast had no barrier. Today, cottonwoods grow along the creek but are too sparse to serve as shelter in inclement weather. Mesquites, yucca, and short grasses dot the hills surrounding the site.

A streamlet runs intermittently around the Triassic sandstone boulders scattered along Rica Creek. It flows mostly in winter but may run in any unusually wet season. In the past, the amount of water in the stream sustained a large number of travelers and livestock.

The 196 artifacts recovered from the area range in age from early Native Americans (prehistoric) to the late nineteenth century, representing Native Americans, Mexicans, military, and civilian travelers. The Fort Bascom–Adobe Walls Road enters the site from the west and veers up a shallow valley to the northeast after it leaves the creek. Erosion has altered the topography at the crossing, leaving it with vertical embankments a few feet high.

The artifacts were at a depth of less than one foot, indicating that the surface of the site has changed little since Carson and his troops camped there.

Fig. 113. Hand-forged S-hooks. Photograph by Wyman Meinzer, 2009.

Fig. 115. Small mule shoe. Photograph by Wyman Meinzer, 2009.

Fig. 114. Metal point and tinkler. Photograph by Wyman Meinzer, 2009.

Table 26.1	Rica Creek Artifact Descriptions. 41HT61	
Artifact Category	**Quantity**	**Description**
Arms and Ammunitions		
Cartridges		
.44-40 caliber	3	EP. Head stamp. none. Ave base dia .47-in/1.20-cm. Ave lgth 1.30-in/3.3-cm.
.44-40 caliber	3	EP. Head stamp. *WRA Co. .44 WCF.* Ave base dia .47-in/1.20-cm. Ave lgth 1.30-in/3.3-cm.
.44 caliber	1	EP. Head stamp. none. Dia .44-in/1.19-cm. Lgth .906-in/2.30-cm. Measurements similar to .44 Smith & Wesson.*[1]
.44 caliber	1	RF. Dia undetermined. Lgth .91-in/2.31-cm. Hole drilled in base (off center).
.45 caliber	15	EP. Head stamp. none. Ave base dia .482-in/1.23-cm. Ave lgth 1.28-in/3.25-cm.
Unfired Bullets		
.44 caliber	1	Percussion bullet. Rough cut on base. Dia .452-in/1.15-cm. Lgth .74-in/1.88-cm. Back of bullet reduced in size.
.52 caliber	2	Sharps percussion bullets. Two ring. One has cone in base while the other has flat base. Ave dia .545-in/1.38-cm. Ave lgth .94-in/2.39-cm. One bullet weighs 450 gr. while the other weighs 433.8 gr.
.58 caliber	3	Minié bullets. Concave base. Three ring. Ave dia .58-in/1.47-cm. Ave lgth .98-in/2.49-cm. Ave wt 481.0 gr.
Fired Bullets		
.36 caliber	1	Low-velocity impact. Flat base. Dia .374-in/.95-cm. Lgth .475-in/1.21-cm. Wt 106.5 gr. Consistent with Colt M 1851 Navy revolver.*
.42 caliber	1	High-velocity impact. Flattened bullet. Dia .425-in/1.08-cm. Wt 189.8 gr. Consistent with Sharps Meacham.*[2]
.42 caliber	1	High-velocity impact. Flattened bullet. Paper patch bullet. Dish base. Dia .426-in/1.08-cm. Wt 366.7 gr. Consistent with Sharps Meacham.*
.42 caliber	1	High-velocity impact. Dia .422-in/1.07-cm. Wt 193.9 gr. Paper patch bullet. Consistent with sharps Meacham.*
.42 caliber	1	Medium-velocity impact. Dished base. Dia undetermined. Wt. 218.1 gr.*

Table 26.1 Rica Creek Artifact Descriptions. 41HT61 (*cont.*)

Artifact Category	Quantity	Description
Arms and Ammunitions		
Fired Bullets (cont.)		
.45 caliber	1	Low-velocity impact. Two rings. Hollow base. Dia .451-in/1.15-cm. Wt 240.3 gr. Post-1875 colt revolver.*
.45 caliber	1	Medium-velocity impact. Two rings. Flat base. Dia 451-in/1.15-cm. Wt 249.8 gr. Post-1875 Colt revolver.*
.50 caliber	1	High-velocity impact. Dia undetermined. Wt 433.3 gr.*
Flattened bullets	4	High-velocity impact. Dia undetermined. Total wt 875.9 gr.
Unfired Lead Ball		
.50 caliber	1	Sprue intact. Dia .527-in/1.34-cm. Wt 221.1 gr.
Fired Lead Ball		
.45 caliber	1	High-velocity impact. Dia undetermined. Wt 152.4 gr.*
Flattened ball	1	High-velocity impact. Dia undetermined. Wt 195.9 gr.
Unfired Cartridge		
.44 caliber	1	Broken. Head stamp. none. Dia .467-in/1.19-cm. Lgth undetermined.
Lead Piece		
Irregular chunk	1	Wt 224.4 gr.
Gun Parts		
Gun screw	1	Raised head with blade slot. Dia .198-in/.502-cm. Lgth .698-in/1.77-cm.
Personal Items		
Buttons		
Four-hole metal button	2	Ave dia .66-in/1.68-cm. Recessed center.
Four-hole metal button	1	Dia .53-in/1.35-cm. Recessed center.
Towers wire fastened	1	Dia .91-in/2.31-cm. Keeper and wire attached. Plating peeling off.
Metal button	1	Dia .636-in/1.62-cm. *McDONALD* ** on front of button. rmdc. Brass fastener on back.
Smooth brass button	1	Dia .75-in/1.91-cm. Flat front. Iron back with bent shank.
Rounded brass button	1	Dia .50-in/1.27-cm. Convex front. Bent shank.

Buttons (cont.)		
Brass button back	1	Dia .56-in/1.43-cm. Small bar on back for sewing to garment.
Military button	1	Dia .754-in/1.92-cm. General Service. Maker's mark. none. Bent shank.
Military button	1	Dia .57-in/1.43-cm. General Service. Maker's mark. *W. LANG BOSTON*. Manufactured by Scoville for Lang in late 1850s.[3]
Suspender Latches		
Broken wire suspender hook	1	Lgth 1.69-in/4.30-cm. Wire dia .06-in/.157-cm.
Suspender latch	1	Lgth .88-in/2.24-cm. Wdth 1.32-in/3.55-cm. Two-prong.
Coins		
1875 dime	1	Dia .709-in/1.80-cm. Front-Seated Lady Liberty. *United states of America* around edge and date at bottom. Back-*ONE DIME* inside of wreath.
1867 nickel	1	Dia .807-in/2.05-cm. Front-*In God We Trust* over shield with date at bottom. Back-*5* surrounded by thirteen stars. *United States of America* around edge with word *CENTS* at the bottom.
Key		
Base of key	1	Lgth .78-in/1.98-cm. Wdth .74-in/1.89-cm.
Footwear		
Boot Heel Plate	1	Lgth 1.4-in/3.56-cm. Max wdth .49-in/1.25-cm. Fragment with two holes.
Fasteners		
Nails		
Complete machine-cut nail	22	Lgth varies 1.73-in/4.4-cm. to 3.04-in/7.73-cm. All tapered on two sides.
Broken machine-cut nail	4	Various sizes. All tapered on two sides.
Short, hand-forged square spike	1	Lgth 1.954-in/4.96-cm. Approximately .43-in/1.09-cm. square below head. All sides tapered. Could be ax head wedge.
Screws		
Wood screws	2	Lgth 1-in/2.54-cm. Head dia .44-in/1.1-cm. Flat head. Blade-type screw.
Bolts, Pins, and Brads		
Broken carriage bolt	1	Lgth 3.35-in/8.50-cm. Dia .20-in/.51-cm. Square shoulders beneath round head.

Table 26.1 Rica Creek Artifact Descriptions. 41HT61 (*cont.*)

Artifact Category	Quantity	Description
Fasteners		
Bolts, Pins, and Brads (cont.)		
One bolt and nut	1	Carriage bolt. Lgth 1.85-in/4.70-cm. Dia .33-in/.84-cm. Round head with square shoulders.
Broken pin	1	Lgth 6.5-in/16.51-cm. Dia .50-in/1.27-cm.
Broken pin	1	Lgth 1.23-in/3.13-cm. Pin dia .34-in/.87-cm. Approx. head dia 1.08-in/2.75-cm. Hand-forged. Irregular head.
Bent and broken pin	1	Lgth 2.216-in/5.63-cm. Dia .54-in/1.37-cm.
Bent and broken brad	1	Lgth 1.42-in/3.61-cm. Dia .32-in/.81-cm. Flattened on one end.
Brads	2	Ave lgth 1.56-in/3.96-cm. Ave dia .25-in/.64-cm. Probably from shovel shank found nearby. One brad has flattened end and washer.
Nuts		
Square nuts	2	Nut (a) .85-in/2.16-cm square. Thk .41-in/1.04-cm. Nut (b) .91-in/2.31-cm. square. Thk .39-in/.99-cm.
Washers		
Flat washer	1	Outside dia .995-in/2.53-cm. Inside dia .61-in/1.55-cm.
Horse Tack and Wagon Hardware		
Horseshoes		
Horseshoes with calks	24	Lgth varies 4.33-in/11.0-cm. to 5.8-in/14.76-cm. Wdth varies 4.29-in/10.90-cm. to 5.56-in/14.2-cm. One of the shoes has a toe guard and 12 shoes are warped.
Horseshoes without calks	5	Lgth varies 4.29-in/10.09-cm. to 5.4-in/13.73-cm. Wdth varies 4.33-in/11.0-cm. to 5.35-in/13.59-cm. Two shoes are warped.
Broken horseshoes	6	Lgth varies 3.82-in/9.71-cm. to 5.5-in/13.97-cm. One shoe has a calk.
Mule Shoes		
Mule shoes with calks	4	Lgth varies 4.64-in/11.79-cm. to 5.32-in/13.51-cm. Wdth varies 3.44-in/8.75-cm. to 4.11-in/10.44-cm. One shoe has a toe guard and one shoe is warped.
Broken mule shoes	1	Lgth 5.21-in/13.23-cm. Shoe has a calk.
Burro shoe	1	Lgth 3.79-in/9.63-cm. Wdth 3.20-in/8.13-cm. Shoe has calks.

Horseshoe Nails		
Complete nails	9	Lgth varies 1.65-in/4.2-cm. to 2.65-in/6.75-cm.
Broken nails	4	Various lgths.
Bridle Bits		
Bit shank	1	Lgth 4.48-in/12.3-cm. Max wdth 1.645-in/4.18-cm. Small flower designs stamped into the metal.
Buckles and Rings		
Roller buckle	1	Lgth 1.217-in 3.1-cm. Wdth 1.613-in/4.1-cm. Tongue fastened on the side.
Roller buckle	1	Lgth 1.50-in/3.81-cm. Wdth 2.62-in/6.66-cm. Broken tongue, fastens on one side.
Small buckle	1	Lgth 1.027-in/2.58-cm. Wdth 1.27-in/3.22-cm. Tongue fastens to middle bar.
Cinch buckle	1	Outside dia 3.59-in/9.12-cm. Tongue lgth 3.69-in/9.37-cm.
Iron saddle skirt ring	1	Bent to slight oval. Lgth 1.42-in/3.61-cm. Max wdth 1.30-in/3.30-cm.
Iron saddle skirt ring	1	Outside dia 1.743-in/4.43-cm.
Chains		
Broken chain link	1	Lgth 1.915-in/4.86-cm. Stock dia .42-in/1.06-cm.
Worn chain link	1	Lgth 3.09-in/7.85-cm. Max wdth 1.027-in/2.61-cm. Stock dia .23-in/.59-cm. Worn through on one end.
Hooks		
Metal hook	1	Lgth 2.58-in/6.56-cm. Wdth 1.6-in/4.06-cm.
Flat S-hook	1	Lgth 4.183-in/1.06-cm. Max wdth 2.18-in/5.54-cm. Max thk .26-in/.66-cm. Hand-forged.
Flat S-hook	1	Lgth 3.36-in/8.54-cm. Max wdth 1.86-in/4.73-cm. Max thk .328-in/.835-cm. Hand-forged.
Picket Pins or Metal Stakes		
Broken metal peg	1	Lgth 6.29-in/16.0-cm. Max wdth of square shaft .39-in/.99-cm. Rounded on end with square shaft.
Leather and Canvas Hardware		
Brass rivet head	1	Bent to oval shape. Lgth .574-in/1.46-cm. Wdth .352-in/.89-cm. Hole torn.
Wagon Hardware		
Wagon bow staple	1	Lgth 2.32-in/5.90-cm. Staple lgths 1.40-in/3.56-cm. Staple is bent and tips broken.

Table 26.1 Rica Creek Artifact Descriptions. 41HT61 (*cont.*)		
Artifact Category	**Quantity**	**Description**
Horse Tack and Wagon Hardware		
Wagon Hardware (cont.)		
Unidentified wagon part	1	Lgth 4.08-in/10.37-cm. Max wdth 2.02-in/5.13-cm. Max thk .633-in/1.61-cm.
Tools		
Shovels		
Two sides of shovel shank	2	Max lgth 6.5-in/16.51-cm. Max wdth 1.4-in/3.56-cm. Maker's mark. *O. AMES STEEL "2".* Two brad holes in each piece.
Broken shovel shank	2	Ave lgth 3.3-in/8.39-cm. Max wdth 1.39-in/3.53-cm. Two pieces.
Camp Utensils		
Cans		
Flattened leaded can	1	Dia 4.0-in/10.17-cm. Ht 4.84-in/12.29-cm.
Lids		
Small metal lid	1	Dia 1.68-in/4.27-cm. Maker's-mark. *SHEPARD & Co. PATD AUG 16-70 OCT. 31-71.*
Small round lid	1	Dia 1.60-in/4.06-cm. Plain top with indented ring.
Metal shaker lid	1	Approx. dia 2.0-in/5.08-cm. Flattened.
Handles		
Round metal handle	1	Lgth 6.75-in/17.5-cm. Dia .275-in/.69-cm. Handle has curved, flat ends.
Skillet handle	1	Lgth 12.75-in/32.39-cm. Max wdth .565-in/1.44-cm. Max thk .28-in/.71-cm. Hand-forged. Spanish-Colonial style loop on end of handle.
Flatware		
Broken fork	1	Overall lgth 3.61-in/9.16-cm. Tine lgth 1.85-in/4.70-cm. Max wdth .58-in/1.47-cm. Two tines. Handle missing.
Bucket		
Bucket bail holder	1	Dia 1.13-in/2.87-cm. Convex on outside with hole in center.
Cup		
Broken metal cup handle	1	Lgth 2.32-in/5.90-cm. Max wdth .79-in/2.0-cm. Rolled edges.

Indian or Mexican Artifacts		
Metal		
Iron metal point	1	Lgth 1.77-in/4.49-cm. Shoulder wdth .657-in/ 1.67-cm. Stem wdth .225-in/.57-cm. Shoulder thk .066-in/.167-cm. Broken stem. No serrations.
Broken parasol rib	1	Lgth 6.63-in/16.84-cm. Rod thk .124-in .315-cm. Possible Indian awl.[4]
Cut-iron metal blade	1	Lgth 2.04-in/5.18-cm. Max wdth .347-in/.88-cm. Sharpened on one side.
Cut-iron metal pieces	12	Lgth varies 1.18-in/3.0-cm. to 4.9-in/12.45-cm. Wdth varies .76-in/1.93-cm. to 1.124-in/ 2.85-cm.
Cut-iron metal tools	2	Max Lgth 1.07-in/2.72-cm. Max wdth .71-in/1.80-cm. One piece curved, the other piece triangular shaped. Both sharpened for cutting tools.
Engraved brass piece	1	Lgth 1.47-in/3.73-cm. Max wdth .48-in/1.2-cm. Max thk .064-in/.16-cm. Ears cut in one end and tie engraved at mid-section. Front is polished.
Small curved oval piece with two holes	1	Lgth .84-in/2.13-cm. Max wdth .61-in/1.55-cm.
Indian brass earring	1	Ave Dia 2.84-in/7.20-cm. Wire dia .111-in/.284-cm. Pointed on one end.
Cut brass rod	1	Lgth 5.1-in/12.94-cm. Rod dia .17-in/.434-cm. Bent on one end. Probably a blank for a bracelet.
Coscojos (Hispanic charms)	2	Overall lgth 2.36-in/5.99-cm. Ave blade wdth .40-in/1.01-cm. Fastened together by small hook though hole. Bottom blade serrated.
Coscojo	1	Overall lgth 1.89-in/4.80-cm. Blade wdth .42-in/1.06-cm. Broken hanger. No decorations.
Miscellaneous Pieces		
Fish hook and lead weight	2	Hook lgth 2.165-in/5.50-cm. Size 5/0. Lead wt. Rolled flat. Wt 134.8 gr.
Spring or small pin	1	Lgth 2.94-in/7.47-cm. Wdth .077-in/.196-cm. Thk .053-in/.137-cm. Curved with loop on one end.

Chapter 27
Rica Creek Site-B and Artifacts

Rica Creek-B (41HT61-B) spreads over nine acres along a ridge about one mile south of Rica Creek (41HT61). Rica Creek, the stream, runs south making a sharp bend to the east before turning back south a short distance below the campsite. A dry gulley borders the southwest boundary of the site before entering Rica Creek. Mesquites and yucca grow intermingled with short grasses along the high ground; sagebrush and skunkberry sumac flourish on the lower terraces. A few cottonwoods grow along the creek.

Fifty-seven artifacts, evenly divided between military and non-military, though few in number, represent a long period of intermittent occupation. Most of the military artifacts came from the south slope and the terrace below it, while most of the Indian artifacts came from the crest of the ridge. The earliest artifacts of

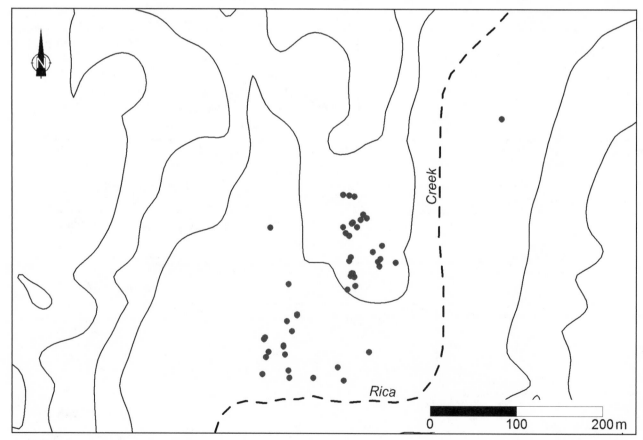

Map 27.1. Rica Creek-B site. Illustration by Brett Cruse, 2010.

Tecovas chert point to early Indian occupation. The more recent metal artifacts were from the middle to late nineteenth century. It is possible that Colonel Andrew Wallace Evans camped there in 1868 as some cartridges match the types found in his winter camp further down the Canadian River.

Fig. 116. Indian awl. Photograph by Wyman Meinzer, 2009.

Fig. 117. Large-bowl spoon. Scan by Lisa Jackson, 2011.

Table 27.1 Rica Creek-B Artifact Descriptions. 41HT61-B		
Artifact Category	**Quantity**	**Description**
Arms and Ammunition		
Cartridge Cases		
.44 caliber Henry cartridge case	1	Head stamp. Raised *"H"* in circle. RF. Double firing pin. Dia undetermined. Flattened case. Lgth .87-in/2.21-cm.
.45 caliber	3	Head stamp. none. EP. Ave dia .48-in/1.22-cm. Ave lgth 1.27-in/3.23-cm.
.50/70 caliber	1	Head stamp. none. IP. Dia undetermined. Lgth 1.77-in/4.49-cm.
Unfired Cartridges		
Spencer	1	Head stamp. *SAW*. RF. Base dia .56-in/1.42-cm. Lgth 1.6-in/4.06-cm.
.50/70 caliber	1	Head stamp. none. Cartridge broken in two pieces. IP. Base dia .561-in/1/43-cm. Lgth undetermined.
Unfired Bullets		
.36 caliber	1	Dia .37-in/.94-cm. Lgth .59-in/1.50-cm. Wt 129.2 gr. Reduced size at rear. Flat base.
.44 caliber	4	Ave. dia .45-in/1.15-cm. Ave. lgth .725-in/1.84-cm. Ave. wt 226.6 gr. Reduced size at rear. Flat base.
Fired Bullets		
.45 caliber	1	High-velocity impact. Dia undetermined. Lgth undetermined. Wt 300.5 gr. Consistent with 1886 Winchester or later gun.[1]
Fired Lead Balls		
.50 caliber	1	Medium-velocity impact. Dia undetermined. Wt 181.3 gr.
.58 caliber	1	Low-velocity impact. Dia .565-in/1.44-cm. Wt 225.7 gr.*
.58 caliber	1	Low-velocity impact. Dia .565-in/1.44-cm. Wt 225.7 gr.*
Percussion Caps		
Hat-type musket percussion caps	2	Ave. dia .24-in/.61-cm. Av. Lgth .25-in/.64-cm. Four flange, flared bottoms.
Gun Tools		
Ram and cleaning rod combination	1	The original rod had four sections of 7 in lgths. Rod is broken into three pieces. Total rod lgth 28.0-in/71.12-cm. Rod dia .23-in/.59-cm. Brass tamping tip on one end with slotted cleaning tip on the other. This is a Winchester 1866 and 1873 carbine and rifle .44 and .38 caliber- cleaning rod.[2]

Personal Items		
Buttons		
Smooth brass button	1	Thin brass. Max dia .67-in/1.70-cm.
Small military button	1	General Service. Shank bent. Maker's mark *EXTRA*QUALITY* dm. .588-in/1.49-cm. Made around 1860.[3]
Military button	1	General Service. Shank bent. Maker's mark. none. Dia .75-in/1.91-cm.
Suspender Latches		
Two-prong latch	1	Wdth 1.22-in/3.1-cm. Lgth .79-in/2.01-cm. Steel.
Military		
Saber Hooks		
Bent brass hooks	2	Ave lgth 2.2-in/5.59-cm. One is broken and the other is twisted.[4]
Fasteners		
Nails		
Complete machine-cut nail	7	All nails are tapered on two sides. Sizes vary 1.53-in/3.89-cm. to 2.0-in/5.08-cm.
Broken machine-cut nail	1	Tapered on two sides. Lgth 1.41-in/3.58-cm. Irregular head.
Tacks		
Iron square tack	1	Tapered on all four sides. Lgth .83-in/2.11-cm.
Bolts, Pins, and Brads		
Square wagon bolt with nut	1	Lgth 4.07-in/10.34-cm. Max bolt width .41-in/1.04-cm. Nut size 1.11-in/2.82-cm square.
Nuts		
Large square nut	1	1.25-in/3.18-cm x 1.26-in/3.20-cm. Thk .56-in/1.43-cm. Center hole dia .50-in/1.27-cm.
Small square nut	1	.70-in/1.78-cm. x .71-in/1.81-cm. Thk .33-in/.84-cm. Center hole dia .32-in/.81-cm.
Horse Tack and Wagon Hardware		
Horseshoes		
Standard horseshoe	1	Calks removed with a chisel. Toe worn. Lgth 5.08-in/12.9-cm. Wdth 5.23-in/13.29-cm.
Draft horseshoe	1	Calks removed with a chisel. Little wear. Lgth 5.90-in/14.99-cm. Wdth 5.56-in/14.12-cm.

Table 27.1   Rica Creek-B Artifact Descriptions. 41HT61-B (*cont.*)

Artifact Category	Quantity	Description
Horse Tack and Wagon Hardware		
Horseshoe Nails		
Complete nails	3	Lgth varies 1.96-in/4.98-cm. to 2.14-in/5.44-cm.
Buckles		
Roller buckle	1	Tongue attached on side. Lgth 1.51-in/3.84-cm. Wdth 1.62-in/4.12-cm.
Wagon Hardware		
Wagon bow staple	1	Overall lgth 2.32-in/5.90-cm. Max staple lgth 1.59-in/4.04-cm. Staple tips broken.
Wagon bow staple	1	Overall lgth 2.43-in/6.17-cm. Max broken staple lgth 1.8-in/4.58-cm.
Wagon bow staple tips	2	Tapered on two sides. Ave lgth 1.21-in/3.08-cm.
Chains		
Broken chain link	1	Connector link. Lgth 3.42-in/6.15-cm. Max wdth .96-in/2.44-cm.
Tools		
Metal Punch		
Flat punch	1	Flat handle with round tip. Broken tip. Lgth 6.25-in/15.9-cm. Max wdth .57-in/1.45-cm.
Camp Utensils		
Spoons		
Large bowl spoon	1	Plain Ware. Overall lgth 7.75-in/19.69-cm. Bowl lgth 3.04-in/7.73-cm. Max bowl wdth 1.68-in/4.2-cm.
Lids		
Small lid	1	Ave dia 1.67-in/4.24-cm. Melted lead on top of lid.
Leaded can lid	1	Dia 3.83-in/9.72-cm. One side cut straight.
Knives		
Utility knife blade tip	1	Lgth 1.69-in/4.29-cm. Max wdth .80-in/2.03-cm.
Mexican and Indian Artifacts		
Non-Metal Artifacts		
Base of point	1	Tecovas chert. Max wdth .946-in/2.4-cm. Max lgth .99-in/2.52-cm.
End scraper	1	Tecovas chert. Lgth 1.53-in/3.89-cm. Max wdth .92-in/2.34-cm.

Metal Artifacts		
Brass tinkler	1	Lgth 1.46-in 3.71-cm. Flared bottom width .50-in/1.27-cm.
Metal awl	1	Lgth 7.88-in/20.02-cm. Max wdth .168-in/ .427-cm. Square rod sharpened on each end. Possible worked parasol rib.
Hatchet blade cutting tool	1	Lgth 2.49-in/6.33-cm. Ht 1.87-in/4.75-cm. Top beaten flat. Chisel marks on the sides.
Chisel-cut metal pieces	19	Greatest lgth 1.08-in/2.74-cm. Shortest lgth .69-in/1.75-cm.
Miscellaneous Pieces		
Box bands	3	Max lgth 5.15-in/13.08-cm. Max wdth .84-in/2.13-cm. Ave. thk .03-in/.078-cm.
Broken hasp latch	1	Lgth 5.17-in/13.13-cm. Max wdth 1.34-in/3.14-cm. Slot lgth 1.85-in/4.7-cm. Slot wdth .42-in/1.07-cm. End curled.
Small metal piece with curled end	1	Lgth 1.83-in/4.65-cm. Wdth .27-in/.69-cm. Spanish-Colonial design.
Twisted metal piece	1	Chisel-cut. Lgth 2.80-in/7.1-cm. Max wdth .42-in/1.07-cm.

Chapter 28
Reimer Arroyo Site and Artifacts

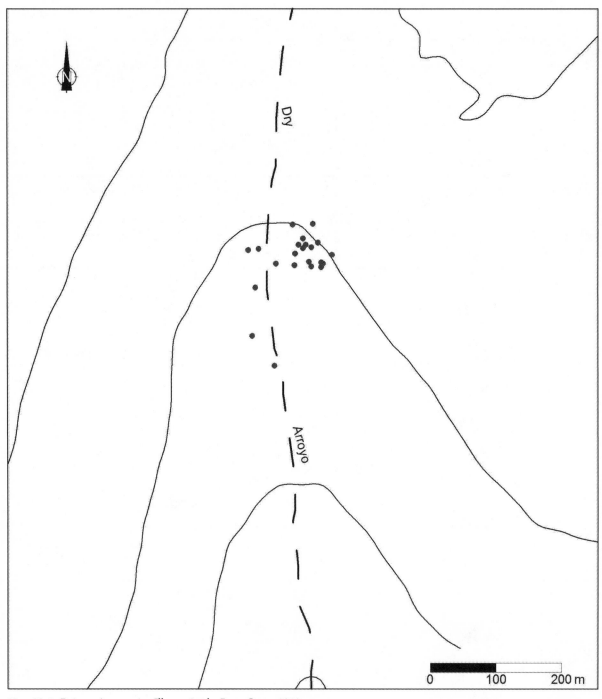

Map 28.1. Reimer Arroyo site. Illustration by Brett Cruse, 2010.

eimer Arroyo camp (HLMO3B) is on a dry ravine one mile north of a large playa lake and is midway between Rica Creek camp and Blue Creek camp. The site extends over one acre along the north and south sides of the Fort Bascom–Adobe Walls Road. Having found only twenty-two artifacts at the site is evidence of a short stay, perhaps a noon stop. One military button and a Remington pistol combination tool represent a military presence. This locale would not have been conducive for an overnight stay as it is on a high plain and affords no protection or wood for fuel. The vegetation is limited to short grasses, a few scattered cholla, and yucca. The large playa lake to the south might have been a source for re-filling water containers and watering stock, especially in the summertime.

Almost one hundred artifacts recovered from the north shore of the lake were from small civilian camps. It is unlikely that a large, military column would have taken the time to move off the trail to the playa lake for camping because Blue Creek was only about ten miles farther down the road and was a more reliable water source.

Fig. 118. Remington combination gun tool. Scan by Lisa Jackson, 2011.

Fig. 119. Hame staple. Scan by Lisa Jackson, 2011.

Table 28.1 Reimer Arroyo Artifact Descriptions. HLMO3		
Artifact Category	**Quantity**	**Description**
Arms and Ammunition		
Cartridge Cases		
.44 caliber	2	Head stamp. none. EP. Dia undetermined. Ave lgth 1.11-in/2.82-cm.
.44-40 caliber	1	Head stamp. none. EP. Dia undetermined. Lgth 1.31-in/3.33-cm. Case torn and flattened.
.45 caliber	1	Head stamp. none. EP. Dia .48-in/1.22-cm. Lgth 1.27-in/3.23-cm.
Unfired Cartridge		
.45 caliber	1	Head stamp. none. EP. Dia .48-in/ 1.22-cm. Overall lgth 1.64-in/4.17-cm.
Fired Bullets		
.00 buckshot	1	Low-velocity impact. Dia .315-in/.80-cm. Wt 51.6 gr.*[1]
.38 caliber	1	Low-velocity impact. Dished base. Two ring. Dia .347-in/.88-cm. Wt 152.7 gr. Consistent with Smith & Wesson revolver.*
.45 caliber	1	Low-velocity impact. Cone base. Two ring. Dia .443-in/1.13-cm. Lgth .723-in/1.84-cm.*
Remington combination tool	1	Long arm lgth 3.097-in/7.87-cm. Short arm lgth 1.42-in/3.61-cm. For use with Remington percussion revolver: Army .44 caliber and Navy .36 caliber.[2]
Personal Items		
Buttons		
Metal button	1	Recessed center. Stippled design. Brass attachment on back. Dia .67-in/1.71-cm.
Military button	1	General Service. Bent Shank. Maker's mark •*SCOVILL MFG Co*• *WATERBURY* rmdc. Dia .775-in/1.97-cm. Manufacture date 1850–1860.[3]
Fasteners		
Nails		
Complete machine-cut nail	3	Lgth varies 1.54-in/3.91-cm. to 2.44-in/6.2-cm. Tapered on two sides.
Broken machine-cut nail	2	Lgth varies 2.01-in/5.11-cm to 2.55-in/6.48-cm. Tapered on two sides.

Bolts, Pins, and Brads		
Carriage bolt	1	Lgth 4.8-in/12.2-cm. Bolt dia .32-in/8.15-cm. Square bolt beneath round head. Bent.
Small carriage bolt	1	Lgth 2.06-in/5.23-cm. Bolt dia .225-in/.57-cm. Square shoulders beneath round head.
Round pin	1	Lgth 1.26-in/3.2-cm. Broken and bent.
Pin with braded washer	1	Lgth 2.28-in/5.79-cm. Ave dia .24-in/.61-cm.
Short pin with cone-shaped head	1	Lgth 1.21-in/3.07-cm. Pin dia .185-in/.47-cm. Head dia .56-in/1.42-cm.
Horse Tack and Wagon Hardware		
Harness Gear		
Hame staple	1	Lgth 1.96-in/4.98-cm. Max wdth 1.06-in/2.69-cm. Bent.
Miscellaneous		
Broken handle	1	Lgth 4.43-in/11.26-cm. Max Thk .52-in/1.32-cm. Hole in one end. Hole dia .59-in/1.50-cm.

Chapter 29
Blue Creek Site and Artifacts

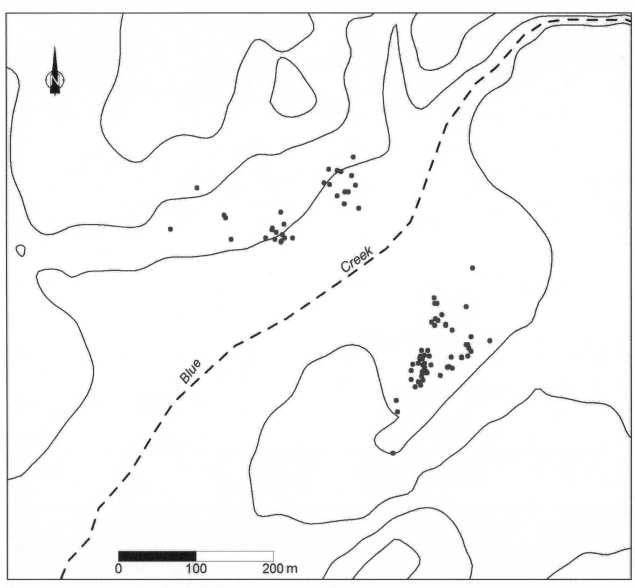

Map 29.1. Blue Creek site. Illustration by Brett Cruse, 2010.

The headwaters of Blue Creek originate at the eastern escarpment of the High Plains. Two dry tributaries meander through deep canyons for four or five miles and converge where they enter into a wide valley.

Carson's troops bivouacked on both sides of Blue Creek (Camp 41MO235) four miles east of the confluence of the two dry branches. A clear stream flowed through the camp and continued eastward below the high bluffs along the north side of the creek. The Bascom–Adobe Walls Road passed to the west of the bluffs and continued to the northeast, out of the valley.

The extent of the site is about fifteen acres. Today, sagebrush, yucca, short and tall grasses, and skunkberry sumac grow on the flat terraces while plum thickets, tall grasses, and cottonwoods abound along the creek. Most of the cottonwoods are young trees, but a few large, older ones exist. At the time Carson camped there, the creek was probably void of trees. Colonel Howe stated that his encampment of July 29, 1866, had good water and grass but no trees.[1] I believe Blue Creek to have been his campsite.

Billy Dixon noted that when he camped on Blue Creek in the fall of 1873, the holes in the creek teemed with fish. He also mentioned seeing old camp remains of Mexican buffalo hunters.[2]

Ninety-six artifacts recovered from Blue Creek camp verify that it was a multi-component camp, dating from early Native American (prehistoric) to late nineteenth century.

Fig. 121. Stopper holder attached to canteen chain. Photograph by Wyman Meinzer, 2009.

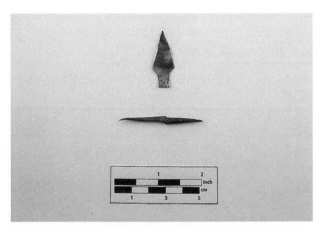

Fig. 120. Brass arrowpoint and an English trade–style (lightning) awl. Photograph by Wyman Meinzer, 2009.

Fig. 122. Small chain swivel. Photograph by Wyman Meinzer, 2009.

Table 29.1 Blue Creek Artifact Descriptions. 41MO235		
Artifact Category	**Quantity**	**Description**
Arms and Ammunition		
Cartridge Cases		
.44-40 caliber	1	Head stamp. none. EP. Dia .47-in/1.20-cm. Lgth 1.26-in/3.2-cm. Case split on one side and shortened.
Maynard .50 caliber	1	Large disk with pin hole on base. Disk dia .77-in/1.96-cm. Lgth 1.21-in/3.01-cm. Pin-fire.
Spencer .56-50 caliber	1	Head stamp. none. RF. Three firing-pin marks. Dia undetermined. Case flattened. Lgth 1.152-in/2.93-cm.
Cartridge case fragment	1	Dia undetermined. Base missing. Lgth .88-in/2.24-cm.
Unfired Cartridges		
56-50 Spencer	1	Head stamp. *SAW*. IP. Dia .56-in/1.42-cm. Lgth 1.59-in/4.04-cm.
56-50 Spencer	1	Head stamp. *SAW*. IP. Dia .56-in/1.42-cm. Lgth 1.76-in/4.24-cm. Bullet chewed by animal.
Unfired Bullets		
.36 caliber	1	Dia .378-in/.96-cm. Lgth .61-in/1.55-cm. Wt 141.6 gr. Flat base. Reduced size at rear of bullet.[3]
.44 caliber	3	Ave. dia .450-in/1.15-cm. Ave. lgth .75-in/1.90-cm. Ave. wt 227.2 gr.
Fired Bullets		
.41 caliber	1	Dia .41-in/1.04-cm. Wt 210.8 gr. Three ring. Flat base. Medium-velocity impact.
Percussion Caps		
Straight-type cap	1	Ht .30-in/.76-cm. Dia undetermined. Flattened.
Personal Items		
Buttons		
Four-hole iron button	3	Ave dia .67-in/1.70-cm. Two buttons have recessed centers and one has stippled design on front.
Decorated brass button	1	Dia .64-in/1.62-cm. Back with shank broken loose from button front.
Buttons with "J&L" on front.	2	Ave dia .74-in/1.88-cm. Back is missing from both buttons.
Military button	1	Dia .78-in/1.98-cm. General Service. Shank missing. Maker's mark **WATERBURY BUTTON CO.*[4]

Buttons (cont.)		
Military button	1	Dia .58-in/1.48-cm. General Service. Maker's mark. *HORSTMAN & ALLIEN NY.* 1850 to post-Civil War. Steele and Johnson produced buttons for Horstman brothers.[5]
Infantry military button	1	Dia .81-in/2.06-cm. Bent shank. "I" on crest. Maker's mark. none.
Brass spool fasteners	2	Ave dia .63-in/1.60-cm. Ave lgth .53-in/1.35-cm.
Brass spool fastener	1	Dia .61-in/1.55-cm. Lgth .68-in/1.71-cm.
Suspenders Fasteners		
Four-prong iron suspender clip	1	Lgth 1.31-in/3.3-cm. Wdth 1.60-in/4.07-cm.
Suspender slide	1	Lgth .83-in/2.11-cm. Wdth 1.0-in/2.54-cm.
Knives		
Pocket knife	1	Lgth 4.09-in/10.39-cm. Wdth .83-in/2.11-cm. One blade. Brass end. Handle cover is missing. Very rusty.
Canteens		
Canteen stopper holder and chain	1	Overall lgth 8.0-in/20.5-cm. Chain lgth 5.8-in/ 14.47-cm. Cork missing.
Canteen stopper holder	1	Lgth 2.61-in/6.63-cm. Stopper and chain missing.
Fasteners		
Nails		
Complete machine-cut nails	24	Max lgth 2.52-in/6.41-cm. Min lgth 1.22-in/3.1-cm. All nails tapered on two sides.
Broken machine-cut nail	1	Lgth .78-in/1.98-cm. Tapered on two sides.
Tacks		
Large-head tack	1	Lgth .9-in/2.29-cm. Head dia .475-in/1.21-cm.
Iron square tack with round head	1	Lgth .91-in/2.31-cm.
Bolts, Pins, and Brads		
Round bolt head	1	Dia 1.12-in/2.85-cm. Lgth .51-in/1.30-cm.
Horse Tack and Wagon Hardware		
Horseshoes		
Complete shoe	1	Lgth 4.85-in/12.32-cm. Wdth 4.64-in/11.78-cm. No calks. Worn toe.
Complete shoe	1	Lgth 4.7-in/11.94-cm. Wdth 4.74-in/12.04-cm. Calks. Worn toe.

Table 29.1 Blue Creek Artifact Descriptions. 41MO235 (*cont.*)		
Artifact Category	**Quantity**	**Description**
Horse Tack and Wagon Hardware		
Mule Shoe		
Broken shoe	1	Lgth 4.53-in/11.51-cm. Calk.
Horseshoe Nails		
Unused nails	5	Max lgth 2.65-in/6.73-cm. Min lgth 2.0-in/5.08-cm.
Used nails	8	Max lgth 1.60-in/4.06-cm. Min lgth .99-in/2.52-cm.
Harness Rings		
Brass D-shaped ring	1	Wdth 1.63-in/4.14-cm. Lgth 1.27-in/3.23-cm. Rod dia .18-in/.46-cm.
Harness ring	1	Max dia 2.87-in/7.29-in. Slightly oval.
Hames		
Broken hame staple	1	Staple lgth 1.98-in/5.03-cm. Wdth 1.38-in/3.51-cm. One side broken.
Chains		
Broken links	4	Max lgth 3.89-in/9.88-cm. Max wdth 2.03./5.16-cm. Min lgth 1.52-in/3.86-cm. Min wdth .93-in/2.16-cm.
Chain swivel	1	Lgth 3.14-in/7.09-cm. Max wdth 1.02-in/2.59-cm. Ball swivel.
Wagon Tools		
Wagon wrench	1	S-wrench. Three size openings on each end. Lgth 7.0-in/18.0-cm. Max wdth 2.6-in/6.6-cm.
Leather and Canvas Hardware		
Copper brads	2	Max dia .38-in/.97-cm. Max lgth .19-in/.47-cm.
Tools		
Needles		
Needle mid-section	1	Lgth .94-in/2.39-cm.
Broken canvas needle	1	Lgth 4.07-in/10.34-cm. Eye lgth .32-in/.82-cm. Needle is flat at point.
Camp Utensils		
Cans		
Sardine can	1	Lgth 4.23-in/10.75-cm. Wdth 3.0-in/7.622-cm. Ht .95-in/2.41-cm. Circle on bottom. Soldered seams. A few rusted holes.
Round can lid	1	Dia 3.14-in/7.97-cm. Lip size .12-in/.31-cm.

Flatware		
Metal fork	1	Overall lgth 7.38-in/1.87-cm. Tine lgth 2.35-in/5.79-cm. Max wdth .68-in/1.73-cm. Three tine fork. Two pin holes for handle cover.
Knife mid-section	1	Lgth .91-in/2.32-cm. Max wdth .65-in/1.65-cm. Bulge in middle of piece.
Cookware		
Broken cast-iron pot fragments	4	Max lgth 2.29-in/5.82-cm. Max wdth .03-in/5.16-cm. Ring around rim fragment.
Hooks		
Ninety-degree, S-shaped hook	1	Lgth 3.5-in/8.89-cm. Wdth 1.44-in/3.66-cm. One side of hook has curled end. Hand-forged. Spanish-Colonial style.
Metal hook	1	Lgth 5.89-in/14.97-cm. Rod dia .25-in/.63-cm. Hook on each end of rod.
Mexican and Indian Artifacts		
Non-Metal		
Alibates scraper	1	Lgth 2.37-in/6.02-cm. Max wdth 1.59-in/4.04-cm.
Broken Alibates bi-face	1	Lgth 1.9-in/3.8-cm. Wdth 1.11-in/2.82-cm. All missing except the base.
Metal Artifacts		
Brass metal point	1	Lgth 1.35-in/3.43-cm. Shoulder width .53-in/1.35-cm. Stem width .275-in/.7-cm. Stem lgth .30-in/.76-cm. Thk .027-in/.069-cm. Chisel-cut.
Cut brass point preform	1	Lgth 1.255-in/3.19-cm. Max wdth .63-in/1.6-cm. Thk .03-in/.078-cm. Probably cut from the same piece of brass as the above point.
Chisel-cut metal	2	Max lgth .86-in/2.19-cm. Max wdth .35-in/.89-cm.
Indian child's brass ring	1	Max dia .59-in/1.5-cm. Wdth .30-in/.77-cm. Open on bottom.
English trading–style (lightning) awl	1	Lgth 1.96-in/4.98-cm. Max wdth .176-in/.45-cm.
Copper tinkler	1	Lgth 1.22-in/3.1-cm. Flattened.
Miscellaneous		
Curved brass piece	1	Lgth 1.75-in/4.45-cm. Max wdth .97-in/2.46-cm. Threaded hole in one end. Broken.
Broken rod	2	Overall lgth .9-in/2.3-cm. Max rod dia .42-in/1.07-cm.
Box band fragment with cut nail	1	Lgth 2.89-in/7.38-cm. Wdth .83-in/2.11-cm. Two small holes-cut nail in one hole.

Chapter 30
Carson's Moore Creek Site and Artifacts

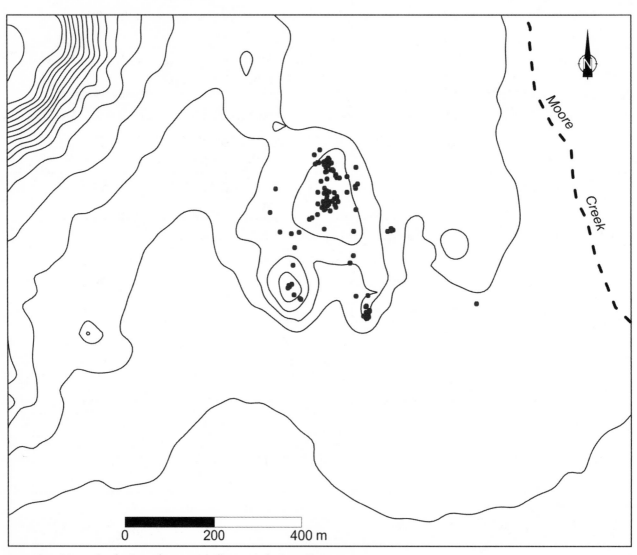

Map 30.1. Moore Creek, Carson's campsite. Illustration by Brett Cruse, 2010.

After a long day's battle at Adobe Walls and the Kiowa village, Colonel Carson marched back up the Canadian River searching for his supply wagons. On a long ridge west of, what is now, Moore Creek, Carson found Colonel Abreu and his contingent holding the wagons. Abreu had chosen a good, defensive position for his camp, on high ground isolated from other hills. On the morning after the battle, Carson moved the entire camp a short distance to the south. Because of the two locations of the wagon, the site number is HLHC7-A&B (*A* to designate the original camp and *B* the re-located camp). Together they cover about sixteen acres.

Vegetation is sparse along the top of the ridge, but a good covering of grama grass grows on all the slopes. A few scrubby mesquites grow around the base of the high ground; cottonwoods thrive along the creek to the east and on the Canadian River to the south.

The deep red pigment of the Permian soil colors all the bluffs around the area. The Kiowa called it *Guadal Doha* (red bluff). A dolomite outcrop caps the magenta soil at the north end of the ridge and the hill at the south end. The Fort Bascom–Adobe Walls Road passes south of the high ground.

With the exception of two bullets from a later time and one Indian quartzite pestle retrieved from the hill, the 135 artifacts recovered date to the time of Carson's campaign. All bullets found were unfired from percussion rifles and pistols of the same calibers as those dropped by Carson's troops near the howitzers at the Adobe Walls battle. The camp appears to be a single-component site of the Carson era.

Fig. 123. Combination gun tool. Photograph by Wyman Meinzer, 2009.

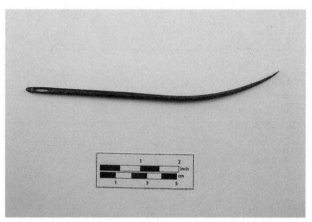

Fig. 124. Canvas needle. Photograph by Wyman Meinzer, 2009.

Fig. 125. Tobacco tin label. Photograph by Wyman Meinzer, 2009.

Table 30.1 Carson's Moore Creek Camp Artifact Descriptions. HLHC7-A&B		
Artifact Category	**Quantity**	**Description**
Arms and Ammunition		
Unfired Bullets		
.36 caliber	4	Ave dia .38-in/.97-cm. Ave lgth .62-in/1.57-cm. Ave wt 136.5 gr. Ringtail. Manufactured by the St. Louis Arsenal for the Navy Colt revolver.*[1]
.44 caliber	10	Ave dia .46-in/1.17-cm. Ave lgth .74-in/1.87-cm. Ave wt 230.4 gr. Flat base. Reduced size at rear.
.52 caliber	22	Ave dia .544-in/1.38-cm. Ave lgth .925-in/2.35-cm. Ave wt. 432.3 gr. Two ring. Flat base with cone.
.52 caliber Ringtail	6	Ave dia .56-in/1.42-cm. Ave lgth 1.02-in/2.58-cm. Ave wt 447.8 gr. Two ring with ringtail base.
.52 caliber Ringtail	1	Dia .568-in/1.44-cm. Lgth .975-in/2.48-cm. Wt. 458.2 gr. Nine rings with ringtail base.
.52 caliber cut bullets	2	Both bullets reshaped with a knife. Ave wt 374.4 gr.
.54 caliber	1	Dia .54-in/1.37-cm. Lgth 1.0-in/2.54-cm. Wt 432.8 gr. Three ring with hollow base.
.58 caliber Minié	2	Ave dia .575-in/1.46-cm. Ave lgth 1.02-in/2.59-cm. Ave wt 462.9 gr. Three ring with hollow base.
Fired Bullets		
.32 caliber	3	Ave dia .352-in/.89-cm. Ave lgth .75-in/1.92-cm. Ave wt 149.8 gr. Concave base. Low-velocity impact.
.45 caliber Colt	1	Dia .451-in/1.15-cm. Wt 250.2 gr. Two rings with cupped base. Low-velocity impact. Consistent with post-1875 Colt revolver.*
Unfired Lead Balls		
.31 caliber	1	Dia .31-in/.79-cm. Wt 41.4 gr.
.38 caliber	1	Dia .382-in/.97-cm. Wt 85 gr.
.50 caliber	1	Dia .52-in/1.32-cm. Wt 210.9 gr.
.54 caliber	3	Ave dia .55-in/1.27-cm. Ave wt 224.3 gr.
Percussion Caps		
Hat-type	10	Ave dia: No measurements. Ave ht .5-in/1.27-cm. Four flanges on bottom.
Straight-type	6	Ave dia .25-in/.64-cm. Ave ht .31-in/.79-cm. Two caps have eagle design on top.

Gun Tools		
1841 U.S. musket wrench	1	Overall lgth 3.69-in/9.37-cm. Max wdth .56-in/1.42-cm. One blade broken but present.[2]
Gun Parts		
Percussion rifle nipples	2	Total lgth .75-in/1.91-cm. Thread lgth .25-in/.64-cm. U.S. musket wrench found nearby fits nipples.
Personal Items		
Buttons		
Four-hole iron button	1	Dia .69-in/1.75-cm. Plain.
Four-hole iron button	1	Dia .50-in/1.27-cm. Plain. Recessed center.
Two-hole plated button	1	Dia .69-in/1.75-cm. Recessed center. Wire fastened.
Towers wire fastened button	1	Dia 1.0-in/2.54-cm. Recessed center.
Military button	1	Dia .63-in/1.60-cm. General service. Maker's mark. _WATERBURY BUTTON Co._ dm. Manufactured 1860s.[3]
Military button	1	Dia .75-in/1.91-cm. General service. Maker's mark _*EXTRA QUALITY*_ dm.[4]
Military button	1	Dia .56-in/1.42-cm. General service. Maker's mark. none.
Tobacco Tag		
Tin tag	1	Oval-shaped with two tabs. Lgth 1.13-in/2.87-cm. Wdth .63-in/1.60-cm.
Knives		
Pocket knife	1	Three-blade knife with one blade open. Handle covers missing. Shield on one side of knife. Handle lgth 3.63-in/9.22-cm. Open blade lgth 2.0-in/5.08-cm. Blade tip missing.
Keys		
Iron key	1	Lgth 1.44-in/3.66-cm. Max loop wdth .75-in/1.91-cm.
Fasteners		
Cut Nails		
Complete machine-cut nail	6	Tapered on two sides. Lgth varies .98-in/2.5-cm to 2.75-in/6.99-cm.
Incomplete machine-cut nail	1	Tapered on two sides. Lgth .98-in/2.5-cm.
Screws		
Wood screws	4	Lgth 1.75-in/4.45-cm. Twelve threads per inch. Head dia .44-in/1.12-cm. Blade-type.
Wood screw	1	Lgth 1.75-in/4.45-cm. Ten threads per inch. Head dia .49-in/1.24-cm. Blade-type.

Table 30.1 Carson's Moore Creek Camp Artifact Descriptions.
HLHC7-A&B (*cont.*)

Artifact Category	Quantity	Description
Fasteners		
Washer		
Large iron washer	1	Outside dia 3.5-in/8.89-cm. Inside dia 2.25-in/5.72-cm. Thk .44-in/1.12-cm. Considerable wear.
Horse Tack and Wagon Hardware		
Horseshoes		
Complete	1	Lgth 5.0-in/12.7-cm. Wdth 4.75-in/12.07-cm. Calks. Two nails.
Mule Shoes		
Incomplete	1	Lgth 5.0-in/12.7-cm. Calk. Three nails.
Horseshoe Nails		
Unused	2	Ave lgth 2.5-in/6.35-cm.
Broken	3	Ave lgth 1.5-in/3.81-cm.
Buckles and Rings		
Sunk-bar harness buckle	1	Lgth 1.63-in/4.14-cm. Wdth 1.0-in/2.54-cm. Tongue attached to center bar.
Small rounded buckle	1	Lgth .88-in/2.24-cm. Wdth .69-in/1.75-cm. Tongue fastened to center bar.
Harness ring	1	Outside dia 3.0-in/7.62-cm. Metal dia .5-in/1.27-cm.
Small iron ring	1	Outside dia .81-in/2.06-cm. Metal dia .13-in/.33-cm.
Chains		
Broken chain link	1	Lgth 3.5-in/8.89-cm. Max wdth 1.5-in/3.8-cm. Metal dia .31-in/.79-cm.
Grommets and Leather Rivets		
One-half brass grommet	1	Dia .44-in/1.12-cm
Grommet	1	Dia .56-in/1.40-cm.
Brass rivets	2	Ave dia .5-in/1.27-cm.
Tools		
Needles		
Sewing needle	1	Lgth 1.63-in/4.14-cm. Dia .042-in/.11-cm.
Canvas needle point	1	Lgth 2.0-in/ 5.08-cm. Max wdth .10-in/.25-cm.

Needles (cont.)		
Broken canvas needle	1	Lgth 2.08-in/5.30-cm. Curved. Point section. Tapered.
Complete canvas needle	1	Lgth 6.75-in/17.5-cm. Curved. Pointed end flattened.
Files		
Triangular file	1	Lgth 6.0-in/15.24-cm. Max wdth .44-in/1.12-cm.
Camp Utensils		
Cans		
1867 leaded can	1	Dia 3.5-in/8.89-cm. Ht 4.63-in. 11.76-cm. Top cut open. Bottom reads *EXCELSIOR CAN PATENTED APR. 22, 1867.* Probably from Carr's nearby 1868 camp.
Buckets		
Bucket bail holder	1	Dia .75-in/1.9-cm. Convex.
Tin Cups		
Cup handle	1	Lgth 4.25-in/10.8-cm. Max wdth 1.0-in/2.54-cm. Rolled edges.
Lids		
Small round lid	1	Dia 1.13-in/2.87-cm. Lip .25-in/.64-cm.
Flatware		
Fork or knife handle	1	Lgth 3.13-in/7.95-cm. Max wdth .75-in/1.91-cm. Bone on one side. Two pins in handle.
Utility knife	1	Overall lgth 7.75-in/19.69-cm. Max blade wdth 1.0-in/2.54-cm. Max handle wdth .75-in/1.91-cm. Two pin holes in handle. Handle covering missing. Tip broken.
Three-tine broken fork	1	Overall lgth 6.5-in/16.5-cm. Handle lgth 2.75-in/6.99-cm. Two tines broken. Three pin holes for handle cover.
Three-tine broken fork	1	Overall lgth 4.63-in/10.9-cm. Max wdth .69-in/1.75-cm. All tines broken. Three pins for handle cover.
Hooks		
Small hook	1	Lgth 1.5-in/3.81-cm. Curved with sharpened point.
Mexican or Indian Artifacts		
Non-metal		
Quartzite pestle	1	Ht 4.7-in/12.0-cm. Base dia 2.95-in/7.5-cm. Top dia 1.97-in/5.0-cm. Bell-shaped. Faint groove at mid-section.
Metal		
Coscojo (Hispanic charm)	1	Lgth 1.5-in/3.81-cm. Blade wdth .38-in/.97-cm. flat type. Serrated on end of blade.

Table 30.1 Carson's Moore Creek Camp Artifact Descriptions. HLHC7-A&B (*cont.*)

Artifact Category	Quantity	Description
Miscellaneous Pieces		
Small strap with holes in each end	1	Lgth 3.44-in/8.74-cm. Wdth .25-in/.64-cm. Thk .075-in/.19-cm.
Metal piece with hole	1	Lgth 3.25-in/8.26-cm. Max wdth 1.25-in/3.18-cm. Hole in small end.
Box band fragment with rivet	1	Lgth 1.5-in/3.81-cm. Wdth .88-in/2.23-cm.
Brass piece with hole	1	Lgth .94-in/2.39-cm. Max wdth .38-in/.97-cm.

Chapter 31
Penrose and Carr's Moore Creek Site and Artifacts

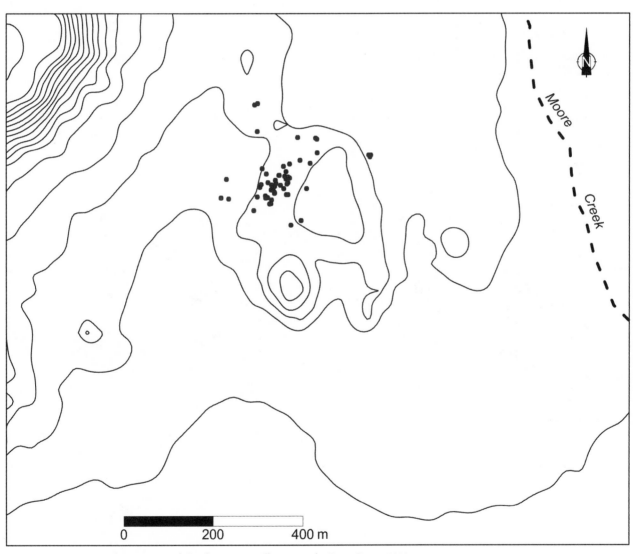

Map 31.1. Moore Creek, Penrose and Carr's campsite. Illustration by Brett Cruse, 2010.

During Sheridan's 1868 winter campaign, Penrose and Carr moved nine companies of troops from North Palo Duro Creek to the Canadian River. They left on Christmas Day and arrived at the Canadian three days later.[1]

Cartographers for the United States War Department, in 1871, drew, in detail, the topography surrounding the site, which matches modern topographic maps of the area. They also marked the site of Penrose and Carr's camp with a cross.[2] Using this information, I had little trouble finding the military camp.

The campsite (HLHC7C) is on the west side of Moore Creek near its confluence with the Canadian River. It is about fifty yards west of where Carson camped in 1864. There is a small outlying camp, probably a picket post, on the east side of the ridge. The site extends over six acres along the grama grass–covered slopes.

With the exception of a leaded can dated 1867, there is no over-lapping of artifacts from the two encampments. I found no brass cartridge cases in Carson's camp and few rifle or pistol percussion bullets in Penrose and Carr's camp.

Of the seventy artifacts recovered at the site, nineteen are 56-50 unfired Spencer cartridges. Seventeen have *SAW* (Sage Ammunition Works) head stamps, one has *JG* (Jacob Goldmark), and the other one has no head stamp. The remaining artifacts are typical of military sites: buttons, bullets, harness buckles, saddle rings, gun tools, cut nails, and camp utensils.

Fig. 126. Unfired 56-50-caliber Spencer cartridges. Photograph by Wyman Meinzer, 2009.

Fig. 127. Sunk-type harness buckles. Photograph by Wyman Meinzer, 2009.

Fig. 128. Horseshoe. Photograph by Wyman Meinzer, 2009.

Table 31.1 Penrose and Carr's Moore Creek Artifact Descriptions. HLHC7-C

Artifact Category	Quantity	Description
Arms and Ammunition		
Cartridge Cases		
.45 caliber	1	Head stamp. none. EP. Dia .48-in/1.22-cm. Lgth 1.27-in/3.23-cm.
.50/70 caliber	1	Head stamp. none. IP. Dia .574-in/1.46-cm. Lgth 1.75-in/4.45-cm.
Unfired Cartridges		
56-50 caliber	17	Head stamps. All but one has SAW. Ave dia .56-in/1.42-cm. Ave lgth 1.59-in/ 4.05-cm.
56-50 caliber, broken	1	Head stamp. *JG*. RF. Lgth and dia not measured.
56-50 caliber	1	Head stamp. *SAW*. RF. Lgth and dia not measured.
Unfired Bullets		
.44 caliber	6	Ave dia .46-in/117-cm. Ave lgth .73-in/1.83-cm. Ave wt. 228.6 gr. Flat bases. Reduced size at rear.
Fired Bullet		
.45 caliber Colt	1	Low-velocity impact. Dia .448-in/1.14-cm. Lgth .71-in/1.80-cm. Wt 244.7 gr. Two ring. Concave base. Consistent with post-1875 Colt revolver.[3]
Gun Tools		
Colt combination tools	2	Long-blade ave lgth 3.13-in/7.90-cm. Short end ave lgth 1.44-in/3.66-cm.[4]
Personal Items		
Buttons		
Four-hole metal button	1	Dia .69-in/1.75-cm. Recessed center. Plain.
Four-hole metal button	1	Dia .63-in/1.60-cm. Recessed center. Plain.
Small military button	1	Dia .56-in/1.42-cm. General service. Maker's mark *SCOVILLS & Co.* EXTRA* dm. Manufactured in 1840s.[5]
Military button	1	Dia .88-in/2.24-cm. General service. Maker's mark •SCOVILL MFG CO• WATERBURY rmdc Manufactured 1855–1860.[6]
Brass spool fastener	1	Dia .81-in/2.06-cm. Spool lgth .56-in/1.42-cm.
Suspender Fasteners		
Iron suspender clip	1	Lgth .88-in/2.24-cm. Wdth 1.13-in/2.87-cm.

Table 31.1 Penrose and Carr's Moore Creek Artifact Descriptions. HLHC7-C (*cont.*)		
Artifact Category	**Quantity**	**Description**
Fasteners		
Cut Nails		
Complete machine-cut nails	4	Lgth varies 2.0-in/5.08-cm. to 3.0-in/7.62-cm. Tapered on two sides.
Horse Tack and Wagon Hardware		
Horseshoes		
Complete shoes	3	No calks. Lgths vary. 5.0-in/12.70-cm. to 5.6-in/13.97-cm. Wdth varies 4.9-in/12.40-cm. to 5.25-in/13.3-cm.
Broken shoes	2	No calk. Lgths vary 4.5-in/11.43-cm. to 5.25-in/13.3-in
Mule Shoe		
Complete shoe	1	Calks. Worn toe. Lgth 5.5-in/13.97-cm. Wdth 4.0-in/10.16-cm.
Horseshoe Nails		
Unused nails	5	Lgths vary 2.0-in/5.08-cm. to 2.63-in/6.68-cm.
Used nails	1	Lgth 2.5-in/6.35-cm. Twisted.
Buckles and Rings		
Roller buckle	1	Lgth .75-in/1.91-cm. Wdth 1.0-in/2.54-cm. Partially deteriorated.
Harness buckle, sunk-type	1	Lgth 2.5-in/6.35-cm. Wdth 1.75-in/4.45-cm. Tongue fastened to center bar.
Harness buckle, sunk-type	1	Lgth 2.0-in/5.08-cm. Wdth 1.25-in/3.18-cm. Tongue fastened to center bar.
Harness buckle, sunk-type	2	Ave lgth 1.5-in/3.81-cm. Ave wdth 1.0-in/2.54-cm. Tongue fastened to center bar.
Saddle skirt ring	1	Iron. Outside dia 1.69-in/4.29-cm. Metal dia .19-in/.41-cm.
Brass saddle guard plates	2	Oval with nail hole in each end. Lgth 1.5-in/3.81-cm. Wdth .88-in/2.24-cm. Rectangular cut-out 2.25-in/.64-cm x .88-in/2.24-cm.
Chains		
Broken chain link	1	Lgth 1.44-in/3.66-cm.

Camp Utensils		
Cans		
Sardine can	1	Flattened. Approx. Lgth 4.0-in/10.16-cm. Approx. wdth 2.5-in/6.35-cm. Approx. height 1.0-in/2.64-cm. Circle dia on lid 1.25-in/3.18-cm.
Miscellaneous		
Bent box band	1	Overall lgth 9.0-in/22.86-cm. Wdth .75-in/1.91-cm. Thk .07-in/.18-cm.

Chapter 32
Kiowa Village Site and Artifacts

In the winter of 1864, Chief Dohäsan and the Kiowa elders selected a choice location for their camp below *Guadal Doha* (the red bluffs) on the north side of the Canadian River. A small clear stream bordered the village on the north while the Canadian River ran along the south edge of the encampment. Sand hills, surrounding the site on the north, east, and west sides, afforded protection from winter winds. The Fort Bascom–Adobe Walls Road ran east-west and crossed the creek between the Kiowa camp and the red bluff.

Skunkberry sumacs, hackberries, short and tall grasses, and plum bushes grow on the site. Cottonwoods, grapevines, willows, and other brush thrive along the creek and the Canadian River to the south.

According to artifact distribution, the Kiowa village covered about fifteen acres, although it may have been

Fig. 129. Joe Faulkenberry and author excavating burned tepee site. Photograph by Wyman Meinzer, 2009.

METAL POINTS

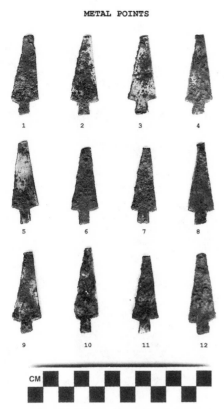

Fig. 130. Metal points from Kiowa village, 1–12. Photograph by author, 2007.

METAL POINTS

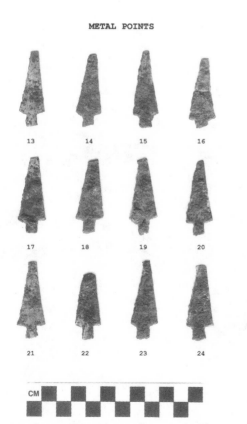

Fig. 131. Metal points from Kiowa village, 13–24. Photograph by author, 2007.

METAL POINTS

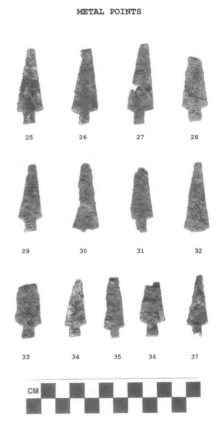

Fig. 132. Metal points from Kiowa village, 25–37. Photograph by author, 2007.

larger. Concentrated areas of burned artifacts indicate that Carson's troops gathered the tepees and paraphernalia into stacks and burned them. An excavated trench revealed charcoal at a depth of around sixteen inches. The charcoal appeared to be from a section of a tepee pole. In addition, sand hills may have encroached into the village area, covering many of the artifacts too deeply to set off a metal detector.

One other discovery supports the stack-and-burn theory. Seventy-four burned items recovered from a small area at a depth from twelve to twenty inches included thirty-eight bullet buttons, sixteen brass tacks, a short chain with rings, one gun sight, one decorated piece, six percussion caps, a flint piece, one .52-caliber fired bullet, two burned *coscojo*s, one spoon bowl, two metal scrapers, one knife blade, cut metal pieces, a melted lead piece, and a cut nail. Of the 218 artifacts recovered from the village, 175 show evidence of burning.

The most significant find at the Kiowa camp was a cache of thirty-eight unfinished, metal points. I surmise that these points came from a leather pouch that burned, leaving them significantly corroded, with many fused together.

All of the specimens were unsharpened pre-forms, straight on one side and chisel-cut on the other. The manufacturer crudely cut the stems, leaving them unfinished with the stem base sloping downward toward the straight side of the point.

One-inch to three-inch metal bands were the raw material for the maker of these pre-forms. In the 1860s, coopers used metal hoops to hold the wooden staves of barrels together when making kegs and barrels. Most of the points found at this site, when placed side-by-side with opposing ends together, measure approximately one inch, the width of a small barrel or keg hoop.

My theory is that the maker of the pre-forms first cut the band into roughly two-inch (5.0-cm.) rectangles and then cut the rough points with a chisel at an angle from near-the-top corner to near-the-opposing bottom

Fig. 135. Metal triangular file used for sharpening metal points. Photograph by Wyman Meinzer, 2009.

Fig. 136. Square metal used as an anvil. Photograph by Wyman Meinzer, 2009.

Production of Metal Points Using Barrel Bands

Preforms Cut from   Barrel Band Section
Barrel Band

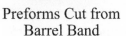

Step 1   Step 2   Step 3

Fig. 133. Production of metal points using barrel bands. Scan by Lisa Jackson, 2011.

Fig. 134. Metal chisel used in producing metal arrowpoints. Photograph by Wyman Meinzer, 2009.

Fig. 137. Broken cast-iron cookware. Photograph by Wyman Meinzer, 2009.

corner. This process created two triangular blanks from which the producer cut two notches from the base to form the stems, thus completing the pre-forms.

One chisel, a file, and a chisel-marked piece of metal found at the site give credence to the method of manufacture of the metal points found at this camp.

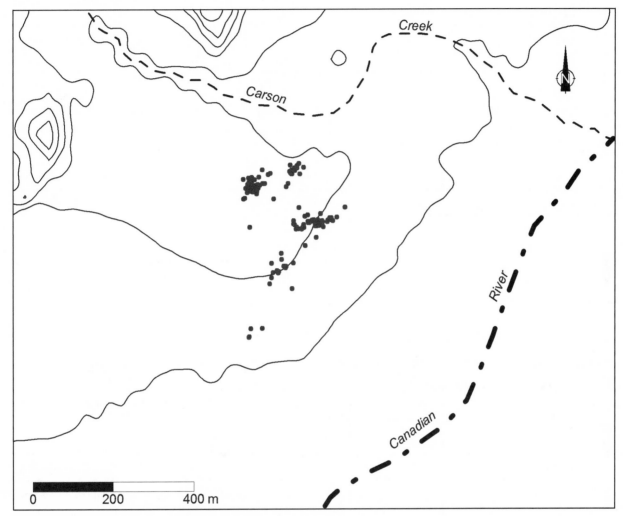

Map 32.1. Kiowa Village site. Illustration by Brett Cruse, 2010.

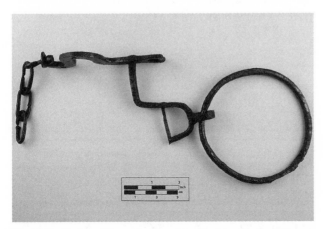

Fig. 138. Broken Hispanic ring bit. Photograph by Wyman Meinzer, 2009.

Fig. 139. Worn wagon bolts. Possibly from Chief Dohäsan's wagon. Photograph by Wyman Meinzer, 2009.

Table 32.1 Kiowa Camp Artifact Descriptions. HLHC6		
Artifact Category	**Quantity**	**Description**
Arms and Ammunition		
Cartridge Cases		
.45 caliber Colt	2	Head stamp. *UMC .45 COLT.* EP. Ave dia .48-in/1.22-cm. Ave lgth 1.27-in/3.22-cm.
Unfired Bullets		
.52 caliber	1	Two rings with ringtail. Dia .55-in/1.40-cm. Lgth 1.02-in/2.59-cm. Wt 446.0 gr.
.58 caliber Minié	2	Three rings with hollow base. Ave dia .575-in/1.46-cm. Ave lgth 1.1-in/2.79-cm. Ave wt. 475.6 gr.
Fired Bullets		
.32 caliber	1	Low-velocity impact. Concave base. Dia .35-in/.84-cm. Lgth .69-in/1.75-cm.
.52 caliber	1	High-velocity impact. Ringtail. Wt 444.0 gr.
Unknown caliber	1	Medium-velocity impact. Two Ring with dished base. Dia .435-in/1.10-cm. Lgth .60-in/1.52-cm. Wt 198.2 gr.
Flattened lead ball	1	High-velocity impact. Wt 181.5 gr.
Lead Pieces		
Lead bar pieces	2	Largest piece .75-in/1.91-cm. x .5-in/1.27-cm. x .25-in/.64-cm. Smallest piece .56-in/1.42-cm. x .5-in/1.27-cm. x .25-in/.64-cm.
Percussion Caps		
Small pistol caps	6	Ave dia .19-in/.48-cm. Ht .19-in/.48-cm. *GD* stamped on top. Burned. Ribbed sides.[1]
Gun Parts		
Ram rod thimbles	3	Ave lgths 1.0-in/2.54-cm. Ave dia 0.5-in/1.27-cm. One thimble has been cut at an angle. Two have pins in flanges.
Gun trigger	1	Lgth 1.63-in/4.14-cm. Wdth 1.19-in/3.02-cm. Hole in upper front of trigger. Burned.
Gun tumbler	1	Lgth .88-in/2.24-cm. Burned.
Brass trigger guard	1	Type of rifle unknown. Two fastening tabs. Lgth 7.5-in/19.1-cm.
Unidentified gun part	1	Lgth 0.5-in/1.27-cm. Small hole on bottom side. Burned.
Gun sight	1	Max wdth 0.63-in/1.6-cm. V sight depth 0.25-in/.64-cm. Top of V wdth 0.25-.64-cm. Burned.

Gun Parts (cont.)		
Gun stock screw	2	Ave lgth 1.0-in/2.54-cm. Blade-type. Head broken on one. Burned.
Gun Tools		
Musket worm	1	Lgth 1.63-in/4.14-cm. Tip of coil broken. Max wdth of coil .68-in/1.73-cm. Fits .69 cal. Probably 1842 U.S. musket. Burned.[2]
Personal Items		
Buttons		
Brass button back	1	Dia 0.75-in/1.91-cm. Missing shank. Burned.
Smooth brass buttons	6	Dia varies .72-in/1.83-cm. to .94-in/2.39-cm. Shanks missing or bent on four buttons.
Brass bullet buttons	38	Ave dia .38-in/.97-cm. Shanks missing from most buttons. Burned.
Small slotted metal button	1	Dia .63-in/1.60-cm. Two slots with four prongs on back. Burned.
Four-hole metal buttons	2	Ave dia .69-in/1.75-cm. Recessed centers. Burned.
Decorated brass button	1	Dia .89-in/2.27-cm. Shank missing. Stamped design on front. Maker's mark. *SCOVILLS & Co. WATERBURY.* Manufactured during the 1840s.[3]
Military button	1	General Service. Dia .81-in/2.06-cm. Bent shank. Maker's mark. none.
Military button	1	General Service. Dia .63-in/1.60-cm. Bent shank. Maker's mark. *WATERBURY BUTTON Co.* Unknown date.
Jewelry		
Small brass bead on wire	1	Approx. bead dia .2-in/.51-cm. Wire and bead lgth .75-in/1.9-cm.
Decorated brass concha	1	Dia 1.0-in/2.54-cm. Two slots. Stamped design on front.
Brass wire bracelet	1	Oval. Lgth 2.88-in/7.32-cm. Wdth 2.25-in/5.72-cm. Burned.
Plain brass conchos	4	Oval with holes in each end. Ave lgth 1.0-in/2.54-cm. Ave wdth .94-in/2.39-cm. Convex front.
Pendant or flattened tinkler	1	Max lgth 2.52-in/6.41-cm. Max wdth 1.0-in/2.54-cm. Small hole in narrow end. Wide end cut angular. Burned.
Brass rings	3	Soft brass. Outside dia varies .75-in/1.91-cm. to 1.0-in/2.54-cm. Slight indention inside of rings.

Table 32.1 Kiowa Camp Artifact Descriptions. HLHC6 *(cont.)*		
Artifact Category	**Quantity**	**Description**
Personal Items		
Jewelry (cont.)		
Painted pendant	1	Shaped like spoon handle end but thinner metal. Red, blue, and yellow paint covered with carbon. Floral design under paint. Lgth 1.64-in/4.16-cm. Max wdth .80-in/2.02-cm. Burned.
Pocket Knife		
Burned knife	1	Knife frame lgth 3.44-in/8.74-cm. Max wdth 1.0-in/2.54-cm. Burned.
Keys		
Small trunk or chest key	1	Lgth 1.38-in/3.51-cm. Loop for handle. Iron. Burned.
Large brass key	1	Lgth 5.63-in/14.30-cm. Oval loop handle wdth 1.75-in/4.45-cm. Key slot tab lgth .75-in/1.91-cm. Three raised ridges around key. Probably from New Mexico. Similar to keys on display in Kit Carson House at Taos.
Fasteners		
Cut Nails		
Complete machine-cut nail	12	All nails tapered on two sides. Sizes vary 1.25-in/3.18-cm to 2.5-in/6.35-cm. All nails burned.
Incomplete machine-cut nail	3	All nails tapered on two sides. Sizes vary 1.75-in/4.45-cm to 2.5-in/6.35-cm. All nails burned.
Various Small Nails and Tacks		
Brass headed nails	11	Ave lgth 1.0-in/2.54-cm. Ave head dia .38-in/.97-cm. All nails burned.
Small iron nails	14	Various sizes up to 1.0-in/2.54-cm. All nails burned.
Brass tacks	23	Lgths vary .30-in/.76-cm to .50-in/1.27-cm. All tacks burned.
Screws		
Wood screws	3	Lgths vary 1.0-in/2.54-cm to 1.25-in/3.18-cm. Blade-type screws. All screws burned.
Bolts and Pins		
Long carriage bolt	1	Lgth 8.0-in/20.5-cm. Dia .37-in/.95-cm. Round head. Burned.
Short carriage bolt	1	Lgth 1.63-in/4.13-cm. Dia .29-in/.74-cm. Round head. Burned.

Bolts and Pins (cont.)		
Broken metal pin	1	Lgth 1.75-in/4.45-cm. Dia .25-in/.64-cm. Burned.
Broken metal pin	1	Lgth 1.0-in/2.54-cm. Dia .19-in/.48-cm.
Horse Tack and Wagon Hardware		
Horseshoes		
Complete	1	Lgth 5.0-in/12.7-cm. Wdth 5.0-in/12.7-cm. Calks. Burned.
Bridle Bits		
Broken ring bit	1	One side shank missing. No port rollers. Lgth 11.14-in/28.28-cm. Max wdth 4.25-in/10.80-cm. Burned.
Ring bit piece	1	Lgth 3.56-in/9.0-cm. Max wdth 2.44-in/6.20-cm. Burned.
German silver-head stall piece	1	Lgth 2.0-in/5.08-cm. Wdth 1.0-in/2.54-cm. Decorated on one end.
Coscojos (Hispanic charms)	2	Coscojos hooked together. Each coscojo lgth 1.25-in/3.18-cm. Ave blade wdth .44-in/1.12-cm. Burned.
Coscojos	2	Coscojos hooked together. Ave coscojo lgth 1.19-in/3.02-cm. Blade-type. Burned.
Buckles		
Harness roller buckles	3	Lgths vary .75-in/1.91-cm to 1.75-in/4.45-cm. Wdths vary .88-in/2.23-cm to 2.5-in/6.35-cm. Burned.
Flat brass harness buckle	1	Lgth 1.38-in/3.5-cm. Wdth 1.38-in/ 3.5-cm. Tongue is iron and fastened on one side. Burned.
Regular harness buckles	4	Lgths vary 1.0-in/2.54-cm. to 1.5-in/3.81-cm. Wdths vary 1.25-in/3.18-cm to 1.75-in/4.45-cm. Burned.
Broken harness buckle	1	Lgth 1.75-in/4.45-cm. Wdth 2.01-in/5.08-cm. Tongue missing. Burned.
Brass Kepi buckle	1	Slide type. Lgth .82-in/2.08-cm. Wdth .94-in/2.39-cm.
Sunk-type buckle	1	Lgth 1.63-in/4.14-cm. Wdth 1.0-in/2.54-cm. Tongue fastened to center bar. Burned.
Harness Rings and Triangles		
Harness triangle	1	Max lgth 2.31-in/5.87-cm. Burned.
Harness ring	1	Outside dia 2.13-in/5.41-cm. Metal dia .31-in/.79-cm. Burned.

Table 32.1 Kiowa Camp Artifact Descriptions. HLHC6 (*cont.*)		
Artifact Category	**Quantity**	**Description**
Horse Tack and Wagon Hardware		
Chains		
Chain with rings	1	Five-link chain with rings on ends. Burned. Total lgth 6.63-in/16.8-cm. (1) Ring dia 2.25-in/5.72-cm. (2) Ring dia 2.0-in/5.08-cm.
Small chain	1	Three S-type links. Links vary in lgth 1.5-in/3.81-cm. to 2.0-in/5.08-cm. Burned.
Harness Snaps		
Two-wire snap	1	Blade-spring type. Lgth 2.5-in/6.35-cm. Burned.
Tools		
Cutting Tools		
Split hatchet head	1	Lgth 3.01-in/7.62-cm. Wdth at blade 1.5-in/3.81-cm. Wdth at top 1.0-in/2.54-cm. Burned.
Split hatchet head	1	Probably the other half to the tool above. Lgth 3.25-in/8.26-cm. Max wdth at blade 1.5-in/3.81-cm. Lgth of side slot .5-in/1.27-cm. Burned.
Serrated metal	1	Lgth 2.0-in/5.08-cm. Max wdth 1.75-in/4.45-cm. Serrations on long edge. Small hole. Dia .13-in/.33-cm. Burned.
Re-worked scissor blade	1	Lgth 2.25-in/5.72-cm. Max wdth .5-in/1.27-cm. Burned.
Scrapers		
Flat metal scraper	1	Lgth 2.0-in/5.08-cm. Wdth 1.0-in/2.54-cm. Curved on one end, sharpened on the other. Burned.
Metal scraper with hole in end	1	Lgth 1.50-in/3.81-cm. Wdth 1.25-in/3.18-cm. Sharpened on end away from hole. Burned.
Metal scraper	1	Lgth 2.0-in/5.08-cm. Wdth 1.63-in/4.14-cm. Sharpened on one side. Burned.
Flesher or scraper	1	Lgth 2.5-in/6.35-cm. Wdth 1.25-in/3.18-cm. Thk .25-in/.64-cm. Made from file. Sharpened on one end. Burned.
Flat Thin metal scraper	1	Lgth 5.5-in/13.97-cm. Max wdth 3.75-in/9.53-cm. Burned.
Metal scraper	1	Lgth 3.5-in/8.89-cm. Wdth 1.25-in/3.18-cm. Made from flattened shovel shank. Hole in one end and the other end sharpened. Burned.

Graters		
Grater fragments	7	Lgths vary 1.0-in/2.54-cm to 2.5-in/6.35-cm. Wdths vary .93-in/2.37-cm. to 1.0-in/2.54-cm. Graters made by driving nail holes in thin metal. All pieces burned.[4]
Metal Anvil		
Metal with chisel marks	1	Lgth 2.0-in/5.08-cm. Wdth 1.63-in/4.14-cm. Thk .13-in/.33-cm. Chisel marks on both sides. Burned.
Files		
Triangular file	1	Lgth 5.63-in/14.30-cm. Burned.
Chisels		
Metal chisel	1	Lgth 3.0-in/7.62-cm. Blade wdth 1.0-in/2.54-cm. Chisel head beaten. Burned.
Punches		
Metal punch	1	Lgth 3.75-in/9.53-cm. Round with flattened base. Burned.
Metal punch	1	Lgth 4.88-in/12.40-cm. Base flattened. Square and tapered. Bent and broken at base. Burned.
Metal Points and Lance Blades		
Metal Points		
Point pre-form	1	Lgth 1.84-in/4.68-cm. Shoulder wdth .59-in/1.5-cm. Stem lgth .34-in/.86-cm. Max stem wdth .33-in/.84-cm. Thk at shoulders .036-in/.09-cm. One side sawed past stem into point. Burned.
Point pre-forms	38	This was a cache of unfinished points. Ave lgth 1.91-in/4.86-cm. Ave shoulder wdth .70-in/1.78-cm. See Table 32.2 for more information. All points burned.
Complete point	1	Lgth 1.88-in/4.78-cm. Shoulder wdth .75-in/1.91-cm. Stem lgth .5-in/1.27-cm. Stem wdth .25-in/.64-cm. Serrated stem with slanted base. Burned.
Complete point	1	Lgth 1.31-in/3.32-cm. Shoulder wdth .5-in/1.27-cm. Stem lgth .25-in/.64-cm. Stem wdth .25-in/.64-cm. Thk at shoulders .035-in/ .089-cm. sloping shoulders. Burned.
Broken point	1	Lgth 2.13-in/5.41-cm. shoulder wdth .75-in/1.91-cm. Thk at shoulders .065-in/.165-cm. Stem missing. Burned.
Broken point	1	Lgth 2.38-in/6.05-cm. Shoulder wdth .69-in/1.75-cm. Thk at shoulders .08-in/.20-cm. Sloping shoulders. Stem missing. Point broken in middle. Burned.
Broken point	1	Lgth 1.88-in/4.78-cm. Shoulder wdth .63-in/1.60-cm. Thk .075-in/19-cm. Sloping shoulders. Stem missing. Burned.

Table 32.1 Kiowa Camp Artifact Descriptions. HLHC6 (*cont.*)		
Artifact Category	**Quantity**	**Description**
Metal Points and Lance Blades		
Lance Blades		
Complete blade	1	Lgth 15-in/38.1-cm. Shoulder wdth 1.19-in/2.86-cm. Stem lgth 3.44-in/8.74-cm. Max stem wdth .38-in/.97-cm. Stem tapered to point on all four sides. Shoulders cut at angles. Appears to be reworked trade blade. Straight ridge down center of blade. Burned.
Broken blade	1	Lgth 7.0-in/17.78-cm. Max wdth .63-in/1.60-cm. sharpened on both sides.
Camp Utensils		
Cast-iron Cookware		
Cookware fragments	35	The 35 cookware fragments represent at least five vessels. Fragment sizes vary. Lgth 1.19-in/3.02-cm. to 6.75-in/16.5-cm. Wdth 1.0-in/2.54-cm. to 3.75-in/9.53-cm. All pieces are burned.
Cast-iron skillet handle	1	Lgth 9.0-in/22.86-cm. Handle wdth .63-in/1.60-cm. Hole in one end. Hole dia .63-in/1.60. Burned.
Cups		
Cup handle fragment	1	Lgth 1.88-in/4.78-cm. Max wdth 1.06-in/2.69-cm. Rolled edges. Burned.
Buckets		
Bucket rim	1	Lgth 7.75-in/19.69-cm. Burned.
Flatware		
Spoon	1	Lgth 7.25-in/18.42-cm. Bowl lgth 2.63-in/6.68-cm. Max bowl wdth 1.75-in/4.45-cm. Heart design on end of handle. Burned.
Spoon handle	1	Lgth 4.75-in/12.07-cm. Max wdth .88-in/2.03-cm. Burned.
Spoon bowl	1	Lgth 3.0-in/7.62-cm. Max wdth .75-in/1.91-cm. Pointed bowl. Burned.
Utility Knives		
Knife handle	1	Lgth 3.5-in/8.89-cm. Max wdth 1.0-in/2.54-cm. One pin hole. Burned.
Broken knife blade	1	Lgth 5.0-in/12.7-cm. Max wdth 1.0-in/2.54-cm. Burned.
Knife blade fragment	1	Lgth 4.75-in/12.1-cm. Badly burned.

Miscellaneous		
Metal Rods		
Small rod	1	Lgth 15-in/38.1-cm. Dia .25-in/.64-cm. Slightly bent. Burned.
Long rod with loop	1	Lgth 21-in/53.3-cm. Dia .31-in/.79-cm. Burned.
Straight rod	1	Lgth 14.25-in/34.2-cm. Dia .32-in/.82-cm. Burned.
Bent rod	1	Lgth 6.75-in/17.5-cm. Bent back 2.0-in/5.08-cm. Dia .31-in/.79-cm. Burned.
Brass Metal		
Brass ring	1	Lgth .75-in/1.91-cm. Outside dia 1.0-in 2.54-cm.
Decorated brass piece	1	Lgth 1.5-in/3.81-cm. Wdth .5-in/1.27-cm. Decorated rim on one side.
Folded brass piece	1	Lgth 1.5-in/ 3.81-cm. Wdth 1.0-in/2.54-cm.
Chisel-cut brass piece	1	Max lgth 2.25-in/5.72-cm. Max wdth 2.0-in/5.08-cm. Irregular shaped piece.
Brass strips with holes	9	Various lgths. Ave wdth .44-in/1.12-cm. All pieces have holes.
Iron Metal Pieces		
Cut metal	5	Lgths vary 1.0-in/2.54-cm to 2.0-in/5.08-cm. Wdths vary .75-in/1.91-cm. to 1.0-in/2.54-cm. Various shapes. Burned.
Cut box band	1	Lgth 4.0-in/10.16-cm. Wdth .88-in/2.23-cm. Burned.

Speciman #	Field #	Point Length	Point Width	Point Thickness	Stem Length	Stem Width	Stem Shape	Serrated	Base
					Table 32.2 Metal Point Properties. HLHC6				
1	164	50.8	19.1	1.5	6.4	7.9	Expanded	No	Slanted
2	165	50.8	19.1	1.4	7.9	7.9	Expanded	No	Slanted
3	166	50.8	19.1	1.4	7.9	7.9	Expanded	No	Slanted
4	167	50.8	19.1	1.4	6.4	7.9	Expanded	No	Slanted
5	168	52.4	19.1	1.4	9.5	6.4	Expanded	No	Slanted
6	169	49.2	17.5	1.5	7.9	6.4	Straight	No	Slanted
7	170	47.6	17.5	1.3	6.4	7.9	Expanded	No	Straight
8	171	52.4	17.5	1.3	7.9	7.9	Straight	No	Slanted
9	172	50.8	19.1	1.3	7.9	7.9	Expanded	No	Slanted
10	173	53.9	15.9	1.3	7.9	7.9	Straight	No	Straight
11	174	49.2	19.1	1.5	7.9	7.9	Expanded	No	Slanted
12	175	50.8	19.1	1.3	6.4	7.9	Expanded	No	Slanted
13	176	49.2	17.5	1.5	7.9	7.9	Expanded	No	Slanted
14	177	49.2	17.5	1.5	6.4	7.9	Expanded	No	Slanted
15	178	50.8	17.5	1.7	7.9	7.9	Expanded	No	Slanted
16	179	47.6	19.1	1.3	6.4	7.9	Broken	No	Broken
17	180	50.8	19.1	1.5	7.9	7.9	Straight	No	Straight
18	181	49.2	19.1	1.7	7.9	7.9	Straight	No	Slanted
19	182	50.8	19.1	1.5	9.5	6.4	Straight	No	Slanted
20	183	50.8	19.1	1.5	7.9	7.9	Straight	No	Slanted
21	184	50.8	19.1	1.7	7.9	7.9	Expanded	No	Slanted
22	185	44.5	17.5	1.7	7.9	7.9	Expanded	No	Slanted
23	186	52.8	19.1	1.4	7.9	9.5	Straight	No	Slanted
24	187	50.8	19.1	1.7	7.9	9.5	Expanded	No	Rounded
25	188	50.8	19.1	1.5	7.9	7.9	Expanded	No	Slanted
26	189	50.8	19.1	1.4	7.9	6.4	Straight	No	Slanted
27	190	54.0	17.5	1.4	7.9	6.4	Straight	No	Slanted
28	191	44.5	17.5	?	7.9	7.9	Straight	No	Slanted
29	192	44.5	17.5	1.3	7.9	7.9	Expanded	No	Slanted
30	193	44.5	19.1	?	?	?	No Stem	?	?
31	194	42.9	15.9	1.5	9.5	6.4	Straight	No	Rounded
32	195	44.5	17.5	1.4	?	?	No Stem	?	?
33	196	?	19.1	?	7.9	9.5	Expanded	No	Slanted
34	197	38.1	14.3	1.7	6.4	7.9	Expanded	No	Slanted
35	198	39.7	14.3	1.1	7.9	7.9	Straight	No	Straight
36	199	?	17.5	1.3	7.9	7.9	Expanded	No	Straight
37	200	41.2	9.5	1.4	7.9	6.4	Straight	No	Broken
Average in Millimeters	——	48.6	17.9	1.4	7.7	7.7	——	——	——

Chapter 33
Red Bluff Military Site and Artifacts

The Red Bluff Military site (HLHC3) spreads over fifteen acres north of Dohäsan's Kiowa village. A dolomite-capped, red bluff forms the north boundary of the site while Carson Creek borders it on the south. Today cottonwoods, willows, hackberries, plums, skunkberry sumacs, and grapevines are abundant along the creek. Sumac grows as a large bush and covers much of the campsite. The Fort Bascom–Adobe Walls Road crosses Carson Creek below the red bluff and meanders eastward for about four miles to Adobe Walls.

Fig. 140. William "Billy" Dixon (1850–1913). Courtesy of Kansas Collection, Spencer Research Library, University of Kansas Libraries.

Fig. 141. Billy Dixon's Medal of Honor. Courtesy of Panhandle Plains Historical Museum.

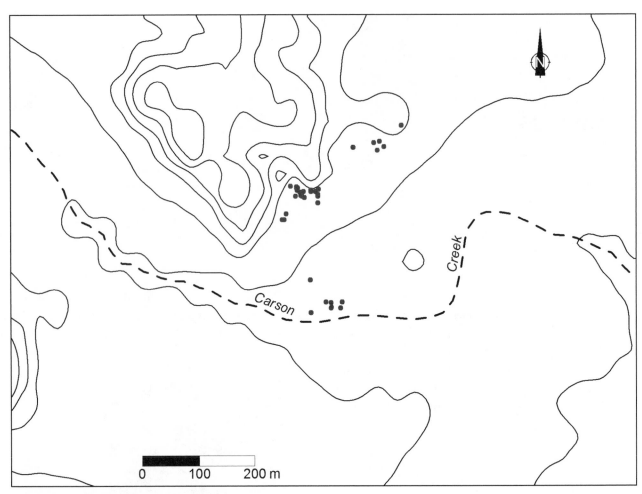

Map 33.1. Red Bluff military site. Illustration by Brett Cruse, 2010.

Fig. 142. Colt .45-caliber cartridges, fired and unfired. Scan by Lisa Jackson, 2011.

Spencer cartridge cases, internal primed .45 cartridges, and military buttons found indicate that this was a multi-component military camp. Troopers from Carr and Penrose's 1868 campaign, most likely, established the camp, and the military used the same site during the Red River War of 1874. It was not one of Carson's encampments, but it has a significant place in the annals of history. It was there, near the red bluff, on Christmas Eve 1874, that General Nelson Miles presented the Congressional Medal of Honor to William "Billy" Dixon. With his slight New England accent resounding across the Canadian River Valley, Miles read his statement crediting Dixon with skill, courage, and indomitable fortitude displayed in an engagement with five others on September 12, 1874, against hostile Indians in overwhelming numbers.[1]

E. A. Brininstool, in his book, *Fighting Indian Warriors,* penned the occasion of Dixon's receiving the medal. Said Dixon, "General Miles had both the heart and the accomplishments of a soldier, and Congress

Fig. 143. Military buttons. Scan by Lisa Jackson, 2011.

voted to each of us the Medal of Honor. He was delighted when the medals came from Washington, and with his own hands pinned mine on my coat when we were in camp on Carson Creek, five or six miles west of the ruins of the original Adobe Walls."[2]

It seems fitting that Dixon received the medal, not at a military fort, but on the hallowed ground near Adobe Walls, a short distance from where Carson engaged the Kiowas and Comanches in 1864 and where Dixon himself fought in the Second Battle of Adobe Walls in June 1874, approximately one mile north of Carson's battle site.

Table 33.1 Red Bluff Military Camp Artifact Descriptions. HLHC3

Artifact Category	Quantity	Description
Arms and Ammunition		
Cartridge Cases		
.44 caliber	1	Head stamp. *.44 WCF WRA CO.* EP. Lgth 1.31-in/3.33-cm.
.45 caliber Colt	4	Head Stamp. none. IP. Ave dia .48-in/1.22-cm. Ave lgth 1.29-in/3.28-cm.
.50/70 caliber	2	IP. Ave dia .564-in/1.43-cm. Ave lgth 1.75-in/4.45-cm.
.50/70 caliber	1	IP. Unfired. Cartridge case cut and bullet removed. Dia .563-in/1.43-cm. Lgth 1.75-in/4.45-cm.
Bullets		
.38 caliber	1	Two ring. Flat base. Low-velocity impact. Dia .357-in/.91-cm. Lgth .675-in/1.71-cm. Weight 139.5 gr.
.45 caliber	1	High-velocity impact. Weight 200 gr.
Unfired Cartridges		
.45 caliber Colt	2	IP. Ave dia .48-in/1.22-cm. Lgth 1.63-in/4.2-cm. Used in the Colt Army Revolver Model 1872.[3]
Personal Items		
Buttons		
Military button	1	Cavalry. Large C in crest. Dia 0.83-in/2.11-cm. Maker's mark. ** EXTRA * QUALITY.* dm. Manufacture date early 1860s.[4]
Military button	1	General Service. Dia 0.78-in/1.98-cm. Maker's mark *•SCOVILL MFG CO•WATERBURY.* rmdc. Manufacture date 1855–1860.[5]
Military button	1	General Service. Shank missing. Dia 0.81-in/2.06-cm. Maker's mark. *•SCOVILL MFG CO•WATERBURY.* rmdc. Manufacture date 1855–1860.[6]
Keys		
Metal key	1	Bent. Lgth 1.7-in/4.32-cm. Max wdth 1.05-in/2.67-cm. Three rings around key. Hole in forward end.
Canteen		
Canteen neck	1	Pewter. Serration around lip. Height 0.9-in/2.29-cm. Bent.
Canteen stopper holder	1	Stopper and washer missing. Loop outside diameter 1.0-in/2.54-cm. Lgth 2.63-in/6.7-cm.

Fasteners		
Nails		
Cut nails	7	Lgth varies from 1.5-in./3.8-cm to 3-in./7.6-cm. All nails are tapered on two sides.
Bolts, Pins, and Brads		
Broken wagon pin	1	Large round head. Head dia 1.56-in/3.97-cm. Pin lgth 4.8-in/12.2-cm. Pin dia 0.75-in/1.91-cm.
Large iron brad	1	Lgth 2.44-in/6.20-cm. Head dia 0.63-in/1.6-cm. Brad dia 0.19-cm./0.48-cm.
Horse Tack and Wagon Hardware		
Horseshoes		
Complete shoe	1	No calks. Six broken nails. Toe guard. Lgth 5.23-in/13.3-cm. Wdth 4.88-in/12.39-cm.
Horseshoe Nails		
Unused nails	3	Varied lgths 2.0-in/5.08-cm. to 2.5-in/6.35-cm.
Buckles and Rings		
Roller buckle	1	Roller missing. Tongue fastened on side. Lgth 2.38-in/3.5-cm. Wdth 1.75-in/4.32-cm.
Iron harness ring	1	Outside dia 1.88-in/4.78-cm. Metal dia 0.19-in/0.48-cm.
Metal Pins and Stakes		
Metal stake	1	Sharpened on one end. Lgth 9.13-in/23.19-cm. Dia 0.78-in/1/98-cm.
Proximal end of metal stake	1	Lgth 0.43-in/1.1-cm. Dia 0.71-in/1.80-cm.
Broken pin	1	Bent. Sharpened on one end. Lgth 9.5-in/24.13-cm. Ave dia 0.26-in/0.66-cm.
Broken pin	1	Bent. Sharpened on one end. Lgth 9.5-in/24.13-cm. Dia 0.38-in/0.97-cm.
Bent pin	1	Lgth 14.5-in/36.83-cm. Dia 0.25-in/0.64-cm.
Tools		
Axes		
Broken ax head	1	Single-bit ax. One side of base missing. Lgth 7.13-in/18.1-cm. Max wdth 4.23-in/10.9-cm. Max thk 1.1-in/2.79-cm.

Table 33.1 Red Bluff Military Camp Artifact Descriptions. HLHC3 (*cont.*)

Artifact Category	Quantity	Description
Camp Utensils		
Flatware		
Large spoon	1	Total lgth 8.25-in/20.96-cm. Bowl lgth 3.0-in/7.62-cm. Max bowl wdth 1.75-in/4.45-cm.
Handles		
Bucket or pot bail holder	1	Two fastener holes and one bail hole. Lgth 2.0-in/5.08-cm. Max wdth 1.75-in/4.45-cm.
Miscellaneous		
Metal Pieces		
Rectangular metal piece	1	Hole in one end. Lgth 3.46-in/8.79-cm. Max wdth 0.66-in/1.68-cm.
Chisel-cut metal band	1	Zinc coated. Lgth 3.0-in/7.62-cm. Wdth 2.1-in/5.33-cm. Nail hole in one end.
Cut metal pieces	1	Zinc coated. Wdth both pieces 0.63-in/1.6-cm. Varied lgths 1.0-in/2.54-cm. to 1.75-in/4.45-cm.

Chapter 34
1864 Adobe Walls Battle Site and Artifacts

The Adobe Walls battle site contains three distinct areas, each with its own site number.

Bent's Trading Post – HLHC2A

When Carson's troops reached Adobe Walls in 1864, the eroding walls were all that remained of Bent's Trading Post. The walls were tall enough to afford protection for horses and for Dr. Courtright's field hospital.

Today, the only evidences of Bent's structure are three flat rocks and some adobe soil that appears to be disintegrated adobe bricks; rusty, cut nails; and scattered glass and crock shards. To this site I assigned the number HLHC2A.

Cannon Hill – HLHC2

Lieutenant Pettis wrote that within a hundred yards of the corralled horses inside Adobe Walls was a symmetrical conical hill of twenty-five or thirty feet elevation. Carson, McCleave, and a few other officers took position near the top of this hill and were there when the artillery battery arrived.[1]

The conical hill mentioned by Pettis is actually the southwest end of a saddleback ridge with a slight rise at the northeast end. It extends approximately 180 yards and covers about two and one-half acres. One small, scrubby mesquite grows atop the grass-covered ridge. I designated this area of the battle site as Cannon Hill, archeological number HLHC2.

According to the location of friction primers found, Pettis placed one howitzer in the saddle of the ridge and the other near the crest to the northeast. Twenty unfired bullets of calibers .36, .52, .54, and .58, dropped by

the soldiers, and several fired percussion caps located along the crest and backside of the ridge, confirm that soldiers were on the hill and Indians were southeast of the hill.

Analysis of fired bullets by Dr. Doug Scott indicates that fifteen lead balls from the south and east side of the hill were fired by Indians in the 1864 battle. Dr. Scott dated twenty-seven fired bullets from the same area to post–Civil War era,[2] too late for use at the First Battle of Adobe Walls.

One .50-caliber and two .44-caliber balls display teeth imprints, probably made by Indians chewing on the lead balls to make them fit their particular firearm. Archeologists working on the Dark Canyon Ranchería Apache/Military Battle Site in New Mexico described chewed lead balls made by Apache Indians.[3]

An unused brass arrowpoint, a *coscojo*, and a child's copper bracelet confirm Indians occupying the high spot before or after the battle. An iron point with a broken stem found at the site was probably from the battle.

Indian Flats – HLHC1

East and south of Cannon Hill is a broad plain that stretches one-half mile south to the Canadian River and extends a half mile to the east along the north bank of the river. It was in this flat where the Indians assembled to attack Carson's troops. Consequently, for archeological purposes, I named that area Indian Flats HLHC1. The battle area spreads out over about one hundred fifty acres of tall grass and weeds.

I recovered only nine artifacts from the battle in this area. Four were fired bullets, one a .69-caliber lead ball, and four cannon ball fragments (parts of two cannon balls). I found cut nails, a spur, and a horseshoe not related to the battle.

I think there are three reasons for finding so few artifacts: (1) The area was too large for one person and his metal detector to cover adequately, (2) tall bunch grass made detecting difficult, and (3) bullets the soldiers fired from a prone position had a high angle of trajectory, carrying them past the field of battle.

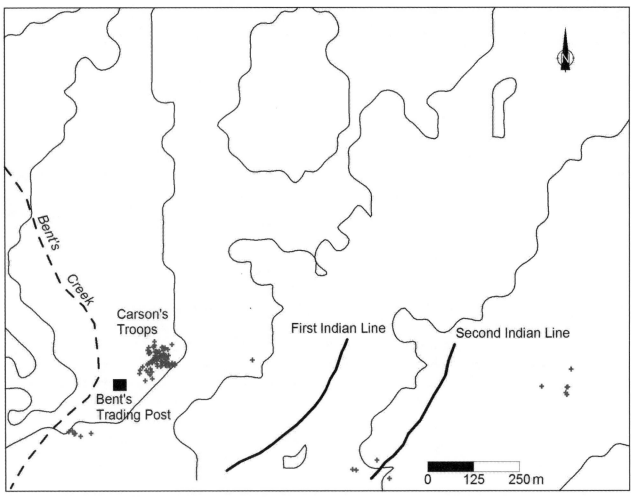

Map 34.1. Adobe Walls battle site. Illustration by Brett Cruse, 2010.

Fig. 144. Unfired bullets dropped by soldiers on Cannon Hill. Photograph by Wyman Meinzer, 2009.

Fig. 145. Lead balls fired by Indians into southeast side of Cannon Hill. Photograph by Wyman Meinzer, 2009.

Fig. 146. Fired pistol and rifle percussion caps. Photograph by Wyman Meinzer, 2009.

Fig. 147. Cannon ball fragments from Indian Flats. Photograph by Wyman Meinzer, 2009.

Fig. 148. Crock and glassware shards from Bent's Trading Post. Scan by Lisa Jackson, 2011.

Table 34.1 Bent's Trading Post Artifact Descriptions. HLHC2-A

Artifact Category	Quantity	Description
Fasteners		
Nails		
Cut nail	1	Broken. Corroded. Lgth 1.38-in/3.5-cm.
Horse Tack		
Buckles		
Harness roller buckle	1	Lgth 1.5-in/3.81-cm. Wdth 1.75-in/4.45-cm. Tongue fastens on side.
Camp Utensils		
Broken Glassware		
White, glazed stoneware	1	Cup handle fragment. Lgth .82-in/2.01-cm. Wdth .35-in/.89-cm.
Milk-glass shard	1	Translucent. Lgth 1.05-in/2.67-cm. Max wdth .68-in/1.73-cm.
White, glazed stoneware shards	2	Max lgth 1.18-in/3.0-cm. Max wdth .89-in/2.26-cm.
Oxidized amethyst glass shards	2	Max lgth 1.95-in/4.95-cm. Max wdth .87-in/2.21-cm.
Oxidized green, glass shards	2	Max lgth 1.50-in/3.81-cm. Max wdth .81-in/2.1-cm.
Brown crock shards	4	Max lgth 1.30-in/3.3-cm. Max wdth .88-in/2.24-cm.
Miscellaneous		
Irregular lead piece	1	Max lgth 2.25-in/5.72-cm. Max wdth 1.5-in/3.81-cm. Wt 490.7 gr.

Table 34.2 Cannon Hill Artifact Descriptions. HLHC2

Artifact Category	Quantity	Description
Arms and Ammunition		
Cartridge Cases		
.44-40 caliber	3	Head stamp. none. EP. Ave dia .47-in/1.19-cm. Ave lgth 1.31-in/3.33-cm.
.45 caliber	1	Head Stamp. none. IP. Dia .48-in/1.22-cm. Lgth 1.25-in/3.18-cm.
.45/70 caliber	1	Head stamp. *WRA Co. .45-70.* EP. Flattened.

Unfired Bullets		
.36 caliber	1	Dia .39-in/.99-cm. Lgth .63-in/1.6-cm. Wt 135.9 gr. Ringtail. Manufactured by the St. Louis Arsenal for the Navy Colt revolver.*[4]
.52 caliber	10	Ave dia .553-in/1.41-cm. Ave lgth .924-in/2.34-cm. Ave wt 439.1 gr. Two ring. Flat base with cone.
.52 caliber Ringtail	5	Ave dia .55-in/1.40-cm. Ave lgth 1.07-in/2.71-cm. Ave wt 445.1 gr. Two ring with ringtail base.
.54 caliber	3	Ave dia. .54-in/1.37-cm. Ave lgth 1.1-in/2.79-cm. Wt 456.9 gr. Three ring with hollow base.
.58 caliber Minié	1	Dia .57-in/1.45-cm. Lgth 1.0-in/2.54-cm. Wt 452 gr. Hollow base.
Fired Bullets		
.30 caliber	3	Ave dia .303-in/.77-cm. Ave lgth .543-in/1.38-cm. Ave wt 84.5 gr. Low-velocity impacts. Winchester hunting rifle.*
.38 caliber	1	Dia .366-in/.93-cm. Lgth .615-in/1.56-cm. Wt 144.7 gr. Post-1875 Colt revolver.*
.44 caliber	4	Ave dia .422-in/1.07-cm. Ave wt 206.0 gr. Henry or Winchester models 1866, 1873, or 1876.*
.44 caliber	2	Ave dia .433-in/1.1-cm. Ave lgth .630-in/1.60-cm. Ave wt 184.0 gr. Smith & Wesson revolver.*
.44 caliber	1	Ave dia .426-in/1.08-cm. Ave wt 180.2 gr. Colt revolver.*
.44 caliber	1	Dia .435-in/1.1-cm. Wt 202.6 gr. Post-1875.*
.44 caliber	3	Ave dia .428-in/1.09-cm. Ave wt 210.9 gr.
.45 caliber	4	Ave dia .449-in/1.14-cm. Ave lgth .72-in/1.82-cm. Ave wt 240.9. Post-1875 Colt.*
.45 caliber	3	Ave dia .445-in/1.13-cm. Ave lgth .720-in/1.83-cm. Ave wt 245.6 gr. Colt revolver.*
.45 caliber	1	Dia .459-in/1.17-cm. Wt 235.7 gr. Post-1875, probably Smith & Wesson.*
.45 caliber	1	Dia .451-in/1.15-cm. Lgth .72-in/1.83-cm. Wt 242.5 gr. 1873 colt revolver.*
Fired Lead Balls		
.38 caliber shot	1	Dia .375-in/.95-cm. Wt. 80.4 gr. .00 Buckshot.*
.40 caliber	1	Dia .402-in/1.02-cm. Wt 121.1 gr. Ramrod impression. Possibly a Colt-revolving rifle.*
.44 caliber	2	Ave dia .427-in/1.12-cm. Ave wt 128.0 gr. One lead ball chewed.*

Table 34.2 Cannon Hill Artifact Descriptions. HLHC2 (*cont.*)		
Artifact Category	**Quantity**	**Description**
Arms and Ammunition		
Fired Lead Balls (cont.)		
.44 caliber	1	Dia .42-in/1.07-cm. Wt 121.9 gr. Colt Walker Dragoon or 1860 Army.*
.44 caliber	1	Dia .448-in/1.14-cm. Wt 122.5 gr. Possible Henry-percussion trade rifle.*
.44 or .45 caliber	1	Dia undetermined. Wt 144.6 gr.*
.45 caliber	1	Dia .46-in/1.17-cm. Wt 143.7 gr. Ramrod impressions.*
.50 caliber	1	Dia undetermined. Wt 160.6 gr.*
.50 caliber	2	Ave dia .493-in/1.25-cm. Ave wt 174.4. One ball has cloth impressions and chew marks. The other has cloth and ramrod impressions.*
.50 caliber	1	Dia .47-in/1.19-cm. Wt 150.9 gr. Ball has cloth impressions and poorly trimmed sprue.*
.50 caliber	1	Dia .483-in/1.23-cm. Wt 160.7 gr. Ball shows some light faceting.*
Percussion Caps		
Hat-type musket percussion caps	21	No measurements taken. Four flanges with some broken. All caps are fired.
Straight-type percussion caps	5	No measurements taken. All caps are fired.
Friction Primers		
Fired primers	4	Primer fragments ranging in lgth from 1.0-in/2.54-cm. to 1.75-in/4.45-cm. Ave tube dia. .19-in/.48-cm.
Fired primer	1	Flat-top primer. Tube lgth 1.5-in/3.81-cm. Tube dia .18-in/.46-cm. Flat-top lgth .88-in/2.24-cm.
Fasteners		
Nails		
Square nail, hand-forged	1	Lgth 2.25-in/5.72-cm. Head dia .75-in/1.91-cm. Off-centered rose head. All sides tapered.
Nuts		
Round brass nut	1	Dia .50-in/1.27-cm. Cross-hashed design on outside of nut.

Horse Tack		
Harness Snaps		
Swivel harness snap	1	Lgth 3.5-in/8.89-cm. Max wdth 1.13-in/2.87-cm.
Camp Utensils		
Flatware		
Three-tine fork	1	Lgth 6.25-in/15.88-cm. Max handle wdth .75-in/1.91-cm. Tines broken. Channel handle.
Broken fork handle	1	Lgth 1.15-in/2.92-cm. Max wdth. .75-in/1.91-cm. Channel handle.
Mexican or Indian Artifacts		
Metal		
Iron metal point	1	Stem missing. Lgth 2.28-in/5.8-cm. Shoulder wdth .67-in/1.7-cm. Thickness at shoulders .03-in/.075-cm. Diameter of hole near one side of point .039-in/0.1-cm. Another rust-filled hole near base.
Brass metal point	1	Lgth 1.59-in/4.04-cm. Shoulder wdth .795-in/2.02-cm. Stem wdth at base .23-in/.58-cm. Stem lgth .50-in/1.27-cm. Thk at shoulders .052-in/1.32-cm. Fine serrations on stem. Straight stem base.
Brass cut pieces	7	Found near brass point. Largest piece has cut *V* that matches the shape of the brass point.
Coscojo (Hispanic Charm)	1	Lgth 1.13-in/2.37-cm. Max blade wdth .34-in/.86-cm. Shows raised finger and has decorations.
Small copper bracelet	1	Three raised areas with cross-marks. Raised area lgths .75-in/1.91-cm. Total lgth 3.38-in/8.59-cm. Bracelet is flattened on both sides and is bent.
Miscellaneous		
Metal rod	1	Lgth 1.38-in/3.50-cm. Approx. dia. .25-in/.64-cm. Broken eye on one end.
Thin metal piece	1	Possible spring. Lgth 2.5-in/6.35-cm. Max wdth in middle .31-in/.79-cm. Thk .05-in/.13-cm.
Cut brass strip	1	Lgth 3.0-in/7.62-cm. Max wdth .44-in/1.12-cm. Thk .06-in/.152-cm.
Broken metal pin	1	Lgth 1.63-in/4.14-cm. Ave dia. .28-in/.71-cm. Small wire through one end.

Table 34.3	Indian Flats Artifact Descriptions. HLHC1	
Artifact Category	**Quantity**	**Description**
Arms and Ammunition		
Bullets		
.45 caliber	1	High-velocity impact. Dished base. No rings. Dia .45-in/1.14-cm. Wt 370.1 gr.
.45 caliber	1	High-velocity impact. Dished base. No rings. Dia .449-in/1.14-cm. Wt 373.5 gr.
.52 caliber Sharps	1	Low-velocity impact. Flat base with cone. Two rings. Dia .527-in/1.34-cm. Lgth .948-in/2.41-cm. Wt 427.2 gr.
.58 caliber Minié ball	1	Medium-velocity impact. Three rings with hollow base. Wt 462.5 gr.
.69 caliber	1	Low-velocity impact. Dia .65-in/1.65-cm. Wt 408.6 gr.[5]
Cannon Ball		
Cannon ball fragment	1	Cast iron. Thk 0.5-in/1.27-cm. Triangular shape. Lgth 4.0-in/10.16-cm. Wdth 2.0-in/5.08-cm.
Cannon ball fragment	1	Cast iron. Thk 0.5-in/1.27-cm. Lgth 3.44-in/8.74-cm. Wdth 2.19-in/5.56-cm.
Cannon ball fragment	1	Cast iron. Thk 0.5-in/1.27-cm. Lgth 2.88-in/7.32-cm. Wdth 2.0-in/5.08-cm.
Cannon ball fragment	1	Cast iron. Thk 0.5-in/1.27-cm. Lgth 3.98-in/10.1-cm. Wdth 3.5-in/8.91-cm.
Personal Items		
Spur		
Spur with wire for a strap	1	Strap buttons turned out. Wdth 6.25-in/15.88-cm. Lgth 5.63-in/14.3-cm.
Fasteners		
Nails		
Cut nails	3	Tapered two sides. Varied lengths 4.13-in/10.49-cm. to 5.63-in/14.3-cm.
Horse Tack		
Horseshoes		
Complete shoe	1	Calks. Five broken nails. Length 4.69-in/11.9-cm. Wdth 5.25-in/13.34-cm.

Epilogue

Historians may debate the overall impact of Col. Carson's 1864 Adobe Walls campaign in the Indian wars of the 1860s and 1870s, but the fact remains that Carson made a significant contribution to Indian warfare by proving the effectiveness of penetrating the heartland of Plains tribes. Carson's expedition was the first military intrusion into Kiowa–Comanche winter camps in the Texas Panhandle to fight a major engagement. His command endured two days of snowstorms on their march to battle, then engaged the Indians against overwhelming odds, yet returned to Fort Bascom with most troopers unscathed. Later military commanders followed Carson's lead by pursuing the Indians into their safe havens along the Canadian, Red, and Washita rivers.

During the decade following the First Battle of Adobe Walls, struggles continued between the United States government and the Indians. Treaties made and broken by both led to continuous conflict. To further aggravate the situation, buffalo hunters, in defiance of treaties but with the blessing of Colonel Richard Irving Dodge, moved into the Canadian River Valley in the summer of 1874.[1] The buffalo hunters set up a trading post they called Adobe Walls about a mile north of Bent's Fort (the first Adobe Walls).[2] Comanches, Kiowas, Cheyennes, and Arapahos retaliated by attacking the hunters, causing them to move back to Kansas for a time. This battle, known as the Second Battle of Adobe Walls, was the catalyst of the 1874 Red River War that followed in the fall and winter.

Columns of blue-coated soldiers entered the Texas Panhandle from all directions in 1874: the Indians found no place of refuge. Everywhere they moved the military hounded them. Even the lush junipers and deep ravines within Palo Duro Canyon failed to conceal them from the persistent pursuit of Lieutenant Colonel Ranald Slidell Mackenzie.

That winter, the Indians were in the last throes of their struggle for liberty to roam freely in the land of their ancestors. By the end of the year, and early in the next, long lines of women, children, old men, and dejected warriors walked eastward toward reservations near Fort Sill, Indian Territory.

A decade earlier, the Kiowas and Comanches fought valiantly against Carson at Adobe Walls. Grassy meadows below the *Guadal Doha* (red bluffs) near Mustang Creek on the Canadian, now stand silent. There are no more Kiowa sun dances, no more winter camps.

With the exodus of the Native Americans and buffalos, a new era dawned, bringing stockmen into the Texas Panhandle. Cattle grazed where tepees once lined fertile valleys. The deteriorating walls of Bent's old fort were the only reminder of the 1864 battle.

Most battle sites and camps suffered little disturbance because ranchers were good stewards of their land. Today, almost one hundred fifty years later, cattle still graze in the valley, but new structures dot the landscape. Two circles of irrigated farmland straddle Carson's retreat route from the battlefield to the Kiowa village. Corrals stand on the slight rise in the terrain that Bent's trading post once occupied. A pump jack southwest of the corrals resonates as it sucks oil from the ground.

The drama of the first Adobe Walls battle still lives through a few early memoirs, soldiers' military reports, and the stories passed down by Kiowa and Comanche elders. Like the Red River War of 1874, Carson's 1864 battle is an integral part of the heritage of the Texas Panhandle. Archeologists, historians, and

Native Americans are making a concerted effort to preserve these historic episodes.

In spring 2007, I accompanied John Carson, great-grandson of Kit Carson, and James Coverdale, great-great-grandnephew of Dohäsan, chief of the Kiowas, to the battle site. Both wore the period dress of their ancestors—John in tan buckskin, and James in colorful regalia. They made a vivid image as they stood on the ground of Dohäsan's Kiowa village near the base of the red bluff. As we walked about the site, the significance of the moment occurred to me. Almost a century and a half earlier, Colonel Carson and Dohäsan fought a battle on this ground, and, here, their descendants stood, not as adversaries, but as fellow historians, discussing the event.

About two years later, I arrived at the Kiowa village site late in the day and stayed until darkness fell—I remembered that early evening when Carson had retreated from Adobe Walls to Dohäsan's village. There in the quietness, my thoughts turned to that long-ago day.

Darkness devoured the light from the landscape as the sun slipped silently behind the hills. The crimson glow reflecting off *Guadal Doha*, faded to gray as sunset, dusk, and finally darkness covered the valley. Night creatures awoke and began their nocturnal prowl. White-tailed deer browsed in a hackberry mott nearby. A near-sighted armadillo dug through the fallen leaves searching for his evening meal. Not a light shown from any direction, and an eerie silence surrounded me as I sat on the ridge where Colonel Carson positioned his howitzers at about this same hour on November 25, 1864. The small cannons belched fire, smoke, and ball into Dohäsan's village where the warriors were trying to retrieve their belongings. In a short time, on that fateful evening, soldiers stacked the tepees, and flames consumed the entire camp.

Northwest of the sand ridge, a small stream wound its way toward the Canadian River. In the twilight, I could barely make out the thick vegetation along the creek and sand hills that offered sanctuary to the Indians. There, northwest of the village, frightened Kiowa women and children huddled while Carson's troops wreaked havoc with their village.

In the quietness of the night, the activities of that evening swept across the canvas in my mind: Kiowa warriors scurrying to salvage what they could; soldiers intent on burning the Indians' winter supplies; women and children peeping from behind trees sadly watching their village erupt into flames.

Leaving the ridge north of the Kiowa village, I retraced Carson's route. Driving westward, my headlights penetrated the darkness as I left behind the Indian camp Carson's troops had torched. I bumped across the two miles of sagebrush flats before passing over the ridge where Carson first spotted the Kiowa tepees. I noted the point at which Ute and Jicarilla Apache scouts captured the Kiowa ponies. Finally, I drove along the creek opposite Abreu's wagon camp.

Leaving the ranch, and the battlegrounds, I wondered if my years of fieldwork and research had been enough to bring life to this epic event—the Adobe Walls Campaign of 1864. Would my written account make it live for others? If not, it wasn't for lack of passion.

Even though the artifacts I found substantiate the trails, camps, Kiowa village, and the battle site, it is exciting to consider what future research and archeological fieldwork might add. I come to the end of my book, but I hope it is not the end of the story.

Notes

Introduction

1. *100 Moore Years: A History of Moore County, Texas* (Moore County Centennial, Inc.), 1992.

2. George H. Pettis, *Kit Carson's Fight with the Comanche and Kiowa Indians, at the Adobe Walls, on the Canadian River, November 25, 1964: Personal Narratives of the Rebellion, being Papers Read Before the Rhode Island Soldiers and Sailors Historical Society.* No. 5. (Providence: Sidney S. Rider, 1878), 29.

3. Col. Kit Carson to Capt. Benjamin C. Cutler, December 4, 1864, in *The War of the Rebellion: A Compilation of the Official Records of the Union and Confederate Armies*, Ser. 1, Vol. 41, Pt. 1, 940.

4. Edwin L. Sabin in his book, *Kit Carson Days,* gives the most complete account of the 1864 Adobe Walls battle.

5. Dr. George S. Courtright, *An Expedition Against the Indians in 1864* (Lithopolis, OH: Privately printed ?, 1911), 8.

6. Rev. A. E. Butterfield, *Comanche Kiawa and Apache Missions: Forty-Two Years Ago and Now, Interesting and Thrilling Incidents* (publisher unknown, 1934), 18.

Chapter 1

1. Leo E. Oliva, *Fort Union and the Frontier Army in the Southwest.* (Division of History, National Park Service, Santa Fe, New Mexico. Southwest Cultural Resources Center Professional Papers No. 41. 1993), 307.

2. Dr. Frances Levine and Martha Doty Freeman, *A Study of Documentary and Archeological Evidence for Comanchero Activity in the Texas Panhandle* (Austin, TX: The Texas Historical Commission, September 30, 1981), 202–208.

3. Josiah Gregg, *The Commerce of the Prairies*, ed. Milo Milton Quaife (Lincoln: University of Nebraska Press, 1967), 200.

4. John Galvin, ed., *Through the Country of the Comanche Indians in the Fall of the Year 1845, The Journal of a U. S. Army Expedition led by Lieutenant James W. Abert of the Topographical Engineers,* (San Francisco, CA: John Howell Books, 1970), 42–43.

5. Lansing B. Bloom, "From Lewisburg (Pa.) to California in 1849; Diary of William H. Chamberlin, I," *New Mexico Historical Review* 20, no. 2 (1945), 46.

6. Charles L. Kenner, *A History of New Mexican-Plains Indian Relations* (Norman: University of Oklahoma Press, 1957), 155.

7. Ibid., 145.

8. Ibid., 140.

9. Oliva, *Fort Union and the Frontier Army*, 296–305.

10. Gen. Carleton to Col. Carson, October 23, 1864, in Condition of the Indian Tribes: Report of the Joint Special Committee Appointed under Joint Resolution of March 3, 1865 (Washington, DC: GPO, 1867).

11. Dewitt Clinton Peters, *The Story of Kit Carson's Life and Adventures* (Hartford, CT: Dustin, Gilmore & Co., 1873), 566.

12. Gen. Carleton to Col. Carson, August 15, 1864, in *The War of the Rebellion: A Compilation of the Official Records of the Union and Confederate Armies*, Ser. 1, Vol. 41, Pt. 2, 723.

13. Gen. Carleton to Mr. Lucien B. Maxwell, September 18, 1864, in *The War of the Rebellion: A Compilation of the Official Records of the Union and Confederate Armies*, Ser. 1, Vol. 41, Pt. 3, 244.

14. Tom Dunlay, *Kit Carson and the Indians* (Lincoln: University of Nebraska Press, 2000), 325.

15. Carleton to Maxwell, September 18, 1864, 244.

16. Gen. Carleton to Col. Carson, September 18, 1864, in Condition of the Indian Tribes: Report of the Joint Special Committee Appointed Under Joint Resolution of March 3, 1865 (Washington, DC: GPO, 1867).

17. Col. Carson to Gen. Carleton, September 21, 1864, in *The War of the Rebellion: A Compilation of the Official Records of the Union and Confederate Armies*, Ser. 1, Vol. 45, Pt. 3.

18. Col. Carson to Gen. Carleton, October 10, 1864, in *The War of the Rebellion: A Compilation of the Official Records of the Union and Confederate Armies*, Ser. 1, Vol. 41, Pt. 3.

19. Gen. Carleton to Col. Carson, October 20, 1864, in Condition of the Indian Tribes: Report of the Joint Special Committee Appointed Under Joint Resolution of March 3, 1865 (Washington: GPO, 1867), 200: Invoice of Ordnance and Ordnance Stores, turned over by M9? R Shoemaker M.S.Q. Com(mandin)g: Union arsenal to Colonel C. Carson New Mexico Volunteers at Fort Union. New Mexico. On the 28 day of October, 1864.

20. Lt. Col. Franco P. Abreu to Capt. B. C. Cutler, October 10, 1864, in *The War of the Rebellion: A Compilation of the Official Records of the Union and Confederate Armies*, Ser. 1, Vol. 41, Pt. 3.

21. Carson to Cutler, December 4, 1864, 939.

22. Fort Bascom was an adobe fort built on a gentle rise in the center of a large meander south of the Canadian River. It was the last tie to civilization and was the jumping-off place for expeditions to the plains. The military built it in 1863 as a deterrent to Confederate troops of Texas moving up the Canadian River into New Mexico. It also served as a barrier to Plains Indian raids and *Comanchero* trade with these Indians.

The fort closed in 1870, but the military continued to use it as a gathering point for Plains campaigns. Nothing remains of the fort today. Like all adobe buildings, the walls eventually deteriorated.

I visited there in 2001 and saw that someone had given the fort a death-blow by bulldozing it to the ground. The brick base of the sutler's store, mounds of dirt, and scattered glass and metal are the only evidence of its existence.

23. Carson to Cutler, December 4, 1864, 939.

24. William F. Dawson, "Ordnance Artifacts at the Sand Creek Massacre Site—A Technical and Historical Report," National Park Service (No date), 20–22.

25. Carson to Cutler, December 4, 1864, 939.

26. William A. Keleher, *Turmoil in New Mexico, 1846–1868* (Santa Fe, NM: The Rydal Press), 232.

27. Chris Emmett, *Fort Union and the Winning of the Southwest* (Norman: University of Oklahoma Press, 1965), 237.

28. Courtright, *Expedition Against the Indians*, 12.

29. Emmett, *Fort Union and the Winning of the Southwest*, 240.

Chapter 2

1. Herbert Eugene Bolton, *Spanish Exploration in the Southwest 1542–1706* (New York: Barnes and Noble, 1946), 252.

2. Carl Coke Rister, ed., "Colonel A. W. Evans' Christmas Day Indian Fight (1868)," *The Chronicles of Oklahoma* 16, no. 3 (September, 1938), 286.

3. Lt. Col. Silus Newton to Bvt. Major Cyrus H. De Forrest, October 3, 1866, Fort Bascom, Letters Sent, from James W. Arrott Collection, New Mexico Highlands University, Las Vegas, New Mexico.

4. Personal interview with Duane Moore of Tucumcari, NM, in spring of 2006. Moore saw the rock crossing while helping survey the Canadian River for construction of Ute Lake in the early 1960s.

5. Pettis, *Kit Carson's Fight*, 9.

6. Maj. C. F. Ruff, R.M.R., Comdg. To AAG U.S. Army, Letters received, Dept. of New Mexico, Hd Qtrs Comanche Expedition, Camp Jackson, Canadian River, N.M. July 30, 1860." Record Group 393, National Archives.

7. Courtright, *Expedition Against the Indians*, 6.

8. Pettis, *Kit Carson's Fight*, 9.

9. Galvin, *Through the Country of the Comanche Indians*, 28.

10. Ibid.

11. Pettis, *Kit Carson's Fight*, 11.

Chapter 3

1. Pettis, *Kit Carson's Fight*, 11.

2. Carson to Cutler, December, 4, 1864, 939.

3. Galvin, *Through the Country of the Comanche Indians*, 29.

4. Ritter Springs (also known as Red River Springs), at the base of the bluff, produces 100 gal./min. Beaver Dam Spring approximately 3/4 mile up river produces 75 gallons/min. Interview with landowner, Matt. Erwin, October, 2005.

5. Galvin, *Through the Country of the Comanche Indians*, 29.

6. The camp Montaignes described was near present day Beaver Dam Springs, a little less than a mile from the small valley at the northeast end of the flat land, see Nancy Alpert Mower and Don Russell, eds., *The Plains . . . by François des Montaignes* (Norman: University of Oklahoma Press, 1972), 105.

7. Galvin, *Through the Country of the Comanche Indians*, 29.

8. Ibid.

9. Ibid.

10. Col. Carson did not report that he spent two days at Red River Springs, but he arrived at his next camp on November 15, which indicates that he stayed an extra day at the springs.

11. Pettis, *Kit Carson's Fight*, 10–11.

12. Harry C. Myers, "Massacre on the Santa Fe Trail—Mr. White's Company of Unfortunates," *Wagon Tracks: Santa Fe Trail Association Quarterly* 6, no. 2 (February, 1992), 21.

13. Ibid.

14. Ibid.

15. Ibid., 22.

16. Ibid.

17. Wm. M. Grier, Captn 1st Drags & Brvt Majr U.S.A. to Lieut. Jno. Adams, 1st Regt Drgs, Actg Adjt., Taos, N. M., *J.M. White Massacre*. Grier Report, Record Group 94, M98/1850, National Archives.

18. Myers, "Massacre on the Santa Fe Trail," 22.

19. Ibid.

20. Peters, *Story of Kit Carson's Life*, 341.

21. Howard Louis Conard, Uncle Dick Wootton: The Pioneer of the Rocky Mountain Region, ed. Milo Milton Quaife (Chicago: The Lakeside Press, R.R. Donnelley & Sons Company, 1957), 193.

22. Peters, *Story of Kit Carson's Life*, 341–342.

23. Myers, "Massacre on the Santa Fe Trail," 23.

24. Peters, *Story of Kit Carson's Life*, 342.

25. Grier's report of six Indians killed was probably most accurate since he was in charge of the expedition.

26. Myers, "Massacre on the Santa Fe Trail," 23.

27. Peters, *Story of Kit Carson's Life*, 343.

28. Ibid., 345.

29. According to Grier's report. I have searched for the burial, but sand hills have encroached into the area around the springs, and have probably covered the grave.

30. Myers, "Massacre on the Santa Fe Trail," 23.

31. Bvt. Brig. Gen. Jno. Gasland to Colonel L. Cooper, April 29, 1858, No. 127, NA Microfilm Publications M1072, Roll 2. MF 1981-1/228. Panhandle-Plains Historical Museum Archives, Canyon, Texas.

32. Myers, "Massacre on the Santa Fe Trail," 23.

33. Gasland to Cooper, April 29, 1858.

Chapter 4

1. Newton to DeForrest, October 3, 1866.

2. Galvin, *Through the Country of the Comanche Indians*, 29.

3. Ibid., 30.

4. Ibid., 29–30.

5. Pettis, *Kit Carson's Fight*, 11–12.

6. Galvin, *Through the Country of the Comanche Indians*, 29–30.

7. Pettis, *Kit Carson's Fight*, 11–12.

8. Rister, "Evans' Christmas Day Indian Fight," 286.

9. Pettis, *Kit Carson's Fight*, 12.

Chapter 5

1. Pettis, *Kit Carson's Fight*, 12.

2. Galvin, *Through the Country of the Comanche Indians*, 30.

3. D. D. Kirkpatrick, Resurvey Texas and New Mexico Boundary, (1911) (Austin, TX: Texas General Land Office archives), 312, 484.

4. Ibid.

5. Galvin, *Through the Country of the Comanche Indians*, 30–31.

6. Hampton Sides, *Blood and Thunder: An Epic of the American West* (New York: Doubleday, 2006), 149–165.

7. Galvin, *Through the Country of the Comanche Indians*, 31.

8. Thomas A. Muzzall, "Across the Plains in 1866," *New Mexico Historical Review* 32, no. 3 (1957), 252.

9. Galvin, *Through the Country of the Comanche Indians*, 30.

Chapter 6

1. Muzzall, "Across the Plains in 1866," 252.

2. Ruff to AAG, U.S. Army, July 30, 1860.

3. Ibid.

4. Ibid.

5. Ibid.

6. Ibid.

7. Ibid.

8. Carson to Cutler, December 4, 1864, 939.

9. John Koster, ed., "The Forty-Day Scout: A trooper's firsthand account of an adventure with the Indian-fighting army in the American Southwest," *American Heritage* 31, no. 4 (1980), 101.

Chapter 7

1. John L. McCarty, *Maverick Town: The Story of Old Tascosa* (Norman: University of Oklahoma Press, 1968), 36–40, 188, 189.

2. Don Culton Collection, Panhandle-Plains Historical Museum, Drawer 1, File 36, Field Notes, 145.

Chapter 8

1. Carson to Cutler, December 4, 1864, 939.

2. McCarty, *Maverick Town*, 15.

3. Ibid., 15–16.

4. W. D. Olmstead, *Survey Notes Volume 3* (1875), Channing, Hartley County, TX., Hartley County Courthouse, 120.

5. Rister, "Evans' Christmas Day Indian Fight," 287.

6. C. E. MacConnell, *XIT Buck* (Tucson: The University of Arizona Press, 1968), 195.

7. Glen F. "Red" Skelton, interview by the author, Channing, Texas, 1995.

8. F. Stanley, *Fort Bascom Comanche-Kiowa Barrier* (Pampa, TX: Pampa Print Shop, 1961), 127.

9. Muzzall, "Across the Plains in 1866," 252.

10. Ibid.

Chapter 9

1. Skelton, interview.

2. Muzzall, "Across the Plains in 1866," 252.

3. I found both .50/70 and Spencer cartridge cases in Evans's 1868 depot on Monument Creek.

Chapter 10

1. Grant Foreman, *Marcy & the Gold Seekers: The Journal of Capt. R. B. Marcy With an Account of the Gold Rush Over the Southern Route* (Norman: University of Oklahoma Press, 1939, second printing, 1968), 231–232.

2. Koster, "The Forty-Day Scout," 101.

3. Ernest R. Archambeau, ed., "Whipple's Transcontinental Railroad Survey Across the Texas Panhandle 1853," *Panhandle-Plains Historical Review* 44, (1971), 87.

4. Sides, *Blood and Thunder*, 131–133.

5. Ibid., 130–133.

6. Gregg, *Commerce of the Prairies*, 212–213.

7. Muzzall, "Across the Plains in 1866," 252.

8. Gregg, *Commerce of the Prairies*, 89–90.

9. Galvin, *Through the Country of the Comanche Indians*, 40.

10. Muzzall, "Across the Plains in 1866," 252.

11. Olive K. Dixon, *Life of "Billy" Dixon: Plainsman, Scout, and Pioneer* (Austin, TX: State House Press, 1987), 105.

12. John R. Cook, *The Border and The Buffalo: An Untold Story of the Southwest Plains* (Austin, TX: State House Press, 1989), 55–58.

Chapter 11

1. Pettis, *Kit Carson's Fight*, 12–13; Carson to Cutler, December 4, 1864, 939.

2. Ibid.

Chapter 12

1. Pettis, *Kit Carson's Fight*, 12.

2. Ibid., 13–14.

3. Ibid., 14.

4. Ibid., 14–15.

5. Ibid.

6. Ibid., 15.

7. Judd and Detweiler, *The U.S. vs The State of Texas*, 2 vols. Supreme Court of U.S., October term, 1894, #4, Original Washington, DC, 429.

Chapter 13

1. Pettis, *Kit Carson's Fight*, 18.

2. Galvin, *Through the Country of the Comanche Indians*, 41.

3. Pettis, *Kit Carson's Fight*, 16.

4. Ibid.

5. Ibid.

6. Carson to Cutler, December 4, 1864, 940; Pettis, *Kit Carson's Fight*, 16.

7. Carson to Cutler, December 4, 1864, 940.

8. Ibid.

9. Carson to Cutler, December 4, 1864, 940.

10. Pettis, *Kit Carson's Fight*, 18–19.

11. Ibid., 19.

12. Ibid., 20.

13. Ibid., 20.

14. Ibid., 259, 263.

15. Catlin quote in James Mooney, *Calendar History of the Kiowa Indians* (Whitefish: MT: Kessinger Publishing, 2006 Reprint), 268.

16. Galvin, *Through the Country of the Comanche Indians*, 46.

17. Mooney, *Calendar History*, 275.

18. Ibid., 314–315.

19. Ibid., 315.

20. Mooney, *Calendar History*, 315; Pettis, *Kit Carson's Fight*, 21.

21. Pettis, *Kit Carson's Fight*, 21.

22. Ibid., 34

23. J. W. Wilbarger, Indian Depredations in Texas (Austin, Texas: Eakin Press State House Books, 1985), 579–581. (Reprint of 1889 edition. Austin, Texas: Hutchinson Printing House.)

24. Maurice Boyd, *Kiowa Voices: Myths, Legends and Folktales*, Volume II (Fort Worth, TX: Texas Christian University Press, 1983), 161.

25. Ibid.

26. Ibid.

27. Letter written in 1933 from C. T. Johnson to Mrs. Millie Durgan Goombi. Fort Sill National Historic Landmark Museum.

28. Courtright, *Expedition Against the Indians*, 7.

29. Mooney, *Calendar History*, 315.

30. Ibid.

31. Carson to Cutler, December 4, 1864, 941.

32. Sherman Chaddlesone (Kiowa from Anadarko, Oklahoma), interview with the author, November 19, 2010; Chaddlesone letter to the author, February 10, 2011.

33. Mooney, *Calendar History*, 315.

34. Pettis, *Kit Carson's Fight*, 22.

35. Ibid.

36. David Lavender, *Bent's Fort* (Garden City, NY: Doubleday & Company, Inc., 1954), 264. Lavender states that Bent and St. Vrain followed soon behind Lt. Abert with adobe brick makers to establish the adobe fort. Abert camped south of there in September 1845 so the adobe building probably was constructed in the fall or winter of that year; see Galvin, *Through the Country of the Comanche Indians*, 17, 71.

37. Mooney, *Calendar History*, 280–81, 283.

38. Ruff to AAG U.S. Army, July 30, 1860.

39. Joe F. Taylor, ed., *The Indian Campaign on the Staked Plains, 1874-1875: Military Correspondence from War Department Adjutant General's Office, File 2815-1874* (Canyon, TX: Panhandle-Plains Historical Society, 1962), 58.

40. Lavender, *Bent's Fort*, 264.

41. Ruff to AAG U.S. Army, July 30, 1860.

42. Lavender, *Bent's Fort*, 331 and endnote 8 page 442. It doesn't seem likely that Jicarilla Apaches would be around Adobe Walls since the Comanches were their adversaries and this was Comanche country.

43. Ibid., 332.

44. Ruff to AAG U.S. Army, July 30, 1860.

45. Pettis, *Kit Carson's Fight*, 22; Courtright, *Expedition Against the Indians*, 9.

46. Pettis, *Kit Carson's Fight*, 23.

47. Ibid., 22.

48. Ibid., 23.

49. Ibid., 23.

50. Ibid., 24.

51. Ibid., 25.

52. Dawson, "Ornance Artifacts," 21–23.

53. Ibid.

54. Ibid.

55. Pettis, *Kit Carson's Fight*, 25–26; Carson to Cutler, December 4, 1864, 940.

56. Ibid., 26; Ibid., 940.

57. Pettis, *Kit Carson's Fight*, 27.

58. Ibid., 29.

59. Ibid., 29.

60. Boyd, *Kiowa Voices*, 226.

61. Courtright, *Expedition Against the Indians*, 11; Pettis, *Kit Carson's Fight*, 31–32.

62. Carson to Cutler, December 4, 1864, 940.

63. Pettis, *Kit Carson's Fight*, 29.

64. Carson to Cutler, December 4, 1864, 940.

Chapter 14

1. George H. Pettis, History of Company K, First Infantry, California Volunteers (Providence, RI: Providence Press Company, Printers, 1885), 52–53.2. Courtright, *Expedition Against the Indians*, 11.

3. Carson to Cutler, December 4, 1864, 941.

4. Ibid.

5. Pettis, *Kit Carson's Fight*, 32–33.

6. Carson to Cutler, December 4, 1864, 941.

7. Pettis, *Kit Carson's Fight*, 33; Carson to Cutler, December 4, 1864, 941.

8. Pettis, *Kit Carson's Fight*, 33–34.

9. Ibid., 33.

10. Carson to Cutler, December 4, 1864, 941; Pettis, *Kit Carson's Fight*, 34.

11. Col. Carson to Gen. Carleton, December 16, 1864, in *The War of the Rebellion: A Compilation of the Official Records of the Union and Confederate Armies*, Ser. 1, Vol. 41, Pt. 1, 943.

12. Carson to Cutler, December 4, 1864, 941; Pettis, *Kit Carson's Fight*, 36.

13. Ibid.

14. Henry M. Stanley, *My Early Travels and Adventures in America and Asia* (London, Gerald Duckworth & Co. Ltd., 2001; First published in 1895 by Sampson Low, Marston and Company Ltd.), 69.

15. Carson to Cutler, December 4, 1864, 941.

16. Pettis, *Kit Carson's Fight*, 36.

17. Ibid., 37.

18. Ibid., 37.

19. Ibid., 38.

20. Carson to Cutler, December 4, 1864, 942.

21. Morris F. Taylor, "The Carr-Penrose Expedition: General Sheridan's Winter Campaign, 1868–1869," *The Chronicles of Oklahoma* 51, no. 2 (1973), 173.

22. Joseph G. Rosa, *They Called Him Wild Bill: The Life and Adventures of James Butler Hickok* (Norman: University of Oklahoma Press, 1964; second ed. 1974), 125; Don Russell, *The Lives and Legends of Buffalo Bill* (Norman: University of Oklahoma Press, 1973), 112.

23. Ibid., 125; Ibid., 120.

Chapter 15

1. Pettis, *Kit Carson's Fight*, 39; Pettis, *History of Company K*, 53.

2. Pettis, *Kit Carson's Fight*, 39; Courtright, *Expedition Against the Indians*, 13.

3. Pettis, *Kit Carson's Fight*, 40.

4. Ibid.

5. Pettis, *Kit Carson's Fight*, 39; Dr. Courtright reported that the Mexican boy gave him the scalp and he gave it to the Indian scouts in Courtright, *Expedition Against the Indians*, 12.

6. Carson to Cutler, December 4, 1864, 942; Pettis, *Kit Carson's Fight*, 40–41; Dunlay, *Kit Carson and the Indians*, 334.

7. Carson to Cutler, December 4, 1864, 942; Dunlay, *Kit Carson and the Indians*, 335.

8. Pettis, *Kit Carson's Fight*, 41.

9. Ibid., 39.

10. Carson to Cutler, December 4, 1864, 942.

11. Carson to Carleton, December 16, 1864, 943.

12. Pettis, *Kit Carson's Fight,* 41.

13. Leonard M. Slesick, "Fort Bascom: A Military Outpost in Eastern New Mexico," *Panhandle-Plains Historical Review* 56 (1984), 18–31.

14. Stanley, *Fort Bascom Comanche-Kiowa Barrier,* 186.

15. Carson to Carleton, December 16, 1864, 943.

16. Invoice of Ordnance and Ordnance Stores turned over by Capt. E. H. Bergmann, First Cav(alr)y New Mexico Volunteers, to Colonel C. Carson Commanding Kiowa & Comanche Expedition, on 11 November 1864. (Taos, NM: Southwest Research Center, University of New Mexico.)

17. No. 2 Invoice of Stores, Received at Fort Bascom New Mexico, this 12th. day of December 1864 of Colonel Christopher Carson, 1st Cavalry, New Mexico Volunteers, the following Ordinance and Ordnance Stores as per Invoice dated 12 December 1864. (Taos, NM: Southwest Research Center, University of New Mexico.)

18. Cpt. Cutler to Col. Carson, December 26, 1864, NA, RG 98, Dept. of NM Ltrs, v. 16, p. 147, New Mexico Highlands University Library, Las Vegas, New Mexico, Arrott Collections: Fort Union.

19. List of Stores Lost in Action, Reported by Col. Carson at Fort Union, New Mexico, December 31, 1864, Kit Carson Historic Museums, Southwest Research Center, Taos; Kit Carson Files.

20. List of Stores Lost in Action at Bent's Old Fort, Canadian River, November 25, 1864, Kit Carson Historic Museums, Southwest Research Center, Taos; Kit Carson Files.

21. Cutler to Carson, December 26, 1864.

22. Carson to Carleton, December 16, 1864, 943.

23. Kenner, *A History of New Mexican-Plains Indian Relations,* 149.

24. Carleton, James H., to Adjutant General U.S.A., Washington, D.C., January 29, 1865, in Condition of the Indian Tribes: Report of the Joint Special Committee Appointed under Joint Resolution of March 3, 1865 (Washington, DC: GPO, 1867).

25. Kenner, *A History of New Mexican-Plains Indian Relations,* 149.

26. Carson to Cutler, December 4, 1864, 942.

27. Gen. Carleton to Col. Carson, Com'dg Expedition Against the Kiowa and Comanche Indians, Fort Bascom, N.M., December 15, 1864, in The War of the Rebellion: A Compilation of the Official Records of the Union and Confederate Armies, Ser. 1, Vol. 41, Pt. 1, 944.

28. Testimony of Col. James Ford, Fort Larned, Kans., May 31, 1865, in Condition of the Indian Tribes: Report of the Joint Special Committee Appointed under Joint Resolution of March 3, 1865 (Washington, DC: GPO, 1867).

29. Pettis, *Kit Carson's Fight,* 44.

30. Carson to Cutler, December 4, 1864, 941.

31. Darlis A. Miller, *The California Column in New Mexico* (Albuquerque: University of New Mexico Press, 1982), 21.

32. *Santa Fe Weekly Gazette,* January 7, 1865, Vol. VI, no. 30.

33. Miller, *California Column,* 21.

34. Frederick Nolan, *Tascosa: Its Life and Gaudy Times* (Lubbock: Texas Tech University Press, 2007), 304 n4.

35. Miller, *California Column,* 21.

36. Ibid.

37. Pettis, *Kit Carson's Fight,* 42

38. *Amarillo Sunday News and Globe,* Golden Anniversary Edition. August 14, 1938, Page 14-Section D.

39. Carson to Cutler, December 4, 1864, 941.

40. Pettis, *Kit Carson's Fight,* 43.

41. Ibid., 34.

42. Stanley, *My Early Travels and Adventures,* 68–69. Stanley reported that Hancock and Custer destroyed 251 Cheyenne and Sioux lodges and it would take 3000 buffaloes to replace the number of hides on the tepees. This averages 12 hides per lodge; see W. W. Newcomb, *The Indians of Texas From Prehistoric to Modern Times* (Austin: University of Texas Press, 1986), 198. Newcomb wrote that 12 buffalo hides covered an average Kiowa tepee with 20 poles. James Coverdale, a Kiowa friend of the author concurred with these numbers of hides.

43. Stanley, *My Early Travels and Adventures,* 69.

44. Stanley, *Fort Bascom Comanche-Kiowa Barrier,* 69.

45. Rister, "Evans' Christmas Day Indian Fight," 299–300.

46. Frank D. Baldwin, "Baldwin's Fight-Sunday, November 8, 1874," Kansas State Historical Society, Topeka Kansas, MS 168 Microfilm, George W. Baird's Papers, 1874–1891.

47. Gen. Carleton to Col. Ford, July 30, 1865, in Condition of the Indian Tribes: Report of the Joint Special Committee Appointed under Joint Resolution of March 3, 1865 (Washington, DC: GPO, 1867).

48. Carleton to Commanding Officer at Fort Bascom, February 21, 1865, OR, Ser. 1, Vol. 48, Pt. 1, 936; Kenner wrote that Morrison, hoped to reap large trade profits from the Comanches; see Kenner, *A History of New Mexican-Plains Indian Relations,* 152.

49. Carleton to Commanding Officer at Fort Bascom, February 21, 1865, OR, Ser. 1, Vol. 48, Pt. 1, 936.

50. Stanley, *Fort Bascom Comanche-Kiowa Barrier,* 78–79.

51. Cutler to the People, May 4, 1865, *Condition of Indian Tribes.*

52. Dunlay, *Kit Carson and the Indians,* 342–406.

53. Marc Simmons, *Kit Carson and His Three Wives* (Albuquerque: University of New Mexico Press, 2003), 141–145.

Chapter 17

1. Carson to Cutler, December 4, 1864, 939.

2. Donald Buck, Andrew Hammond, Thomas Hunt, David Johnson, and John Maloney, *Mapping Emigrant Trails-MET Manual* (Independence: MO: Office of National Historic Trails Preservation; Oregon-California Trails Association, 1993), 3.

3. Randolph B. Marcy, *The Prairie Traveler* (Bedford, MA: Apple Wood Books, Reprint 1993), 27.

4. Herschel C. Logan, *Cartridges* (New York: Bonanza Books, 1959), 136–137.

5. All bullet identifications with an asterisk (*) after the statement were analyzed by Dr. Doug Scott, National Park Service, Lincoln, Nebraska.

6. Warren K. Tice, *Uniform Buttons of the United States 1776–1865* (Gettysburg, Pennsylvania: Thomas Publications, 1997), 32–36.

7. Ibid., 34–36.

8. Jay D. Edwards and Tom Wells, *Historic Louisiana Nails: Aids to the Dating of Old Buildings.* Geoscience Monograph 2 (Department of Geography and Anthropology, Louisiana State University, Baton Rouge, 1993), 54–56, 67.

Chapter 18

1. Nancy Alpert Mower and Don Russell, eds., *The Plains . . . by François des Montaignes* (Norman: University of Oklahoma Press, 1972), 105.

2. Map and field notes, April 30, 1881, Township No. 14 North—Range No. 35 East. Surveyors General Land Office, Santa Fe New Mexico.

3. Logan, *Cartridges*, 134.

4. Frank C. Barnes, *Cartridges of the World* (Chicago: Follett Publishing Co, 1965), 110.

5. Ibid., 31. Dr. Edward Maynard, in 1859, received a patent for a full metal cartridge. Maynard's first cartridges had steel base disks, but he soon replaced them with brass. It is easy to recognize early Maynard cartridges because they have a wide, thin-rimmed base with a small hole to permit the flame from a percussion cap or Maynard's tape primer to enter the case and ignite the black powder.

6. All bullet identifications with an asterisk (*) after the statement were analyzed by Dr. Doug Scott, National Park Service, Lincoln, Nebraska.

7. Paul McSpadden works in restoration of firearms at Panhandle-Plains Historical Museum, Canyon, Texas.

8. Tice, *Uniform Buttons of the United States*, 34–35.

9. Tice, *Uniform Buttons of the United States*, 464. Gerald D. Saxon and William B. Taylor, eds., *Narrative of the Texan Santa Fe Expedition*, Vol. 1 (Dallas: William P. Clements Center For Southwest Studies, Southern Methodist University,

2004), 134–135. I believe the Red River Springs camp where I found the *TEXAS* button is the first camp on the Canadian River by The Texan Santa Fe Expedition on September 8, 1841.

10. Gary Schild, *Tobacco Tin Tags* (Meriden, CT: John L. Prentiss & Co., 1972), 9.

11. Stanley S. Phillips. *Excavated Artifacts From Battlefields and Campsites of the Civil War 1861–1865* (Chelsea, MI: Book Crafters, Inc., 1980), 165.

12. Ibid., 7.

Chapter 19

1. Pettis, *Kit Carson's Fight*, 11–12.

2. All bullet identifications with an asterisk (*) after the statement were analyzed by Dr. Doug Scott, National Park Service, Lincoln, Nebraska.

3. Phillips, *Excavated Artifacts*, 165.

4. Francis A. Lord, *Civil War Collector's Encyclopedia: Vol. IV* (Edison, NJ: Blue & Grey Press, 1995), 87.

Chapter 21

1. All bullet identifications with an asterisk (*) after the statement were analyzed by Dr. Doug Scott, National Park Service, Lincoln, Nebraska.

2. James B. Shaffer, Lee A. Rutledge, and R. Stephen Dorsey, *Gun Tools: Their History and Identification* (Eugene, OR: Collectors Library, 1992), 155.

3. Ibid.

4. Tice, *Uniform Buttons of the United States*, 31.

5. Ibid., 50.

Chapter 22

1. Douglas D. Scott, "Analysis of Lead Bullets, Percussion Caps, and a Cartridge Case from a Series of West Texas Sites," (Department of Anthropology, University of Nebraska–Lincoln, May 7, 2009), 3.

2. Barnes, *Cartridges of the World*, 106.

Chapter 23

1. All bullet identifications with an asterisk (*) after the statement were analyzed by Dr. Doug Scott, National Park Service, Lincoln, Nebraska.

2. Tice, *Uniform Buttons of the United States*, 32.

Chapter 25

1. Logan, *Cartridges*, 69.

2. All bullet identifications with an asterisk (*) after the statement were analyzed by Dr. Doug Scott, National Park Service, Lincoln, Nebraska.

3. Tice, *Uniform Buttons of the United States*, 31–32.

4. Ibid., 34, 43.

5. Ibid., 50.

6. Ibid., 46.

7. Ibid., 32.

Chapter 26

1. Logan, *Cartridges*, 91.

2. All bullet identifications with an asterisk (*) after the statement were analyzed by Dr. Doug Scott, National Park Service, Lincoln, Nebraska.

3. Tice, *Uniform Buttons of the United States*, 38.

4. J. Brett Cruse, *Battles of the Red River War: Archeological Perspectives on the Indian Campaign of 1874* (College Station: Texas A&M University Press, 2008), 214–216.

Chapter 27

1. All bullet identifications with an asterisk (*) after the statement were analyzed by Dr. Doug Scott, National Park Service, Lincoln, Nebraska.

2. Shaffer, Rutledge, and Dorsey, *Gun Tools*, 303.

3. Tice, *Uniform Buttons of the United States*, 34.

4. Phillips, *Excavated Artifacts*, 183.

Chapter 28

1. All bullet identifications with an asterisk (*) after the statement were analyzed by Dr. Doug Scott, National Park Service, Lincoln, Nebraska.

2. Shaffer, Rutledge, and Dorsey, *Gun Tools*, 206.

3. Tice, *Uniform Buttons of the United States*, 32.

Chapter 29

1. Muzzall, "Across the Plains in 1866," 252.

2. Dixon, *Life of "Billy" Dixon*, 95–96.

3. James E. Thomas and Dean S. Thomas, *A Handbook of Civil War Bullets & Cartridges* (Gettysburg, PA: Thomas Publications, 1996), 2.

4. Tice, *Uniform Buttons of the United States*, 50.

5. Ibid., 46.

Chapter 30

1. All bullet identifications with an asterisk (*) after the statement were analyzed by Dr. Doug Scott, National Park Service, Lincoln, Nebraska.

2. Shaffer, Rutledge, and Dorsey, *Gun Tools*, 155.

3. Tice, *Uniform Buttons of the United States*, 32.

4. Ibid., 34.

Chapter 31

1. Taylor, "The Carr-Penrose Expedition," 173.

2. Untitled Map. The National Archives, Washington D.C. *Records of the War Department*, Office of the Chief of Engineers Q161. Manuscript map with no title. Shows the Panhandle of Texas west to 102° 45' and south to the Red River. Drawn by Adolph Hunnius, Feb. 1871.

3. This bullet was identified by Dr. Doug Scott, National Park Service, Lincoln, Nebraska.

4. Shaffer, Rutledge, and Dorsey, *Gun Tools*, 203.

5. Tice, *Uniform Buttons of the United States*, 31.

6. Ibid., 32.

Chapter 32

1. Scott, "Analysis of Lead Bullets," 4. Dr. Scott cites two sources as to the **GD** head stamp on the percussion caps: Hunt (1989: 356) is of the opinion that the **GD** may be an indication of size as well as manufacturer. Thomas (2003: 210–234) attributes the GD head stamp to the Joseph Goldmark Company.

2. Shaffer, Rutledge, and Dorsey, *Gun Tools*, 102.

3. Tice, *Uniform Buttons of the United States*, 31.

4. James Coverdale (Kiowa) from Perryton, Texas, told me that arrow makers used these graters to remove the bark from arrow shafts.

Chapter 33

1. C. M. Neal, *Valor Across the Lone Star* (Austin: Texas State Historical Association, 2002), 167–168.

2. E. A. Brininstool. *Fighting Indian Warriors: True Tales of the Wild Frontiers* (New York: Bonanza Books, 1952), 208.

3. Logan, *Cartridges*, 92. This was a popular cartridge used by the military during the 1874 Red River Indian War.

4. Tice, *Uniform Buttons of the United States*, 34.

5. Ibid., 32.

6. Ibid., 32.

Chapter 34

1. Pettis, *Kit Carson's Fight*, 23.

2. Scott, "Analysis of Lead Bullets," 12–14.

3. Christopher D. Adams, David M. Johnson, and Diane E. White, *Dark Canyon Rancheria Apache/Military Battle Site, Lincoln National Forest, New Mexico* (Alamogordo, NM: Lincoln National Forest Heritage Program, November 2000), 37–38.

4. All bullet and lead ball identifications with an asterisk (*) after the statement were analyzed by Dr. Doug Scott, National Park Service, Lincoln, Nebraska.

5. Dean S. Thomas, *Round Ball to Rimfire-A History of Civil War Small Arms Ammunition, Part One* (Gettysburg, PA: Thomas Publications, 1997).

Epilogue

1. T. Lindsay Baker and Billy R. Harrison, *Adobe Walls: The History and Archeology of the 1874 Trading Post* (College Station: Texas A&M University Press, 1986), 10.

2. Baker and Harrison, *Adobe Walls,* 140. There were two Adobe Walls. Charles Bent, in the mid-1840s, built the true adobe buildings where Carson fought his battle in 1864. The second Adobe Walls, built by buffalo hunters in 1874, was one mile north of Bent's Trading Post. The hunters and traders constructed the buildings of various materials: pickets and plaster, sod, logs, and adobe.

Bibliography

Books

Adams, Christopher D., Diane E. White, and David M. Johnson. (2000a). *Dark Canyon Rancheria Apache/Military Battle Site, Lincoln National Forest, New Mexico*. Alamogordo, New Mexico: Lincoln National Forest Heritage Program.

Adams, Christopher D., Diane E. White, and David M. Johnson. (2000b). *Last Chance Canyon 1869 Apache/Cavalry Battle Site, Lincoln National Forest, New Mexico*. Alamogordo, NM: Lincoln National Forest Heritage Program.

Albert, Alphaeus H. (1976). *Record of American Uniform and Historical Buttons, Bicentennial Edition, 1775–1976*. Alexandria and Fairfax, Va.: O'Donnell and SCS Publications.

Babb, T. A. (1923, Second Edition). *In the Bosom of the Comanches*. Dallas: Hargreaves Printing Company.

Ball, Durwood. (2001). *Army Regulars on the Western Frontier, 1848–1861*. Norman: University of Oklahoma Press.

Barnes, Frank C. (1965). *Cartridges of the World*. (1st ed.). Chicago: Frank C. Barnes and the Gun Digest Company.

Bartlett, Wallace A. (1956). *Cartridge Manual: An Illustrated Digest*. Union City, TN: Pioneer Press.

Billings, John D. (1993). *Hardtack & Coffee: The Unwritten Story of Army Life*. Lincoln: University of Nebraska Press.

Brewerton, George Douglas. (1930). *Overland with Kit Carson: A Narrative of the Old Spanish Trail in '48*. New York-Chicago: A. L. Burton Company.

Brinckerhoff, Sidney B. (1972). *Metal Uniform Insignia of the Frontier U.S. Army 1846–1902: Museum Monograph No. 3*. Tucson, AZ: Arizona Historical Society.

Buck, Donald, Andrew Hammond, Thomas Hunt, David Johnson, and John Maloney. (1996). *Mapping Emigrant Trails, MET Manual*. Independence, MO: Office of National Historic Trails Preservation Oregon-California Trails Association.

Coates, Earl J. and Dean S Thomas. (1990). *An Introduction to Civil War Small Arms*. Gettysburg, PA: Thomas Publications.

Conrad, Howard Louis. (1957). *Uncle Dick Wootton: The Pioneer Frontiersman of the Rocky Mountain Region*. Chicago: The Lakeside Press.

Cook, John R. (1989). *The Border and the Buffalo: An Untold Story of the Southwest Plains*. Austin, TX: State House Press.

Crawford, Isabel. (1998). *Kiowa: A Woman Missionary in Indian Territory*. Lincoln: University of Nebraska Press. (Reprint with a new Introduction by Clyde Ellis.)

Cruse, J. Brett. (2008). *Battles of the Red River War: Archeological Perspectives on the Indian Campaign of 1874*. College Station: Texas A&M University Press.

Dary, David A. (1974). *The Buffalo Book: The Saga of an American Symbol*. New York: Avon Books.

Davis, W. W. H. (1938 Reprint). *El Gringo, or New Mexico and Her People*. Santa Fe, NM: Rydal Press.

Dixie Gun Works. (1989). *Black Powder Guns, Shooting Supplies, and Antique Gun Parts*, Catalogue 145. Union City, TN: Author.

Dixon, Olive K. (1987 Reprint). *Life of "Billy" Dixon: Plainsman, Scout, and Pioneer*. Austin, TX: State House Press.

Dunlay, Tom. (2000). *Kit Carson and the Indians*. Lincoln: University of Nebraska Press.

Edwards, Jay Dearborn. (1993). *Historic Louisiana Nails: Aids to the Dating of Old Buildings*. Baton Rouge, LA: Geoscience Publications, Department of Geography and Anthropology, Louisiana State University.

Edwards, William B. (1962). *Civil War Guns*. Harrisburg, PA: The Stackpole Company.

Ellis, Edward S. (1889). *Kit Carson: Hunter, Trapper, Guide, Indian Agent and Colonel U.S.A.* New York: The American News Company.

Emmett, Chris. (1965). *Fort Union and the Winning of the Southwest*. Norman: University of Oklahoma Press.

Fergusson, Erna. (1973). *New Mexico: A Pageant of Three Peoples*. Albuquerque: University of New Mexico Press.

Foreman, Grant. (1939. Reprint 1968). *Marcy & the Gold Seekers: The Journal of Capt. R. B. Marcy With an Account of the Gold Rush Over the Southern Route*. Norman: University of Oklahoma Press.

Fowler, Jacob. (2000). *The Journal of Jacob Fowler*. Coues, Elliott. (Ed.) Fairfield, WA: Ye Galleon Press. (Reprint of 1898 edition. New York: Francis P Harper.)

Fox, Richard W. (1977). *Soil Survey of Hartley County, Texas*. United States Department of Agriculture, Soil Conservation Service, in Cooperation with the Texas Agricultural Experiment Station.

Fuller, Claude E. (1958). *The Rifled Musket*. Harrisburg, PA: The Stackpole Company.

Galvin, John. (Ed.). (1970). *Through the Country of the Comanche Indians in the Fall of the Year 1845: The Journal of a U.S. Army Expedition led by Lieutenant James W. Abert of the Topographical Engineers*. San Francisco, CA: John Howell Books.

Garavaglia, Louis A. (1984). *Firearms of the American West 1803–1865*. Albuquerque: University of New Mexico Press.

Gard, Wayne. (1960). *The Great Buffalo Hunt*. New York: Alfred A. Knopf.

Garrad, Lewis H. (1955). *Wah-to-Yah and the Taos Trail*. Norman: University of Oklahoma Press.

Geiger, Luther C. (1975). *Soil Survey of Moore County, Texas*. United States Department of Agriculture, Soil Conservation Service, in Cooperation with the Texas Agricultural Experiment Station.

Gluckman, Arcada. (1956). *United States Martial Pistols and Revolvers*. New York: Bonanza Books.

Gonzales, Samuel Leo. (1993). *The Days of Old*. Albuquerque, NM: Author.

Goodman, George J. (1995). *Retracing Major Stephen H. Long's 1820 Expedition*. Norman: University of Oklahoma Press.

Greene, Jerome A. and Douglas D. Scott. (2004). *Finding Sand Creek: History, Archeology and the 1864 Massacre Site*. Norman: University of Oklahoma Press.

Greene, Jerome A. (2007). *Indian War Veterans: Memories of Army Life and Campaigns in the West, 1864–1898*. New York and California: Savas Beatie.

Gregg, Josiah. (1967). *The Commerce of the Prairies*. Milo Milton Quaife (Ed.). Lincoln: University of Nebraska Press.

Gregg, Kate L. (1952). *The Road to Santa Fe*. Albuquerque: University of New Mexico Press.

Guild, Thelma S. (1984). *Kit Carson: A Pattern for Heroes*. Lincoln: University of Nebraska Press.

Halaas, David F. (2004). *Halfbreed: The Remarkable True Story of George Bent*. Cambridge, MA: Da Capo Press.

Hammond, George P. (1949, Reprint 2003). *Campaigns in the West, 1856–1861: The Journal and Letters of Colonel John Van Deusen Du Bois with Pencil Sketches by Joseph Heger*. Tucson: Arizona Pioneers Historical Society.

Hanson, Charles, Jr. (1960). *The Plains Rifle*. Harrisburg, PA: The Telegraph Press.

Hanson, James A. (1975). *Metal Weapons, Tools, and Ornaments of the Teton Dakota Indians*. Lincoln: University of Nebraska Press.

Hoig, Stan Edward. (2000). *The Kiowas and the Legend of Kicking Bird*. Boulder: University Press of Colorado.

Hoig, Stan Edward. (1993). *Tribal Wars of the Southern Plains*. Norman: University of Oklahoma Press.

Hoyem, George A. (1981). *The History and Development of Small Arms Ammunition* (Vol 1). Missoula, MT: Armory Publications.

Hughes, Elizabeth A. (1993). *The Big Book of Buttons*. Sedgewick, ME: New Leaf Publishers.

Hunt, Aurora. (1958). *Major General James Henry Carleton, 1814–1873: Western Frontier Dragoon*. Glendale, CA: Arthur H. Clark Co.

Hutton, Paul Andrew. (1987). *Soldiers West: Biographies from the Military Frontier* (1st ed.). Lincoln: University of Nebraska Press.

Hyde, George E. (1976). *Indians of the High Plains: From the Prehistoric Period to the Coming of Europeans*. Norman: University of Oklahoma Press.

Hyde, George E. (1967). *Life of George Bent: Written From His Letters*. Norman: University of Oklahoma Press.

Israel, Fred L. (1993). *1897 Sears, Roebuck & Co. Catalogue: 100th Anniversary Edition*. Philadelphia: Chelsea House Publishers.

Jacobsen, Jacques Noel. (1989). *Horstmann Bros. and Co. Catalogue of Military Goods for 1877*. Union City, TN: Pioneer Press.

Jones, Bruce. (2002). *Historical Archeology at the Village on Pawnee Fork, Ness County, Kansas*. Lincoln, NE: United States Department of the Interior, National Park Service, Midwest Archeological Center.

Kaufman, Henry J. (1960). *The Pennsylvania-Kentucky Rifle*. Harrisburg, PA: The Stackpole Company.

Keleher, William A. (1952). *Turmoil in New Mexico, 1846–1868*. Santa Fe, NM: The Rydal Press.

Kendall, George Wilkins. (1929). *Narrative of the Texan Santa Fe Expedition*. Chicago: The Lakeside Press.

Kenner, Charles L. (1969). *A History of New Mexican-Plains Indian Relations*. Norman: University of Oklahoma Press.

Knowles, Tom. (1993). *The West That Was*. Avenel, NJ: Wings Books.

Laubin, Reginald and Gladys Laubin. (1971). *The Indian Tipi: Its History, Construction, and Use*. New York: Ballantine Books.

Lavender, David. (1954). *Bent's Fort*. Garden City, NY: Doubleday & Company, Inc.

Levine, Dr. Francis and Martha Doty Freeman. (1981). *A Study of Documentary and Archeological Evidence for Comanchero Activity in the Texas Panhandle*. Austin, TX: The Texas Historical Commission.

Logan, Herschel C. (1959). *Cartridges*. New York: Bonanza Books.

Lord, Francis A. (1995). Civil War Collector's Encyclopedia: Volumes III, IV, & V (Unabridged). Edison, NJ: Blue & Grey Press.

Lummus, Charles Fletcher. (1925). *The Land of Poco Tiempo*. New York: Charles Scribner's Sons.

MacConnell, Charles E. (1968). *XIT Buck*. Tucson: The University of Arizona Press.

Mayhill, Mildred P. (1965). *Indian Wars of Texas*. Waco, TX: Texian Press.

Mayhill, Mildred P. (1971). *The Kiowas*. Norman: University of Oklahoma Press.

McCarty, John L. (1968). *Maverick Town: The Story of Old Tascosa*. Norman: University of Oklahoma Press.

Mead, James R. (2008). *Hunting and Trading on the Great Plains, 1859–1875*. Wichita, KS: Rowfant Press.

Meketa, Jacqueline Dorgan. (1986). *Legacy of Honor: The Life of Rafael Chacón*. Albuquerque: University of New Mexico Press.

Melton, Jack W. and Lawrence E. Pawl. (1994). *Guide to Civil War Artillery Projectiles*. Kennesaw, GA: Kennesaw Mountain Press, Inc.

Miller, Darlis A. (1982). *The California Column in New Mexico*. Albuquerque: University of New Mexico Press.

Miller, Darlis A. (1989). *Soldiers and Settlers: Military Supply in the Southwest, 1861–1885*. Albuquerque: University of New Mexico Press.

Mooney, James. (2006. Reprint). *Calendar History of the Kiowa Indians*. Whitefish, MT: Kessinger Publishing.

Moore, Nancy Alpert and Don Russell (Eds.). (1972). *François des Montaignes: The Plains*. Norman: University of Oklahoma Press.

Morris, John Miller. (1997). *El Llano Estacado*. Austin: Texas State Historical Association.

Murphy, Lawrence R. (1983). *Lucien Bonaparte Maxwell: Napoleon of the Southwest*. Norman: University of Oklahoma Press.

Neal, Charles M. (2002). *Valor Across the Lone Star*. Austin: Texas State Historical Association.

Newcomb, W. W. (1986). *The Indians of Texas: From Prehistoric to Modern Times*. Austin: University of Texas Press.

Noble, David Grant. (1989). *Santa Fe: History of an Ancient City*. Santa Fe, NM: School of American Research Press.

Nolan, Frederick. (2007). *Tascosa: Its Life and Gaudy Times*. Lubbock: Texas Tech University Press.

Nye, William Sturtevant. (1962). *Bad Medicine and Good: Tales of the Kiowas*. Norman: University of Oklahoma Press.

Oliva, Leo E. (1967). *Soldiers on the Santa Fe Trail*. Norman: University of Oklahoma Press.

Otero, Miguel Antonio. (1935). *My Life on the Frontier 1864–1882*. New York: The Press of the Pioneers.

Peters, Dewitt Clinton. (1873). *The Story of Kit Carson's Life and Adventures*. Hartford, CT: Dustin, Gilmore and Co.

Pettis, George H. (1878). *Kit Carson's Fight With the Comanche and Kiowa Indians at the Adobe Walls on the Canadian River, November 25, 1864*. Providence, RI: S. S. Rider.

Phillips, Stanley S. (1974). *Excavated Artifacts from Battlefields and Campsites of the Civil War 1861–1865*. Chelsea, MI: BookCrafters, Inc.

Pringle, Fred B. (1979). *Soil Survey of Oldham County, Texas*. United States Department of Agriculture, Soil Conservation Service, in Cooperation with the Texas Agricultural Experiment Station.

Rathjen, Frederick W. (1998). *The Texas Panhandle Frontier*. Lubbock: Texas Tech University Press.

Ross, Woodrow James. (1974). *Soil Survey of Tucumcari Area, New Mexico: Northern Quay County*. United States Department of Agriculture, Soil and Conservation Service, in Cooperation with the New Mexico Agricultural Experiment Station.

Russel, Carl P. (1967). *Firearms, Traps, & Tools of the Mountain Men*. New York: Alfred A. Knopf.

Russell, Don. (1973). *The Lives and Legends of Buffalo Bill*. Norman: University of Oklahoma Press.

Russell, Marian. (1981 Reprint). *Land of Enchantment: Memoirs of Marian Russell along the Santa Fe Trail*. Albuquerque: University of New Mexico Press.

Sabin, Edwin. (1995). *Kit Carson Days 1809–1868, Volume. 2*. Lincoln: University of Nebraska Press. (Reprint of 1935 edition. New York: Press of the Pioneers.)

Schild, Gary. (1972). *Tobacco Tin Tags*. Meriden, CT: John L. Prentis & Co.

Schuyler, Hartley & Graham. (1985 Reprint). *Illustrated Catalog of Civil War Military Goods: Union Weapons, Insignia, Uniform Accessories and Other Equipment*. New York: Dover Publications, Inc.

Sellers, Frank. (1978). *Sharps Firearms*. North Hollywood, CA: Beinfeld Publishing, Inc.

Shaffer, James B., Lee A. Rutledge and R. Stephen Dorsey. (1992). *Gun Tools: Their History and Identification*. Eugene, OR: Collectors Library.

Shinkle, James D. (1970). *New Mexican Ciboleros of the Llano Estacado*. Roswell, NM: Hall-Poorbaugh Press, Inc.

Sides, Hampton. (2006). *Blood and Thunder: An Epic of the American West.* New York: Doubleday.

Simmons, Marc. (2003). *Kit Carson and His Three Wives.* Albuquerque: University of New Mexico Press.

Smith, Graham. (1996). *Military Small Arms.* London: Salamander Books Limited.

Spivey, Towana (Ed.). (1979). *A Historical Guide to Wagon Hardware & Blacksmith Supplies.* Lawton, OK: Museum of the Great Plains.

Stanley, F. (1968). *Satanta and the Kiowas.* Borger, TX: Jim Hess Printers.

Stanley, Henry M. (2001). *My Early Travels and Adventures in America and Asia.* London: Gerald Duckworth & Co. Ltd. (First published in 1895 by Sampson Low, Marston and Company Ltd.)

Steffen, Randy. (1978). *The Horse Soldier. Volume II: The Frontier, the Mexican War, the Civil War, the Indian Wars, 1851–1880.* Norman: University of Oklahoma Press.

Stringer, Billy R. (1974). *Soil Survey of Hutchinson County, Texas.* United States Department of Agriculture, Soil Conservation Service, in Cooperation with the Texas Agricultural Experiment Station.

Taylor, Joe F. (Ed.). (1962). *The Indian Campaign on the Staked Plains, 1874-1875: Military Correspondence from War Department Adjutant General's Office, File 2815-1874.* Canyon, TX: Panhandle-Plains Historical Society.

Thomas, Dean S. (1997). *Round Ball to Rimfire: A History of Civil War Small Arms Ammunition, Part One.* Gettysburg, PA: Thomas Publications.

Thomas, James E. (1996). *A Handbook of Civil War Bullets and Cartridges.* Gettysburg, PA: Thomas Publications.

Tice, Warren K. (1997). *Uniform Buttons of the United States, 1776–1875.* Gettysburg, PA: Thomas Publications.

Tiller, Veronica E. (2000. Revised). *The Jicarilla Apache Tribe.* Albuquerque, NM: BowArrow Publishing Company.

Twitchell, Ralph Emerson. (1909). *The History of the Military Occupation of the Territory of New Mexico from 1846 to 1851 by the Government of the United States, Together with Biographical Sketches of Men Prominent in the Conduct of the Government during that Period.* Denver, CO: The Smith Brooks Company.

Utley, Robert M. (1962). *Fort Union National Monument, New Mexico.* Washington, DC: National Park Service Historical Handbook Series NO. 35.

Utley, Robert M. (1967). *Frontiersmen in Blue: The United States Army and the Indian, 1848–1865.* Lincoln: University of Nebraska Press.

Wallace, Ernest and E. Adamson Hoebel. (1952). *The Comanches: Lords of the South Plains.* Norman: University of Oklahoma Press.

Walton, George. (1973). *Sentinel of the Plains: Fort Leavenworth and the American West.* Englewood Cliffs, NJ: Prentice-Hall, Inc.

Articles

Archambeau, Ernest R. (1946). Spanish Sheepmen on the Canadian at Old Tascosa. *Panhandle-Plains Historical Review, 19.*

Ayers, John. (1949). A Soldier's Experience in New Mexico. *New Mexico Historical Review, 24(4).*

Bloom, Lansing B. (1945). From Lewisburg (Pa.) to California in 1849; Diary of William H. Chamberlin, I. *New Mexico Historical Review, 20(1), 46.*

Brown, William R. (1988). Natural History of the Canadian River, 1820–1853. *Panhandle-Plains Historical Review, 61.*

Hanson, Charles, Jr. (1970, Fall). The Mexican Traders. *Museum of the Fur Trade Quarterly, 6(3).*

Harrison, Lowell H. (1965). Three Comancheros and a Trader. *Panhandle-Plains Historical Review, 38.*

Hutton, Paul Andrew. (2007, April). Kit Carson's Rescue Ride: The Haunting Tale of a Noble Frontier Scout and a Pioneer Woman Kidnapped by Apaches. *Wild West: The American Frontier, 30–37.*

Keleher, William A. (1952). Texans in Early Day New Mexico. *Panhandle-Plains Historical Review, 25.*

Morgan, Phyliss. (2010, August). Mirages on the Santa Fe Trail. *Wagon Tracks: Santa Fe Trail Association Quarterly, 24(4), 8–11.*

Morgan, Phyliss. (2010, November). Mules on the Santa Fe Trail. *Wagon Tracks: Santa Fe Trail Association Quarterly, 25(1), 8–12.*

Myers, Harry C. (1992, February). Massacre on the Santa Fe Trail: Mr. White's Company of Unfortunates. *Wagon Tracks: Santa Fe Trail Association Quarterly, 6(2), 18–25.*

Oliva, Leo E. (1993). Fort Union and the Frontier Army in the Southwest. *Professional Papers, 41.* Santa Fe, NM: National Park Service.

Remiger, L. (2007, Winter). The Buffalo Range: The Story of Don Manuel Jesus Vasques—Cibolero and Comanchero. *The Black Powder Cartridge News, 14–16.*

Scott, Douglas D. (2009). Analysis of Lead Bullets, Percussion Caps, and a Cartridge Case from a Series of West Texas Sites. Lincoln: University of Nebraska.

Slesick, Leonard. M. (1984). Fort Bascom: A Military Outpost in Eastern New Mexico. *Panhandle-Plains Historical Review, 56.*

Smith, R. B. (1992, April). Biggest Indian Fight. *Wild West: The American Frontier, 26–32.*

Taylor, Anna J. (1997). Hispanic Settlement of the Texas

Panhandle Plains, 1876–1884. *Panhandle-Plains Historical Review, 70.*

Taylor, Morris F. (1973, Summer). The Carr-Penrose Expedition: General Sheridan's Winter Campaign, 1868-1869. *The Chronicles of Oklahoma, 51(2),* 158–177.

Documents

Condition of the Indian Tribes: Report of the Joint Special Committee Appointed under Joint Resolution of March 3, 1865. Washington, DC: G.P.O., 1867.

Dawson, William F. Ordnance Artifacts at the Sand Creek Massacre Site: A Technical and Historical Report. National Park Service, No date.

"Field Survey Notes: Various Surveyors and Field Books." County Clerk's Office, Hartley County Courthouse, Channing, Texas, Late 1800s.

"Field Survey Notes: Field Book C." County Clerk's Office, Moore County Courthouse, Dumas, Texas, Late 1800s to early 1900s.

"Field Survey Notes: Various Surveyors and Field Books." County Clerk's Office, Oldham County Courthouse, Vega, Texas, Late 1800s to early 1900s.

"Field Survey Notes: Various Surveyors and Field Books." County Clerk's Office, Hutchinson County, Stinnett, Texas, Late 1800s to Early 1900s.

Fort Bascom, Letters Sent-Roll 8. Rodgers Library, New Mexico Highlands University. Las Vegas, NM: National Archives, District of New Mexico Letters, 1866.

J. M. White Massacre: Grier Report. Record Group 94, M98/1850, National Archives, 1850.

Judd and Detweiler. The U.S. vs The State of Texas, 2 Vols. Washington, DC: Supreme Court of U.S., October, 1894.

Letters Received, Department of New Mexico, United States Army Commands. Records Group 393. Washington, DC: National Archives, 1860.

Notes by John Greiner on various subjects. San Diego, CA: RI541(A), Hunnington Library, Various years.

The Kiowa-Comanche War of 1864-65 and the Battle of Adobe Walls, Nov, 25, 1864. Santa Fe, NM: United States Department of the Interior, National Park Service, Southwest Region, 1962.

The War of the Rebellion: A Compilation of the Official Records of the Union and Confederate Armies, Volume 41. Washington, DC: Government Printing Office, 1893.

Newspapers

Amarillo Sunday News and Globe: Golden Anniversary Edition
Boise City News
Dodge City Daily Globe
Santa Fe Weekly Gazette

Archival

Amarillo Public Library
    Bush/Fitzsimon/McCarty Southwestern Collections
American Baptist Historical Society, Atlanta, GA
    Isabel Crawford Collection
Center for Southwest Research, University of New Mexico
    William A. Keleher Collection
Cornette Library, Canyon, TX
    Special Collections
Department of the Army: U.S. Army Military History Institute, Carlisle, PA
    Meketa Collection
New Mexico Highlands University, Special Collections and University Archives
    Arrott Collection
Kit Carson Historic Museums, Southwest Research Center, Taos, NM
    Kit Carson Files
New Mexico State University, Archives and Special Collections
    Rio Grande Historical Collection
Panhandle-Plains Historical Museum, Canyon TX
    Dan Culton Collection
    Leonard M. Slesick Fort Bascom Collection
    W. D. Howren Collection
Spencer Research Library, University of Kansas Libraries
    Kansas Collection
Texas General Land Office
    Sketch Files of Oldham, Hartley, Moore, and Hutchinson Counties

Maps

Duke, J. K. and L. W. Jelinek. (1902-1903). Hartley County Map. Austin, TX: General Land Office.

Gillespie, M. G. (1876). Sheet No. 2 Western Territories. Archives and Manuscripts Division, Oklahoma Historical Society. Oklahoma City, OK: Corp. of Engineers.

Hunnius, A. (1871). Manuscript Map with No Title. Shows the Panhandle of Texas, west to 102 45' W Longitude and south to the Red River. The National Archives, Washington, DC: Records of the War Department, Office of the Chief of Engineers.

Map of Parts of Indian Territory, Texas, and New Mexico. (1874). Chicago: United States War Department, Lithographed at Head Quarters, Mil. Div. of the MO. by Askenvold & Roy.

Moore County. (July, 1884). Austin, TX: General Land Office.

Roeser, C. (1882). Territory of New Mexico. Department of the Interior, General Land Office.

Index

Page numbers in *italics* refer to figures.

About the Author

Alvin R. Lynn grew up on a farm along the Pease River in rural Motley County, Texas. He is a retired social studies and science teach and coach. With a lifelong passion for archaeology and history, he now serves as a steward for the Texas Historical Commission. He and his wife Nadyne live in Amarillo, Texas.

Kit Carson and the First Battle of Adobe Walls: A Tale of Two Journeys is
Texas Tech University Press's inaugural Judith Keeling Book.

The Judith Keeling Book, established in recognition of a lifetime of achievement in and
dedication to scholarly publishing, honors books that are undertaken through careful
research and assiduous attention to detail, that investigate questions posed by any
inquiring mind, and that make a valuable, perhaps otherwise unnoticed, contribution
to the scholarly community and to the literary culture of Texas and the American West.